NEW DOG

NEW DOG

CHOOSING WISELY AND ENSURING A HAPPY EVER AFTER

Dr Bruce Fogle DVM MRCVS

with Patricia Holden White

MITCHELL BEAZLEY

For Macy

New Dog
Bruce Fogle DVM MRCVS
with Patricia Holden White

First published in Great Britain in 2008 by Mitchell Beazley,
an imprint of Octopus Publishing Group Ltd,
2–4 Heron Quays, London E14 4JP
An Hachette Livre UK Company
www.octopusbooks.co.uk

A CIP catalogue record for this book is available from the
British Library.

ISBN: 978 1 84533 323 2

Commissioning Editor Helen Griffin
Senior Editors Suzanne Arnold and Leanne Bryan
Art Director Tim Foster
Senior Art Editor Juliette Norsworthy
Designer Phil Gilderdale
Copy-Editor Candida Frith-Macdonald
Proofreader Sands Publishing Solutions
Picture Researcher Giulia Hetherington
Senior Production Controller Lucy Carter

Set in Univers and Goudy

Colour reproduction by United Graphics
Repro House, Singapore
Printed and bound by Toppan, China

Contents

Introduction

So you're getting a new dog, are you? Do you realize what you're in for, how much precious time you'll have to invest in the hairy monster? More likely, you've already done the deed. As the gimlet-eyed tearaway disrupts your life, are you wondering how on earth you'll ever get your sanity back?

Some of you know I've written quite a few books about dogs – their history, variety, health, and nutrition; about how they think; and why, when training one, it's vital to understand how its mind works. These books are published around the world, so some of the information in them must seem useful, but when (for the first time ever) I found myself e-mailing chapters of *New Dog* to clients, before I'd even sent what I'd written to my editor, I knew this would be a really practical book, especially for people who think they're getting a new dog but are, in fact, getting a new puppy, which is an utterly different species.

New Dog could equally be called *New Dog Owner* because what follows is as much about us as it is about dogs. I did my seven years of veterinary training but realized the blindingly obvious only after I'd entered clinical practice: that almost everything about a dog, especially its health and behaviour, is intertwined with us. The luckiest dogs end up in homes with people who understand that they have to invest time, up front, to earn the extraordinarily wonderful rewards that come from living with a canine companion. That's why I've devoted the start of the book to decision-making. Are you sure that a dog can fit into your present or anticipated lifestyle? If your life can accommodate a dog, are you thinking about the right type for you and your family? Rather than just winging it, when getting a new pup or a recycled, rescued dog, have you done your homework, prepared your home, and planned how to integrate your new dog into your home, your family, your neighbourhood, your life?

I'm not bashful about admitting that I love dogs. I've been a clinical vet for almost 40 years, so I'm a bit of a silverback male. I've got a warm, close family and all the rewards that go with that good luck, but even so, dogs wondrously augment life. There's something about the immutable constancy and fidelity of a dog that's deeply reassuring. Dogs are honest – sometimes painfully so – with their emotions. You can trust their integrity, believe what you see in their expressive eyes. I guess I'm a true

dogaholic because, to me, even a smelly, wrinkled, stiff-legged old-timer has a natural dignity, even beauty, about him.

During the time I've been a vet I've watched the intensity of our relationship with dogs heighten. The reasons for our increasing dependency upon the rewards that dogs give us are another story, but if you think this bond of friendship is a product of modern Western affluence, think again. It's an integral part of human nature that all people are suckers for puppies. In 1828, a major in the British Army visiting Stradbroke Island off the coast of Queensland, Australia, saw a dingo pup he admired for its unusual dark colour, and he tried to buy it from its Aborigine owner. Major Lockyer wrote in his diary: "I was very anxious to get one of the wild native breed of black colour, a very handsome puppy, which one of the men had in his arms. I offered him a small axe for it; his companions urged him to take it, and he was about to do so, when he looked at the dog and the animal licked his face, which settled the business. He shook his head and determined to keep him."

We're all suckers for the lick on the face. That's a puppy behaviour we've intentionally perpetuated into adulthood in many dogs. My own Golden Retriever, Macy, was never much of a face-licker but filled our lives in other ways. Indoors she was a quiet and reassuring presence. Outdoors she was my own personal window into the natural world, the perfect stalker, hunter, and retriever. I use the past tense because, as I neared the finish of this book, she died unexpectedly. At first I was too cut up by her loss – she was only six years old and developed a devastating form of cancer – to do much more than stick to our old routines. I still got up early each morning and went for a 45-minute walk in the park. But soon after, I found myself phoning the rescue secretaries of Golden Retriever clubs, and then the breeder's jungle telegraph took over and some started phoning me, commiserating with my loss and saying that when I was in the market for a new dog, they were there to help.

So, quite unexpectedly, I find myself in exactly the same situation you're in. I'm getting a new dog, and I can't tell you how useful it's been to have Patricia Holden White remind me about the nuances of new dog training. For over 30 years, I've referred new dog owners and their dogs to Patricia. During the evenings, she runs the local dog-training club. During the day, Patricia is a literary agent – mine.

Publishers love to say that a book contains "everything you will ever need to know" about a subject. I'm proud to say that neither my publishers, nor Patricia, nor I claim that this book contains everything you need to know. When it comes to dogs, that sort of claim is just silly. *New Dog* gives you a head-start, a leg-up, the best first steps for living with, playing with, and caring

for your new dog. It sets you on the right course. You can refer back to it and point out what we've written to other members of the family, but it doesn't replace puppy classes or one-to-one lessons from a dog trainer who uses positive reinforcement training techniques, or advice from your veterinarian on your new dog's health and nutrition. I can't wait to have a new dog in my home. I hope you have as much enjoyment from yours as I know I'll have from mine.

20 essential tips for a new dog

1 Start socializing and training your new dog as early as possible. Older dogs can be taught new tricks, but what's learned earliest is learned quickest and easiest. The older the dog, the more bad habits will need to be "un-learned" before new ones can be learned in their place.

2 Train your dog gently and humanely, using positive, motivational methods. Keep obedience sessions upbeat and short, so that the training process is enjoyable for both of you. If training your pooch is a drudge, that means you or your dog will be bored. Rev it up. Try "play training" by using non-adversarial games such as "go find" and "hide and seek" in your training sessions.

3 How well your dog responds to you at home inevitably affects how it will behave outdoors. If your dog doesn't respond reliably to commands at home, where distractions are minimal, it certainly won't respond to you properly outdoors, where temptations are more exciting.

4 Don't let your dog treat you or anyone else in the family like "hired help". Don't let it treat your furniture like its private gymnasium. You make the rules, not your dog. The whole family should be consistent in what your dog may and may not do. Ensure it has its own personal place to chill out.

5 Brush up on your local "dog laws". These vary with where you live, but virtually all require dogs to be identified and under your control, usually by collar and lead. Cleaning up your dog's mess may be the law; it's also at the heart of being a good neighbour.

6 Don't let your dog beg at the table or eat leftovers from your plate. If you utterly hate waste, give the leftovers in the feeding bowl. Give a tasty chew toy to concentrate on rather than letting your dog try to scrounge from the dinner table.

7 Establish a greeting pattern when visitors arrive and stick to it. Giving a rewarding alternative job to do, such as sitting on command or chewing on a tasty treat, prevents jumping up on visitors. Visitors need instructions on how to greet your dog as well.

8 Don't let your dog demand your attention by annoying you to death. Even negative attention such as a good scolding can be rewarding for some dogs. Give a behaviour command like "sit" before it earns your attention.

9 Never give a command you can't enforce. All that will do is train your dog to ignore your commands. Most dogs need refresher courses in basic commands, especially when they become "teenagers" at around 8 to 18 months of age.

10 Dogs are brilliant at understanding your body language. It is more important than the actual words you use. Keep your body language friendly, fresh, and crisply clear.

11 Telling your dog to "sit, sit, sit, sit!" is neither efficient nor effective. Repeating commands tunes your dog out and teaches it that the first several commands are a bluff. Give your dog a single "sit" command, and if it fails to respond, gently place or lure it into the sit position, then reward.

12 Avoid giving incompatible combined commands, such as "sit down", which confuse your dog. Say either "sit" or "down". The command "sit down" doesn't exist.

13 When giving your dog a command, don't shout. Even if your dog is especially independent or unresponsive, your tone of voice when issuing an obedience command should be calm and authoritative, rather than harsh or loud.

14 Before blaming the dog when it doesn't respond to a command, determine whether your dog really knows what you want, knows how to comply, and is not being unresponsive because of fear, stress, or confusion.

15 Use your dog's name positively and stick to one name only. Don't use it with reprimands, warnings, or punishment. Your dog should know that when it hears its name or is called to you, good things happen. Its name should be a word it responds to with enthusiasm, never hesitancy or fear.

16 Good motivational training is based on good communication. After-the-fact discipline does NOT work. Avoid the pitfall of "getting even" for misbehaviour by, for example, banishing your dog from your sight for a protracted time when you find a mess during housetraining or chewed articles when you have left it alone.

17 When training your dog, whether praising or correcting, good timing is essential. A dog should be appropriately rewarded the instant it does something right. Always keep small, tasty training treats at hand. As your relationship grows, your praise will come to mean as much as treats.

18 Don't train one dog when another is watching or listening. Not only is another dog a distraction for you and your dog, it is also learning to actively disregard your spoken or hand-signal commands.

19 Let your dog know what you want, rather than what you don't want. If your dog receives lots of attention when it misbehaves, even negative attention, such as shouting and pushing off when it jumps up on you, its behaviour is reinforced and is likely to be repeated.

20 Keep a lid on your anger. Never train your dog when you're tired, feeling grouchy, or impatient. Earning your dog's respect is never accomplished by yelling, hitting, or handling your dog in a harsh manner. Fear and stress in dogs inhibits their ability to concentrate and learn.

Chapter 1
Choosing
a new dog

What is a dog?

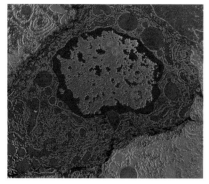

Mitochondria – the elongated orange areas in this skin cell – hold unique maternal DNA.

A dog is a dog. No more, no less. To you it may be a deeply affectionate and loving "fur-person" with some extraordinarily disgusting habits and dreadful personal hygiene. To evolutionary biologists it may be the brilliantly successful descendant of an ancient family of Asian wolves. To animal behaviourists it may be the most successful ever member of the canine family, from which it inherits both its range and its limitations of behaviour, but to me a dog is simply a dog. It is a unique species, which has a spectacular and unrivalled ability to understand humans and get along with us.

Genetic evidence of origins

Mapping of the canine genome was completed in 2006, but even before that, DNA studies were answering questions about what a dog is, where it came from, and how it evolved.

Mitochondria are ancient structures, contained in all living cells and with their own DNA. Mitochondrial DNA is passed from generation to generation on the female side of the family, and each line of mitochondrial DNA has a unique "signature". By studying mitochondrial DNA in wolves and in dogs, geneticists determined that the two species diverged between 40,000 and 100,000 years ago. Most, but not all, experts estimate that our relationship with the dog began around 15,000 years ago. Archaeological evidence of a dog–human relationship certainly dates back no further than that. If this is so, the genetic event that created the "dog" occurred long before it moved into ancient human settlements.

Early selective breeding

The wolf and the dog still share almost all of their DNA, and, of course, matings between the species produce healthy litters. Regardless of exactly when the dog diverged from the wolf, it is, in its origins, self-domesticated. All that was needed was a slight but significant change in the biofeedback mechanism, in the "fight, flight, or freeze" response in a family of wolves. This allowed them to move successfully into a new environment not already exploited by other wolf packs, the human ecological niche, where it scavenged off human waste and ate the smaller mammals attracted by human food. In its new environment, it was protected from larger predators, already cleared from the region by people. This "wolf-dog" adapted to its new environment. Eventually it became smaller. Its teeth became more crowded. Curiously and inexplicably, the frontal sinuses in its skull became larger. And – I'm sorry, but there's no way to deny this – its brain also shrank by one third.

Breeding for utility

It's very likely that some wolf-dog pups were captured by people. Most ended up in the stewing pot, but a pup's endearing behaviour was no different then from what it is now. Nor are we. Even what we think of today as ancient peoples with ancient customs are still enamoured with puppy behaviour.

Small comforter dogs emerged long before terrier types, and today most terrier breeds are "repurposed" as companions.

Humans intuitively respond to a pup's charms. This New Guinea Singing Dog pup has been dressed as part of the family.

for specific coat colours. It was not until the 1700s, however, that a combination of wealth, increased leisure time, and urbanization led to the selective breeding of dogs for coat colour and length, for conformation, and for beauty. By the 1800s, genealogical canine registries existed and became today's kennel clubs, which "guarantee" the genetic purity of the world's hundreds of breeds of dogs. For many, an unregistered dog without a pedigree – a mutt – became unfashionable.

Dogs and us

There's a simple reason why dogs became our best friends and most popular animal companions. Dogs are better than any other species, including all the primates, at reading our intention movements. They are brilliant observers, and they quickly learn to anticipate our moves, our wants, our desires. Dogs are on our wavelength. They vary in size and shape more than any other domesticated or wild species, but regardless of what a dog looks like or what breeders say about their breed, all dogs have more in common with each other than they have differences. A dog is unique. A dog is a dog.

It is only when they mature that dogs risk being ignored, abused, or eaten. Some pups, probably the most sociable and the most aware, survived and were able to breed. Their superior hearing and sense of smell made them useful sentinels, warning humans of potential danger. Some accompanied men on hunts, and their ability to track and attack became apparent. The most efficient of these dogs were allowed to breed, but now under our auspices.

We had intervened in natural breeding, and the modern dog was created. By 7,000 years ago we had created sleek, fast hunting dogs; by 5,000 years ago, massive warrior and guarding dogs and small comforter dogs; and by 1,700 years ago, short-legged, slow hunting dogs. Around 1,300 years ago retrievers and water spaniels were developed, and only 100 years later, "earth dogs", the ancestors of today's terriers, were evident in Europe.

DNA studies published in 2005 revealed that three out of four dogs are descended from a single female wolf ancestor. On three further occasions additional wolf genes were added, giving four small groups of ancient breeds. All later breeds have been created from these groups during the last 300 years.

Breeding for fashion

For most of the dog's existence, it bred on its own or was bred for practical purposes. You could argue that breeding for fashion started over 2,000 years ago in China's imperial court, where the ancestors of the modern Pekingese were selectively bred. Or that European hounds, pointers, setters, and retrievers were bred for fashion, in that they were sometimes bred

---

BRUCE'S TIPS ON SHORT-TAILED DOGS

Some of my clients believe breeds such as Boxers (*see* page 33) and Dobermanns (*see* page 52) have short, stubby tails. We're so used to seeing these dogs without their tails that it's hard to picture them with them. But they are born with wonderfully expressive tails. We thoughtlessly amputate them for cultural and fashion reasons. The fashion began almost 2,000 years ago, when the first European text on dog care recommended biting off puppies' tails to

prevent them from contracting rabies. The fashion for modifying a dog's appearance peaked in 19th-century Germany, where a wide variety of working breeds had their tails and ears amputated. These are no more than fashion statements. The tail evolved to help balance and signal intent, and there are no biological reasons why a pet dog should lose its tail.

Are dogs human?

It may surprise you that the consensus among neuroscientists is that only humans experience consciousness. Do they really mean that dogs do not have internal, personal feelings – what you and I call emotions: joy or sadness, jealousy or anger, contentment, frustration or attraction? Is it completely impossible for dogs to have a sense of fun? Is it really true that they can only react to stimuli, without experiencing the emotions we humans have?

We see human feelings and emotions in dogs' eyes. We think we understand their thoughts.

The roots of consciousness

The most important anatomical clue that this isn't true, that you and your dog both share the same feelings, is that brain studies consistently show that the roots of these emotions are not in the neocortex, the most advanced part of the human brain, but rather in discrete regions of one of the most primitive parts of the brain (technically called the sub-neocortical limbic regions) – a part of the brain that we humans share with all other mammals.

Studies of that part of the brain show that both you and your dog have the same basic emotional network, consisting of seven different systems. It's just evolutionary common sense that these emotional systems, with similar anatomical origins in people and in dogs, evolved in both species for the same reason, and that the neurochemical activities in the brain, which are the basis of emotions, are shared between you and your dog. They evolved as a feedback system to tell you or your dog how well or how badly things are going.

Rewarding emotions

Some of the drugs humans are inclined to abuse are very similar to natural brain chemicals called neurotransmitters, while others stimulate the secretion of those same neurotransmitters.

Engaging in physical activities can also trigger the release of satisfying brain chemicals. For example, my son Ben likes challenges, such as a seven-day marathon run across the Sahara or rowing the Atlantic; his reward is a release of the neurotransmitter dopamine in his brain, giving him a feeling of pleasure. His dog Maggi, a Border Collie-Labrador cross,

To most people, this dog is "kissing" its owner. To us, the lick is a kiss; to the dog, it is more a sign of emotional dependence.

will chase, catch, and retrieve tennis balls until she loses consciousness from exhaustion, if given the chance, because her "seeking" activity is similarly driven by dopamine.

Fear and panic

Among the most troublesome emotions we have to contend with in our dogs are fear and panic. Uncontrolled fear or panic can lead to a dog becoming either aggressive or destructive. Separation anxiety is one of the most common problems in newly rescued dogs, and recent studies show that "sadness" in people and "separation anxiety" in other animals share remarkably similar brain regions. Those of us familiar with puppies know that their distress when separated from their mother is alleviated by our touch. What neuroscientists have shown is that touch triggers the release of brain chemicals called endorphins. Dogs are "human" in their biological need to be touched. It's a potent reward, and the easiest to use in training.

Living in the moment

Dogs have rich mental lives – richer than some people are willing to accept. What they do not seem to share with us is the ability to "step back" mentally and reflect on these emotions. A dog left alone, for example, cannot consciously think about how to react or decide to make the best of things: it lives in the moment of its emotions. This makes our responsibility towards them all the greater.

The owner's responsibility

If we acknowledge that animals do have rich mental lives and share emotions such as joy and sadness, this places a great burden upon us to ensure that their lives are emotionally as well as physically fulfilling. A dog needs to live a natural life. It needs the fulfilment of behaving as it evolved to behave, as an emotional

individual. The variations in our dogs' emotions are not as complex as ours, but the basic range is similar. If you're thinking about getting a new dog and assume it's simply an attractive, cosmetic addition to the home, think again. A dog is a new member of the family, with a complete emotional life of its own. Dogs share their emotions with us; in return we have the "parenting" responsibility to ensure their lives are fulfilling and free from undue stress.

Dogs thrive on shared activities and give us all their attention. They make us feel important.

EMOTIONAL RANGE

Emotional system	Feelings/emotions	Human varients	Dog varients
SEEKING	Motivation, frustration, motor patterns	Desire to win, obsessions, cravings, addictions	Herding, heeling, pointing, retrieving
RAGE	Anger, irritability	Hatred, contempt	Snappishness
FEAR	Anxiety, panic, phobias	Worry	Panic, phobias, fear-induced aggression
PANIC	Separation distress, sadness	Shyness, shame, embarrassment, guilt	Separation anxiety, sadness
LUST	Erotic feelings	Jealousy	Jealousy
CARE	Attraction, nurturing	Love, romance	Need to be with you, licking, touching

What is a dog person?

The "ideal" dog, who waits quietly for us to interact with him when we choose, is a myth.

I imagine you already have a life. A job? A family? Hobbies? I bet you also enjoy going on holiday. And now you'd like a dog. Have you asked yourself why? Do you want a dog to wag his tail when he sees you, look at you with love in his eyes, and go on walks with you? Have you thought that he might eat your home, excavate the garden, fall erotically in love with your best friend's knee, or jump off a cliff because he hasn't worked out it's quite a dumb thing to do? Honest dog people anticipate all these things.

The need to be needed

The need to be needed is a uniquely human desire. In most, if not all, other species, the need to parent, to care for their young, is transient, lasting for a finite time after birth. In dogs, it lasts for less than six months. We're different; we have a lifelong need to nurture. In women it is fairly consistent throughout life; in men it can be muted in early life, not flowering until other needs such as power and control are dimmed. Some people satisfy their need to nurture through gardening. Dog people satisfy it by caring – truly caring – for dogs.

Dogs take time

Dog people understand – through their experience of living with dogs, or through what dog-owning friends tell them, or even through what they read in books like this – that dogs take up time. You have no idea how much time a new dog takes! When it's older and settled in

to your routines, you'll get your life back, but a new dog takes time to train, time to exercise, time to care for, time to groom, and time to worry over. For some people dogs are time-wasters. For dog people, dogs are satisfying time-fillers.

Dogs are dirty

There are some prissy dogs that hate to get dirty or wet, but they are a very small club. A typical dog wants to wallow in mud, dig in dirt, get covered in snow, bog snorkel, and roll in the most disgusting things that nature offers. Moreover, dogs have hair, and hair doesn't just get dirty. Parasites live and love in it; dander, the shedding skin we can be allergic to, gets caught in it. And both doggy smells and those captured by rolling on decomposing

animals or faeces are held in it. Dog people, with resignation, put up with a dog's curious habits. Some are even fascinated by their dogs' behaviours. A small tribe of dog people understand that living with a dog gives them a unique ringside seat on the natural world, to be a welcomed observer of nature.

Dogs take space and cost money

Dogs may be useful to us, and we may be useful to dogs, but they cost more than you think. The daily cost of accessories, food, holiday lodgings, preventive veterinary care, and health insurance may be no more than a daily Frappuccino, but over 12 years that's a five-figure sum!

Dogs take space too – both physical and emotional space. It's not hard to fit a dog

BRUCE'S TIPS ON ASSESSING YOUR SUITABILITY

If you don't know whether you're a dog person and would like to find out, visit a dog training class. The trainers are "dogaholics", a unique class of dog people. Don't examine them (although do talk to them about your dog quest). Instead, look at the people who have brought their dogs to the class. These are true dog people, individuals who are willing to make the investment, in both time and money, to improve their relationship with their dogs. If you feel comfortable with them, if you can see in yourself similar aspirations to theirs, then you're a dog person in the making.

Dog people understand that a puppy is a completely different species from a dog.

comfortably into a small home, but the emotional space is considerable. When our dog Macy recently lost most of her sight, my wife and I greeted each other by first asking how Macy was coping that day. Dogs can tear your heartstrings.

Age is important
The age of a dog when you acquire it will influence how it behaves. Pups under 12 weeks are the most impressionable; older dogs get set in their ways. Mature dogs have mature habits, and training may involve breaking those habits, then creating new ones. That's why only dog

people should rescue dogs from shelters. Dog novices should acquire young pups, ideally around eight weeks old, to allow a month in their new home while their minds are still open. Dog people know that sex is a fact of life with dogs, that various behaviours are influenced by sex hormones, and that early neutering is beneficial (*see page 19*).

Dog people are realistic
There is always a gap between owner expectations and the reality of living with a rambunctious new puppy, no matter how adorable it is. Dog people

QUESTIONS AND ANSWERS

Is it fair to keep a dog in an apartment?

Of course. The only difference between a house and an apartment is the ease with which you can take your dog outside. Even the size of a dog need not preclude it from living in an apartment. Exercise needs are not related to a dog's size: some large breeds need less exercise than some small ones. A dog can live a wonderful life in an apartment, as long as it is taken outdoors several times daily, for toileting needs, exercise, and socializing with its own kind.

know that dogs reach physical maturity long before emotional maturity, and that some puppies never grow up (they're called Boxers). But they also know that nature is capable of the most fabulous trick: given time, and with the right encouragement, a puppy will one day become a reliable, faithful, constant, immutable dog – a wonder of evolution.

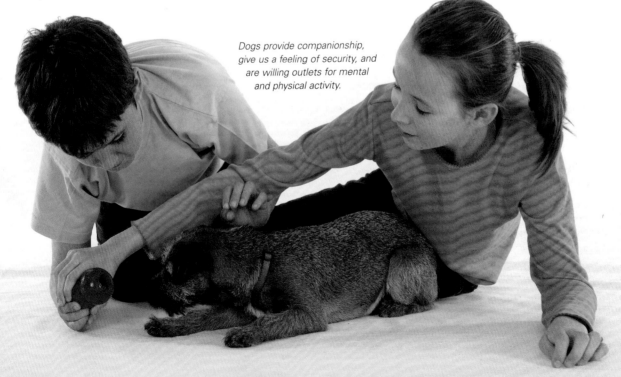

Dogs provide companionship, give us a feeling of security, and are willing outlets for mental and physical activity.

What is a dog breed?

You may criticize my taste in music, my favourite sports team, my idea of a holiday, even my choice of spouse, but you may never, ever say anything even remotely negative about my dog! Or her breed. Dog owners suffer a total lack of sense of humour or irony about our dogs. I know you'll choose a dog because it looks like Dougal, or its bark reminds you of your uncle's cough, or your hydrangea plant just died. But just in case your choice is susceptible to logic, here's some pragmatic information.

Millions of varieties

There are over 400 breeds to choose from, but they make up only a minority of the world's 200 million plus canines. Most dogs are a mix of two or more breeds, or individuals with no known registered antecedents. The latter are the world's mutts, mongrels, or bitsers – or, as the French so eloquently call them, *bâtards*. Pure-breds may be good for us, because we know what that dog tends to be like, physically and mentally, but not

HOW DOGS ARE CLASSIFIED

All pure-bred dogs are categorized by kennel clubs into groupings according mainly to how each breed was used (for instance, for hunting or herding) at the time that kennel club was set up. Usage varies from country to country, so the groupings vary. For instance, the name "Dachshund" sounded like the English "hound", so Dachshunds are considered hounds in the UK and the USA. But the rest of the world thinks dachshunds are in a category of their own.

United Kingdom		North America		Europe	
				1	Spitz and primitive dogs
1	Hound	**1**	Hound	**2**	Scent and related hounds
				3	Sighthounds
				4	Dachshunds
2	Working and Swiss Cattle Dog	**2**	Working	**5**	Pinschers, Schnauzers, Molossoid
		3	Terrier		
3	Terrier	**4**	Toy	**6**	Terrier
4	Toy	**5**	Sporting	**7**	Companion and Toy
5	Gundog			**8**	Retriever, Flushing, Water
		6	Non-sporting	**9**	Pointers
6	Pastoral	**7**	Herding	**10**	Sheep and cattle dogs except Swiss Cattle Dog

so good for the dog, because the very definition of a pure-bred means its gene pool has been closed. No fresh genetic material can be introduced. Once a breed is recognized by a kennel club, only dogs registered with that club can be used in breeding. This preserves the breed's looks but increases the problems of potentially damaging genes locked into the limited gene pool. Inherited medical conditions, such as hip dysplasia, blindness, heart disease, or itchy skin, are more common in some pure-breds than in mutts. When picking a pure-bred, bear in mind the genetic problems of your chosen breed. If you're interested in behaviour, all dogs loosely fall into three groups: those bred to work with people, those bred to work alone, and those bred not to do much.

What are you looking for?

Why do you want a particular type of dog? Familiarity is an excellent reason, because you know what to expect; but

The larger the dog, the more you spend on food, veterinary expenses, and kennel costs.

the behaviour of the breed of your childhood may differ from that breed's behaviour today. Are you choosing for looks? Bear in mind how much time you can invest to maintain those looks. Are you choosing a breed to make a personal statement? Are you going for something unusual to say that you too are different, that you stand out from the crowd? Be honest about why you like a breed and about whether its needs fit your lifestyle.

Size and sex
There's a simple rule in dogdom. Females are almost invariably easier than males. They don't cock their legs everywhere or sneak off to tattoo studios to get LOVE and HATE tattooed on their feet. Early neutering of females prolongs lifespans by 18 months on average. Neutering males doesn't prolong life but almost invariably produces a more manageable individual, especially for the first-time dog owner. The main issue with size is cost; drug bills

can be enormous. Choose a breed by its energy demands and the local exercise area, rather than size. A giant, longhaired breed may be aromatic in a small space, but as long as it is exercised, the question is whether you want to live with a hulk.

Time. Time. Time.
Think about the time you have to invest for the next 12 to 15 years. Some breeds take far longer to train or need much more exercise than others. Some have shorter-than-average lives and take vast amounts of emotional as well as physical time. I can't overemphasize this: a new dog is an enormous investment in time. Most people vastly underestimate how much time they have to devote to their new dog before it becomes what you want: always there, always reliable, a true part of the family.

BREED TRAITS

In the Facts and figures boxes on the following pages, each breed is rated from 1 to 10 according to several characteristics. The figures given come from insurance actuarial statistics.

Excitability means how easily and quickly a dog responds to sights and sounds, and how quickly it recovers an acceptable demeanour. Generally speaking, small dogs (especially terriers) are more excitable than large dogs and score high.

Trainability means ease of obedience training. This is influenced as much by a dog's early environment as it is by its breed. Breeds that were developed to work with us, such as the German Shepherd Dog and Border Collie, are more trainable than those that evolved to live more independent lives, so they score high.

Playfulness means retaining a puppy-like joy in play activity. The higher the score, the more likely it is that the breed will enjoy playing games, with you or other dogs, for its entire life. Poodles score high on playfulness.

Barking means excessive barking. Beagles and a variety of small dogs score high. The higher the score, the more likely it is that the breed barks a lot. This trait might not mean much to you, but it can make or break your relationship with your neighbours!

Pushiness means a breed's natural inclination to dominate its human family. Breeds that are naturally more likely to accept a low position in the family hierarchy, such as the Golden Retriever, score low. These are usually the best breeds for first-time dog owners.

Life expectancy means median life expectancy – the age the majority of the breed should reach. Many live longer.

Labrador Retriever

"Grow up? Me? Grow up?" This is the most popular canine companion in North America, Australia, and Britain by an overwhelming three-to-one ratio, and for good reason. These affectionate dogs can take years to mature, and many, if not most, never do, remaining Peter Pans – lifelong joyous juveniles. Some say they're "nice but dim", but it's more accurate to say that this is a classic "half full" breed, always seeing the positive in life, rather than the negative.

Quiet in repose. Gleeful by nature.

Natural water dogs

The Labrador's seemingly biological need to get wet can be traced to its origins in the Canadian province of Newfoundland. No one knows how the St John's Dog or Lesser Newfoundland developed; it was possibly from the interbreeding of dogs brought to Newfoundland by Portuguese, Basque, Irish, and English cod fishermen. In the early 1800s, some of these water retrievers were brought to English fishing ports and sold to landowners, who

WHAT TO EXPECT

Personality

Labs have a relatively relaxed attitude to life but are extremely energetic, especially when young. They cope well with the unexpected, including children's behaviour, and love affection, asking for it frequently, sometimes plaintively. Labradors are less aggressive than most canines, unlikely to try to dominate you, and relaxed with other dogs. However, they may be miserable watchdogs.

Health

More than 25 inherited medical conditions occur in the Labrador, of which hip, shoulder, or elbow problems are the most common. All reputable breeders use screening to monitor these conditions and check for hereditary eye conditions. Immune-mediated problems, including skin and gut allergies, are increasingly common. Labs can also suffer from an inherited form of juvenile epilepsy. Some lines are susceptible to adverse drug reactions, including reactions to the popular non-steroid anti-inflammatory, Carprofen.

Time taker

Labs shed. A lot! Year round. They wag their tails. A lot! At coffee-table level. They don't mean to knock over coffee cups or grannies, but they do. Unless you match your wardrobe, your home's colour scheme, and your furnishing to your dog, you may find you spend considerably more time house cleaning. Labs also eat. A lot! Twenty-four hours a day if allowed to. Unless you intervene and control their outrageous ability to eat absolutely anything, your dog will end up looking like a giant, waddling, shiny, contented brick, and you'll spend time walking off that weight.

insulating, waterproof down. This is ideal for swimming, an activity all Labradors live for, even if the pool is no more than a water-filled wheel rut.

Breeds for inexperienced owners:
Cavalier King Charles Spaniel
Norfolk and Norwich Terriers
Miniature Schnauzer
Labrador Retriever
Golden Retriever
Yorkshire Terrier

Thumping waggers

This is a breed that lives to please. Because of its relatively calm, adult demeanour, it's a good listener and responds well to obedience training, but be prepared for potential thumping waggers. Labradors with working-dog temperaments have limitless energy. If tail wagging doubles in speed and amplitude when you touch a Lab's head, you've got a high-octane canine whose life-long mantra will be: "Me. Me. Me. Pay attention to happy, smily me."

Don't let that calm puppy to the left fool you. This is what you should expect from a Labrador: a compact, muscular mass of vitality that thrives on activity. Labradors can have apparently boundless energy.

trained them for gun work. Within a few decades, the aristocratic owners of these dogs were so successful in their breeding programmes that the new sporting breed, now called the Labrador, had a written standard and was used throughout the UK. In the later 20th century, the Lab moved from the fields onto our sofas. Whether owned by American, Russian, or French presidents, Swedish, British, or Dutch royalty, it lives to get-wet and then shake itself on its owners.

Show dogs and workers

When choosing a Lab, always check on the family history. Most are bred for show or companionship, but large numbers are also bred for working to the gun or in field trial work. These are almost invariably smaller, lankier individuals with higher energy levels, generally demanding more time to satisfy their higher activity needs.

Colour differences

Breeding Labradors can be genetically tested to determine what colours their pups will be, even whether yellow or chocolate pups will have lightly or heavily pigmented noses. Breeders say yellow Labs are slightly more likely to be destructive or whine when left alone than black ones, although the differences are minimal. The coat consists of shiny guard hair over a dense undercoat of

FACTS AND FIGURES

Height:	55–62cm (21½–24½in)
Weight:	25–36kg (55–80lb)
Life expectancy:	12.6 years
First use:	Gun dog
Country of origin:	Canada/United Kingdom
Colour:	Black, yellow (including shades from almost white to red), chocolate (light or dark)
Excitable:	2–9
Trainable:	8
Vocal:	4
Playful:	8
Pushy puppy:	3–6

75cm (29½in)	
50cm (19¾in)	Adult
25cm (9¾in)	Puppy
0	

German Shepherd Dog

The Labrador Retriever (*see* pages 20–1) may be the Anglo-Saxon world's most popular breed, but elsewhere the imperious German Shepherd Dog wins the popularity sweepstakes by a mile. Even in the UK and USA, the German Shepherd always ranks within the top-five most numerous breeds. Worldwide they number in the millions, all descendants of a small number of working farm dogs in northern Germany – the brilliant success story of possibly the greatest ever canine entrepreneur and publicist, Max von Stephanitz.

Perfect Shepherds

There is often a great difference between what a German Shepherd Dog should be and what you see when you meet one. There is, to my mind, no better dog than one from a reliable line of (often longhaired) working German Shepherds: easy to train and reliably obedient, very playful and dependably good with children, and willing to accept accidental pokes and prods. That's what good Shepherds are like, but unfortunately I see more German Shepherds, always from show lines, that are highly strung, wary worriers, clingy, fearful dogs that turn into fear-biters when approached by strangers. It's such a shame.

Superb promotion

Max von Stephanitz developed the modern German Shepherd Dog just over 100 years ago, from shepherd dogs in northern Germany and adjacent Belgium and the Netherlands. There are still seven recognized varieties of regional shepherd dog breeds in those countries, to give you an accurate picture of the variety he had to work from.

At the outbreak of World War I, he offered dogs to the German military service for free, and they quickly replaced the other breeds, mostly foreign, that were used at the time by Germany's armed forces. By the end of the war, 48,000 German Shepherd Dogs had served as guard dogs, message carriers, and even telephone-cable layers. Some of these were captured or bought by soldiers from Britain, North America, Australia, and New Zealand. Within a year of the war ending, German Shepherd Dogs were to be found around the globe.

In anti-German Britain after World War I, the German Shepherd Dog was renamed the Alsatian; although its international name was adopted in Britain more than 25 years ago, many people still use the name Alsatian.

Hitting Hollywood

In the USA, the noble-looking German Shepherd caught the attention of

FACTS AND FIGURES	
Height:	54–66cm (22–26in)
Weight:	28–44kg (62–97lb)
Life expectancy:	10.3 years
First use:	Guarding
Country of origin:	Northern Germany
Colour:	Black and tan, black, sable, white
Excitable:	3–8
Trainable:	9
Vocal:	5–8
Playful:	5–7
Pushy puppy:	8

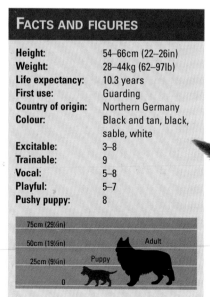

75cm (29½in)
50cm (19½in)
25cm (9¾in)   Adult
                Puppy
         0

One or both ears may lop down temporarily during puppyhood.

Breeds for active, involved owners:
German Shorthaired Pointer
Working Labrador Retriever
English Springer Spaniel
Working Cocker Spaniel
Australian Shepherd
Belgian Shepherds
German Shepherd
Newfoundland
Border Collie
Brittany

Hollywood, and through screen dogs such as Strongheart and Rin Tin Tin, the breed entered the public's consciousness as the epitome of canine reliability, constancy, security, and devotion. The German Shepherd's popularity may ebb and flow just a little, but for the last 50 years it has consistently been the world's favourite guard breed.

Training is essential

Regardless of its name, this is a breed that desperately needs orderly obedience training. Trained well – and they train easily – Shepherds are superb at search and rescue, contraband detection, guarding, guiding the blind, or being a handsome canine addition to the human family. Untrained, they present a real problem, because this is a breed with a naturally high level of aggression toward other dogs and an inclination to want to control you.

Mature dogs like this one are often available from canine rescue centres.

WHAT TO EXPECT

Personality
Think twice about taking the cowering puppy in the corner. German Shepherd Dogs are near the top of the pile when it comes to destructive ability. Separation anxiety (*see* pages 156–7) is particularly common in rescued individuals, and they can redecorate a room faster than you can say "I'll never leave you alone again, my baby." Nervous Shepherds are nothing more than extremely good looking, extremely large lap dogs. They genuinely want to sit on your lap. And will try.

Health
While hip dysplasia is a well-known problem within the breed, the most important cause of the Shepherd's relatively short life expectancy is an inherited loss of use of the hind limbs called degenerative myelopathy, which affects one out of every 50 dogs. Shepherds are also susceptible to inherited digestive disorders and an unpleasant immune-mediated condition causing severe soreness around the anus.

Time taker
Both standard and longhaired Shepherds shed copious quantities of hair, but much of it is coarse and easy to vacuum away. Training is simple but needs constant reinforcement. When exercising your Shepherd, it is important to remain alert and be aware of possible aggression toward or from other dogs. Medical problems are, unfortunately, not uncommon. Expect to spend time finding the right diet, as well as giving a Shepherd the amount of exercise their brains and bodies need.

English Cocker Spaniel

Novice dog owners need to concentrate here, because this breed's official name changes from country to country. In the UK and Europe, it's simply the Cocker Spaniel, but in other parts of the world that's the name of its successful descendant, described opposite. To complicate matters further, the (English) Cocker Spaniel is really two very divergent breeds in the same club, the "show" Cocker and the "working" Cocker. They look considerably different, and each has distinctive behavioural qualities.

This tan and white coat may darken with age.

Smelly affection

What loving dogs all Cockers are: friendly with people and other dogs, and always ready for – in fact, always needing – affection, this is the UK's second most popular breed. They also trail water, snow, and mud through their homes and have droopy lower lips prone to infections that can make them smell like decomposing fish. Cockers have dense coats and are susceptible to a variety of skin conditions. As a consequence, dander and various pollens and spores collect in their coats – factors that are not good for homes with allergy sufferers. As a first dog, they are easy to manage but need routine bathing, grooming, and clipping to control doggy odours.

Working dogs

Breeding lines for working Cockers are often completely different from show-dog lines, although they are sometimes mixed. These are smaller dogs, with less domed heads, shorter ears, and oodles more energy, bred for field work. They are closer in temperament to the original Cockers, developed more than 200 years ago in southwestern England to flush and retrieve woodcock. Just as affection-demanding as their show cousins, working Cockers are generally more active and playful and easier to train, but need much more constant and routine mental and physical stimulation. They have less feathering than show Cockers and so require less trimming.

FACTS AND FIGURES

Height:	38–41cm (15–16in)
Weight:	13–15kg (29–33lb)
Life expectancy:	12.5 years
First use:	Gun dog
Country of origin:	UK
Colour:	More than 30 varieties
Excitable:	5–8
Trainable:	5–9
Vocal:	6
Playful:	5–8
Pushy puppy:	4–10 (Jekyll-Hydes)

50cm (19¾in)
25cm (9¾in)
Adult
Puppy
0

WHAT TO EXPECT

Personality
This is a dog to invest love in, but beware the possibility of a Jekyll/Hyde: a solid blond, red, or black with "avalanche of rage" syndrome, a form of dominance aggression.

Health
Cockers develop heart disease and cancers less frequently than average, yet they live shorter than average due to a high incidence of immune-mediated disorders.

Time taker
Training is simple but body maintenance and grooming time is considerable, as is time spent at the vets. Working cockers need more daily exercise than 'show' types.

American Cocker Spaniel

Thick coat requires daily grooming.

In the 1930s, Cocker Spaniel breeders in the USA who wanted to breed for working qualities broke away to form the English Cocker Spaniel Club. This left the original club free to breed for smaller heads, a more dramatically sloping top line, and silkier coats. From then until 1985, this breed was North America's firm favourite; its popularity has gently waned.

Touch me! Touch me!

The American Cocker Spaniel shares a number of attributes with the English Cocker Spaniel. It's a serious affection hound that thrives on being petted and stroked. American Cockers have a low inclination to fight with other dogs and, once they leave their puppy years, can become relaxed but keen observers of the natural world around them. Except for the occasional solid-coloured individual who has inherited "avalanche of rage" syndrome, a form of dominance aggression, they make gentle, loving companions and form deep bonds with their human families.

Dense forests of hair

The conflict within the Cocker Spaniel club in the USA that created this breed was over glamour and drama. The new "Americanized" Cocker Spaniel, with its long, dense, silky coat, was an enormous success, but this heavy coat also has its drawbacks. Unwittingly, a skin condition called seborrhoea has been increased within the breed. In its dry form this looks like heavy dandruff, and in its oily form it creates a greasy coat; in either form it leads to bacterial skin infections and other skin problems. Thick, dense hair on the ear flaps can also prevent air circulating in the ear canals, leading to ear infections. Heavy hair on the feet acts as a magnet for plant seeds, which can penetrate between the toes.

Solid golden or red colour is sometimes associated with dominance concerns.

FACTS AND FIGURES

Height:	34–39cm (13½–15¼in)
Weight:	11–13kg (24–29lb)
Life expectancy:	12.5 years
First use:	Companion
Country of origin:	USA
Colour:	More than 30 varieties
Excitable:	6
Trainable:	7
Vocal:	6
Playful:	6
Pushy puppy:	4–10

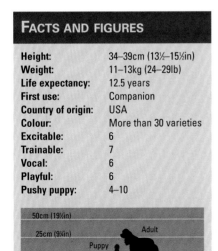

50cm (19½in)
25cm (9¾in)
0
Adult
Puppy

WHAT TO EXPECT

Personality
The American Cocker, while easy to train, is not as rapid a learner as the English Cocker, especially a working English Cocker. It doesn't consider guarding the home as its reason for being; what it wants is to be with you, or on you.

Health
Breeding dogs should be checked for an inherited eye condition called retinal dysplasia. More than 25 inherited conditions occur in the breed, including allergic dermatitis and a serious form of immune-mediated haemolytic anaemia.

Time taker
Maintenance is extensive for this breed. Full body inspections for debris (*see* pages 172–3), especially in ears and between toes, are needed every time a dog walks through dry vegetation.

Golden Retriever

Disclaimer: I have been owned and operated by Golden Retrievers for almost 40 years. I am putty in their paws. It is up to you whether or not you believe what follows. The sun shines out of every single part of a Golden Retriever's gorgeous body. Every little bit. They never roll on disgusting things, never get smelly and wet, and always finish their homework on time. All right, none of that is necessarily true, but Goldens genuinely are highly trainable, playful, and affectionate, and all of mine have told me their only reason for living is to please humanity.

Mature males develop the densest coats.

Biddable best friend
I don't know why this calm, composed breed is sliding in popularity. In the USA it has fallen to fourth place in annual breed registrations, and in the UK it has fallen to seventh place. The Golden thrives in large families and remains the ideal first or family dog for those who want a large companion. I've met Goldens from across Europe, and their owners share an enthusiasm for the outdoors, a willingness to put up with moulting golden hair, and enjoy having a dog as a buddy, rather than as a weapon, a status symbol, or a fashion icon.

Two different breeds
While American standards call for "rich, lustrous golden" hair, British standards allow for cream, and these champagne-coloured dogs have been winning at shows in the UK for the last few decades. One result is that it's now easy to distinguish American and British dogs; another is that temperaments are diverging. In the UK, behaviourists say that this is the breed they see most often for possessive aggression, and most of those referred are very pale. Even so, this is one of the breeds least likely to pick fights with you or other dogs. Two of mine have been great woofers and excellent watchdogs.

FACTS AND FIGURES

Height:	51–61cm (20–24in)
Weight:	27–36kg (59–80lb)
Life expectancy:	12 years
First use:	Gun dog
Country of origin:	UK
Colour:	Dark golden to creamy white
Excitable:	2
Trainable:	9
Vocal:	2–5
Playful:	9
Pushy puppy:	1–3

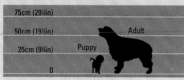

75cm (29½in)
50cm (19½in) — Adult
25cm (9¾in) — Puppy
0

The ears are first to show adult colour.

WHAT TO EXPECT

Personality
Hide your knickers if you have a Golden; it will want to parade them when you have visitors. This breed needs to retrieve and carry, and its need to do things has made it the world's favourite assistance dog.

Health
Breeding dogs should have had their hips and elbows X-rayed for dysplasia and be cleared for inherited eye problems, such as progressive retinal atrophy. Allergy, manifesting as itchy skin or loose stools, is another concern, as are moist skin infections.

Time taker
The coat needs routine brushing and occasional tidying. Obedience and retrieve training is easy, and dogs thrive on advanced training. Rain or shine, assume two hours of daily outdoor activity.

English Springer Spaniel

This is UK's third most popular breed, and it is rapidly increasing in numbers in North America. It is not unlike a turbocharged Golden Retriever in temperament: it loves to be loved and is playful, but desperately needs to think and to do. This very active dog is a common sight at ports of entry, where it has become the most popular breed for contraband detection.

A working-class background

In the late 1800s, British Spaniels were divided into smaller Cockers, for flushing woodcock, and larger Springers for bigger game. In turn, Springers divided into two classes: the smaller Welsh variety, now rather uncommon, and the larger English Springer. This is an excellent first dog, if you put in the work and give it plenty of mental and physical exercise. It's playful, reliable, and as easy to obedience train with kids as the Golden Retriever. It's differentiated by its smaller size and far greater compulsive need to do stuff. Some English Springers vie with Border Collies (*see* page 54) and working Cocker Spaniels (*see* page 24) in their obsessive need to play games, especially retrieve games.

Creative minds

I'm seeing "size creep" in this breed. Over the decades they're getting longer and a little heavier, and today I see individuals as long as small Golden Retrievers. This is not a breed prone to obesity – rather, the opposite: given a choice of food or games, many choose the latter. Pups mature into adults between 18 and 24 months – earlier than many other breeds. Like the Border Collie, this breed thrives on sports, and a caveat is that it creates its own games when bored or home alone (*see* pages 152–3). Its ability to destroy interiors can be breathtaking and wallet-shrinking.

Also available in striking black and white.

(*see* page 54)(*see* page 24)(*see* pages 152–3)

WHAT TO EXPECT

Personality
Even those English Springers bred solely for companionship retain the ability to work. This is a great breed if you're looking for a hunting companion as well as a household pet. English Springers thrive when given additional work, such as search-and-rescue training.

Health
Parents should have been X-rayed for hip dysplasia and had their eyes certified free from signs of inherited lens or retinal disease. As with Cocker Spaniels, seborrhoea is a not-uncommon inherited condition.

Time taker
You have a simple choice: either invest several hours each day in exercising your dog's body and brain, or it will eat all your carpets, curtains, and cushions. Grooming needs are regular brushing and some occasional tidying.

FACTS AND FIGURES

Height:	48–51cm (19–20in)
Weight:	22–24kg (48–53lb)
Life expectancy:	13 years
First use:	Gun dog
Country of origin:	UK
Colour:	Black and white, liver and white
Excitable:	7
Trainable:	9
Vocal:	6
Playful:	10
Pushy puppy:	2

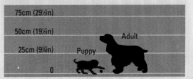

75cm (29½in)
50cm (19½in)
25cm (9¾in)
0

Adult
Puppy

Cavalier King Charles Spaniel

This lustrous chestnut-and-white coat is called "Blenheim".

If ever there was a girly breed, this is it: bashful eyes, an affectionate disposition, looks great in fashionable winter-wear. The tolerant, compliant Cavalier is perennially popular throughout Europe and increasingly popular in North America. And what's curious is that, given the chance, it's not girly at all. Treated like a dog rather than a doll, the Cavalier is robustly confident. Males can be surprisingly cocky, in every sense, with other dogs, even bold enough to challenge much larger ones.

Super city dogs

In my experience there is no better small dog for the first-time dog owner than this responsive, affable, unobtrusive breed. It is easy to obedience train, virtually never challenges for authority, thrives on affection, and settles into a family as one of the kids. A superb urban breed, the Cavalier is as happy on a couch watching natural-history shows as it is in the park chasing squirrels or playing with other dogs. It is almost invariably friendly with strangers, and only those that have not been well socialized when young are wary of other dogs. But there are problems.

Heart-rending health concerns

The male Cavalier's propensity to urine mark every tree trunk, shrub, table corner, or vet's leg is a relatively minor concern. Neutering always dramatically reduces or eliminates this. The real problems are with health. This breed's life is, on average, almost three years shorter than others of this size, almost wholly as a result of a high incidence of heart disease. Almost half of all British Cavaliers have audible heart murmurs by the age of five years. Medication begun at the first sign of heart failure prolongs life by around 18 months, but this distressing and progressive problem is like watching a friend suddenly age a decade in a year. Good breeders avoid lines with early heart disease, raising the age of onset.

WHAT TO EXPECT

Personality
This is a soft-eyed, cuddly, teddy bear of a dog. It is minimally destructive, very playful, good with kids, and won't challenge you for leadership.

Health
As well as heart disease, up to 40 per cent of the breed also suffer varying forms of what can be a painful head and neck condition called syringomyelia. Mild conditions cause scratching near to the ear, as though the dog is playing air guitar. Diagnosis is by MRI scan.

Time taker
Cavaliers are average time takers but most relaxed and happy in the presence of people.

Tan is minimal in tricolours.

FACTS AND FIGURES

Height:	31–33cm (12–13in)
Weight:	5–8kg (11–18lb)
Life expectancy:	10.7 years
First use:	Companion
Country of origin:	UK
Colour:	Chestnut and white (Blenheim), tricolour (black, white and tan), black and tan, solid red (ruby)
Excitable:	4
Trainable:	6
Vocal:	5
Playful:	9
Pushy puppy:	1

50cm (19½in)
25cm (9¾in)
Adult
Puppy
0

Shetland Sheepdog

The remote Shetland Islands off the north coast of Scotland are small. Shetland sheep are small. And so too is the indigenous Shetland Sheepdog. This is, in essence, a miniature Rough Collie, and even though it has been primarily a companion for more than 20 generations, it still retains the aptitudes and abilities of an efficient sheep herder. Shelties are easy to obedience train, and they thrive if given the chance to participate in advanced training, such as agility trials.

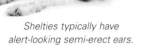
Shelties typically have alert-looking semi-erect ears.

FACTS AND FIGURES	
Height:	35–37cm (14–14½in)
Weight:	6–7kg (13–15lb)
Life expectancy:	13.3 years
First use:	Herding
Country of origin:	UK
Colour:	Tricolour, various bicolours, blue merle
Excitable:	3
Trainable:	9
Vocal:	6–7
Playful:	9
Pushy puppy:	1

50cm (19¾in)

25cm (9¾in) Puppy Adult

0

Fashionable coats

Photographs from the Shetland Islands 150 years ago show dogs similar in size to the modern Sheltie but with far less hair. Their luxurious modern coats are a result of selective breeding for the show ring rather than for their utilitarian activity as sheep herders. Nevertheless, this reserved, sometimes wary breed retains a working dog's mental and physical agility. It learns obedience very easily and has no desire to challenge you or other dogs to see who's the boss. Shelties' retiring disposition makes them inclined to be a little nippy when handled unexpectedly or roughly by strangers or children.

Mental stimulation

Shelties take up little space and are less inclined than some other breeds to destroy your home if left alone. They just curl up and appear sad. Even so, if all the household adults work, think about having someone give your Sheltie daily agility or obedience training (*see* Chapter 3), even showing it in beauty contests – what breeders call "dog show confirmation classes". It needs broad socialization as a pup to ensure it's not frightened by new encounters or events later in life. If you're a new dog owner, puppy parties are virtually compulsory for both you and your dog.

WHAT TO EXPECT

Personality
Like the Cavalier King Charles Spaniel, this is an excellent breed for a first-time dog owner, easy to train and naturally willing to show its pleasure in your company.

Health
Conscientious breeders have their stock certified free of two inherited conditions: Collie eye anomaly and progressive retinal atrophy (PRA). Deafness is associated with some blue merles.

Time taker
Shelties may be small, but they moult vast amounts of hair and need routine, time-consuming grooming. Obedience training is usually fast; consider advanced training.

Pup has a dense undercoat.

West Highland White Terrier

Even in early puppyhood, the Westie's body looks sharp and alert.

Try this word-association test: the next time you meet a vet, ask what's the first word that comes to mind when you say "Westie". Chances are it will be "itchy". The West Highland White is a solid bundle of playful, yappy muscle, an active participant in all activities, a joyous family companion that wants to be one of the kids. But whenever it's not doing something with you, it's likely to be doing something to itself, and that's scratching an itch.

WHAT TO EXPECT

Personality
Westies want to be in your face, actively investigating life. Although some individuals can be nippy, they're wonderful pets for responsible children.

Health
Itchy skin (atopy) and a condition called seborrhoea are common in many lines within the breed. So too is dry eye (keratoconjunctivitis sicca) and, later in life, a chronic, serious cough commonly called "Westie lung disease". All of these are immune-mediated conditions.

Time taker
Not unexpectedly, white Westies are prone to looking a bit grubby. Frequent bathing is essential – not just to keep them clean, but to keep itchiness at bay. Assume you'll spend considerable time on obedience training.

Hunter turned good-looker
While waiting for the ferry to the Isle of Mull a few summers back, I started talking with another man in the queue, accompanied by his two elderly Westies. It was only when he invited my wife and me to visit him at his home, Duntrune Castle, that I realized I was talking to Robin Malcolm, chief of the Clan MacCallum and great-grandson of the man who created the breed snoring in the back of his car. Like most small terriers, the Westie is a bit of an exhibitionist, but it has serious and sober origins. Where these old dogs were now snoozing, Colonel E D Malcolm, out hunting in the late 1800s, mistook his favourite Cairn Terrier for a rabbit and accidentally shot it. Wheaten-coloured Cairns occasionally produced white pups, and from these Colonel Malcolm produced the more visible West Highland White terrier.

Chronically itchy skin
In the UK, the Westie is as popular as the Golden Retriever (*see* page 26), while elsewhere in Europe and North America its numbers are lower, although it is often the most popular terrier. These are little white dynamos – diggers; delvers; bouncy, happy clowns – but as with so many other white-coated breeds, there is a predisposition to both food- and environment-induced itchy skin conditions. You'll get to know your vet well when you live with a Westie.

All shades of white typically occur.

FACTS AND FIGURES

Height:	25.5–28cm (10–11in)
Weight:	7–10kg (15–22lb)
Life expectancy:	12.8 years
First use:	Rabbit hunting
Country of origin:	UK
Colour:	White
Excitable:	10
Trainable:	3
Vocal:	9
Playful:	8
Pushy puppy:	8

50cm (19½in)

25cm (9¾in)   Puppy   Adult

0

Border Terrier

Over the past decade this leggy terrier has galloped out of nowhere and is now one of the ten most popular breeds in the UK; numbers are increasing elsewhere too, and rightly so. Perhaps propitiously, it is a popular pet among vets. This is a "what you see is what you get" dog – a natural athlete that can keep up with horses, let alone joggers. It's uncomplicated, healthy, and, for a terrier, trainable.

Breeds for families with ample spare time:
Old English Sheepdog
Jack Russell Terrier
Siberian Husky
Border Terrier
Border Collie
Weimaraner
Boxer

Standard conformation
Only recently there were considerable differences in the temperaments and looks of Borders bred near the border between Scotland and England and those bred in the south of England. Northern Borders were feistier and lankier, while the southern Borders were more relaxed and had slightly shorter legs. With dramatically increasing popularity, those differences are rapidly disappearing.

Lacking all pretensions
Unlike the Westie, the Border Terrier has rather prosaic origins. They developed willy-nilly from the relatively small dogs living in the border region, dogs that gamely and successfully chased rabbits and foxes into their holes. That they were never fashionably popular saved them from being bred only for looks. The result is a "doggy" dog, a breed without pretensions. Their hard coat is not only dense and waterproof, it also gives a little extra protection from animal bites. Those I see in my practice are reasonably relaxed compared with many other terriers; this makes them more likely to listen to you when you're training them – the most important factor in successful training.

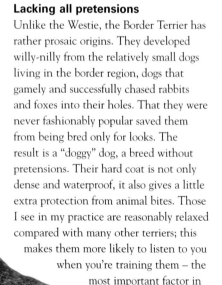

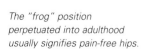
The "frog" position perpetuated into adulthood usually signifies pain-free hips.

FACTS AND FIGURES

Height:	25.5–28cm (10–11in)
Weight:	5–7kg (11–15lb)
Life expectancy:	13.8 years
First use:	Rabbit hunting
Country of origin:	UK
Colour:	Wheaten, tan, red, blue and tan, grey (grizzle)
Excitable:	8
Trainable:	5
Vocal:	6
Playful:	9
Pushy puppy:	6

50cm (19½in)
25cm (9¾in)   Adult
Puppy
0

WHAT TO EXPECT

Personality
This breed's rapid climb in popularity is a reflection of its good health and its unpretentious looks, but perhaps most of all of its equable temperament. Borders fit well into almost any style of family unit.

Health
As their popularity increases, breed-specific inherited medical conditions will emerge, but because the Border terrier evolved almost naturally from a large genetic base, it has the longest life expectancy of all terriers.

Time taker
Borders are self-operating individuals. Training is often a little easier than it is with other terriers, visits to the vet are generally fewer, and grooming the hard coat is fast and simple. Like all terriers, they thrive on plenty of exercise.

Staffordshire Bull Terrier

The Staffie is the most wrongly discriminated-against indigenous breed in Europe. In the UK it is as numerous as the German Shepherd (*see* pages 22–3), and statistics show it causes no more bites than the German Shepherd, but it is banned in many parts of continental Europe, including Germany. Breed-specific legislation is deeply flawed. The Staffie is not a dangerous dog, but some people want to turn theirs into one. Far better to have mandatory classes for expectant owners than the present "breedist" legislation.

Females can be as muscular as this male.

Dual-personality canines

The larger a dog is, the easier it is to turn it into a potentially lethal weapon. The British Staffie is relatively small; much more popular in North America are American Staffordshires, at up to 23kg (51lb), while American Pit Bull Terriers, bred from the American Staffie, are up to 36kg (79lb). All descend from dogs bred for dog fighting, and that predisposition is still there. A faithful, devoted Staffie, affectionate with people, can regress to its dog-fighting ways when another dog appears and, small though it is, can be difficult to control.

Unlimited energy

Staffies are as excitable as dogs come, whirling dervishes thrilled with rough-and-tumble play, in dog heaven when chewing obsessively or chasing and "killing" toys. They are powerfully built, with thigh and jaw muscles that look like the result of steroid abuse. As lovable as their smiling faces are, they do best with experienced owners. Obedience training can be frustrating but is essential. Staffies think the most important part of their job description is pulling on the lead.

Personality
Staffies are playful and affectionate with their family, but their very reactive temperaments can trigger unexpected behaviour. Obsessions and compulsive behaviours are not at all uncommon.

Health
The breed is less pain-sensitive than many others but is prone to hip dysplasia. Caesarians are often needed because of large puppy heads. The bane of all mature, intact male dogs is prostate enlargement. Staffies can also develop prostatic cancer.

Time taker
Early, professional training is essential; walking-on-the lead training (*see* pages 136–7) can be very time consuming. Some individuals benefit from head halters, others from harnesses. Grooming is minimal.

FACTS AND FIGURES

Height:	36–41cm (14–16in)
Weight:	11–17kg (24–38lb)
Life expectancy:	10 years
First use:	Fighting
Country of origin:	UK
Colour:	Any colour except liver, with or without black
Excitable:	10
Trainable:	3–5
Vocal:	7
Playful:	9
Pushy puppy:	8

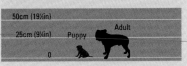

50cm (19½in)
25cm (9¾in) Puppy Adult
0

Pups grow into their surplus skin.

Boxer

What do you call a puppy that never grows up? A Boxer, of course. Reliably one of the top ten breeds in Europe and North America, Boxers show a marked difference in temperament between females and males. Females and neutered

Ears signal calm and contentment.

males live up to their living-catapult reputation and think that it's very, very funny to knock people over then smile; entire males can be more circumspect, even suspicious of strangers.

FACTS AND FIGURES

Height:	53–63cm (21–25in)
Weight:	25–32kg (55–70lb)
Life expectancy:	10.4 years
First use:	Fighting
Country of origin:	Germany
Colour:	Fawn and white, fawn, brindle, occasionally white
Excitable:	8
Trainable:	5
Vocal:	5
Playful:	9
Pushy puppy:	6

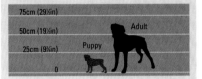

75cm (29½in)	
50cm (19½in)	Adult
25cm (9¾in)	Puppy
0	

Life is for living

This is a high-energy breed that thrives on play and physical activity. It may have developed from an ancient biting breed, the Brabant Bullenbeisser, but its inclination to box with other dogs is no greater than that of others its size. Boxers are boisterous clowns, and females in particular make excellent children's companions. Until only 80 years ago, most Boxers were predominantly white, but when that colour was forbidden (or just frowned upon) in the show ring, it almost ceased to exist. Recently I've seen it start to return.

Controversial ears and tails

The Boxer has been, and still is, as much a victim of fashion as any other breed. The German habit of amputating parts of ears and tails was exported with breeds such as Boxers, Dobermanns (*see* page 52), Schnauzers (*see* page 39), and Great Danes (*see* page 43). Ear amputation, or "cropping", stopped almost at once in many places, although it's still common, particularly in the USA. Tail docking remains pervasive, although technically banned in most of Europe. The procedure leaves a stub of a tail that wags like a demented metronome. When vets X-ray Boxers more than five years old, we see the damaging consequences of this high speed vestige-wagging: extensive, protective new bone formation.

WHAT TO EXPECT

Personality
Boxers are often fearless risk-takers, keen on extreme canine sports of their own making. They need responsible owners to cool their excessive natures.

Health
Boxers' life expectancy is around two years shorter than many other breeds this size. There is a higher-than-average incidence of various dangerous skin cancers and a breed susceptibility to a heart disease called dilated cardiomyopathy or DCM, in which the heart wall thins and the lower chambers dilate.

Time taker
Grooming is minimal, but training can be exasperating with a dog that is too distracted to listen. Ideally, two hours a day should be devoted to exercise when a Boxer is in its physical prime.

Pups are very gangly but rapidly mature into balletic, sometimes demonic athletes.

Yorkshire Terrier

The Yorkshire Terriers of my youth (my family had three) were radically different to those of today. Ours were immutable terriers, bundles of mayhem, fearless in confrontations with porcupines, skunks, and muskrats. Since the 1950s, Yorkies have been dramatically bred down in size, and while "fearless" is still the middle name of many, I see almost equal numbers of worriers – dogs that need a strong cappuccino to help them through each day.

Breeds for homes with allergy sufferers:
Miniature and Toy Poodles
Yorkshire Terrier
Chinese Crested
Chihuahua
Bichon Frise

FACTS AND FIGURES

Height:	23–24cm (9–9½in)
Weight:	Up to 3.2kg (7lb)
Life expectancy:	12.8 years
First use:	Ratting
Country of origin:	UK
Colour:	Black and tan
Excitable:	10
Trainable:	3–5
Vocal:	10
Playful:	8
Pushy puppy:	7

50cm (19½in)
25cm (9¾in)
Puppy   Adult
0

The world's favourite small dog

Yorkshire Terriers had their origins in Scotland but were developed as ratting terriers and acquired their modern name when Scottish mill workers moved to the new mills in Yorkshire, taking their dogs with them. The Yorkie is a classic example of how the breed of your childhood may not be the same breed you meet today. In the 1960s, Yorkies started to replace the then most popular toy dog, the Miniature Poodle (*see* page 44). Today the Yorkie is not only North America's second most popular breed after the Labrador (*see* pages 20–1), it is the world's favourite lapdog. Inevitably, increasing popularity was accompanied by indiscriminate breeding. It didn't help that breed standards placed a low ceiling on breed size. Larger, more laid-back Yorkies dropped from the pool of breeding individuals; small size became their most important selling point, and nervousness gradually became a common characteristic within the breed.

Size still varies

The shrinkage of the Yorkie is such a recent event that it is still not unusual for two small parents to produce a pup that grows to twice their size. Breeders who do not breed for the show ring are happy to perpetuate these larger dogs.

WHAT TO EXPECT

Personality
Even those Yorkies that lack confidence meeting people or other dogs outdoors are natural defenders of your home, yapping dementedly to warn you of visitors. Because of their small size, exercise can be taken on small areas of open land.

Health
Slipping kneecaps are extremely common, and a soft windpipe susceptible to collapse is also frequent. All Yorkies should be walked with harnesses, not collars and leads, to avoid putting pressure on the windpipe.

Time taker
Coats vary from thick and wavy to shiny and thin. Show Yorkies have an exaggerated coat, but pets are usually routinely clipped. In all cases, daily grooming is essential. Teeth need routine brushing to avoid gum disease.

While black and tan is typical, many Yorkies mature to silver and tan.

Chihuahua

This is the breed growing fastest in popularity where I work. And you know what? I don't mind. There was a time when the Chihuahuas I met were all hyper-aggressive little loudmouths, but just as the Yorkie is no longer the breed it once was, so too the Chihuahua has changed, and here the improvements have been excellent. Show breeders prefer very small individuals, but I am seeing many solid, biddable individuals, calm in their demeanour. Although they are still not easy to train, they make reliable tiny companions.

Little Napoleons

They bark a lot, but less than Yorkies. They're excitable, but less than Yorkies, and playful, but less than Yorkies. With a little concentration on your part, they are also trainable, about as trainable as Yorkies. Like so many small breeds, there's a bit of a Napoleon complex within the Chihuahua's mind, which means it often shows its authority through displays of snappy aggression toward other dogs, strangers, or even you.

While longhaired individuals have better thermal insulation, both they and their shorthaired relatives suffer from cold. This is one of the few breeds – Yorkies and Boxers (see page 33) are others – that genuinely benefit from wearing cold-or-wet weather attire.

Mysterious origins

Although the Chihuahua officially comes from Mexico, the breed we know today is likely to have been developed after the arrival of Europeans in that country, by breeding the small indigenous Mexican dogs with brachycephalic imports from Europe. The ancestor usually suggested is the ancient Techichi, although that breed's reputed silence has been lost. However they developed, the first Chihuahuas were exported to the USA in the 1850s, from the neighbouring Mexican state from which they take their name. Chihuahuas are content to be keen observers of the natural world, willing to be transported in shoulder bags by what they consider to be their human slaves.

FACTS AND FIGURES

Height:	15–23cm (6–9in)
Weight:	1–2.7kg (2¼–6lb)
Life expectancy:	13 years
First use:	Companion
Country of origin:	Mexico
Colour:	Any colour
Excitable:	8
Trainable:	3–4 (longhairs more biddable)
Vocal:	8
Playful:	3
Pushy puppy:	8

50cm (19¾in)

25cm (9¾in)

Puppy   Adult

0

WHAT TO EXPECT

Personality
If you are house proud, this is an excellent breed. They are not into destruction, and they housetrain reasonably easily. Their preferred position is on furniture, with you.

Health
Slipping kneecaps are common, as is gum disease, but the Chihuahua's greatest medical threat is trauma from accidentally being stepped on. Their thin bones are very fragile.

Time taker
Longhaired coats need daily brushing, as do the teeth. Exercise can be taken in small open areas. Chihuahuas are happy to be observers rather than participants, and they enjoy owners who take them on their daily visits to coffee shops.

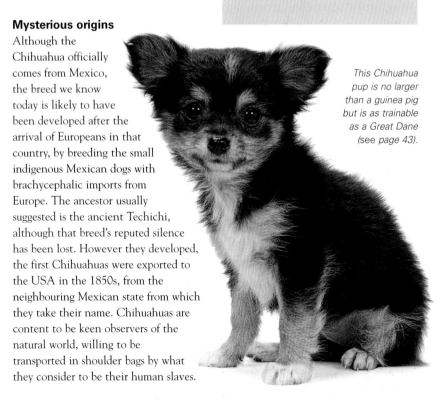

This Chihuahua pup is no larger than a guinea pig but is as trainable as a Great Dane (see page 43).

Pug

One of the best nurses I have at the veterinary clinic is Beatrice, a black Pug. I kid you not. Admittedly, Bea doesn't arrive on her own, she accompanies her veterinary-nurse owner to work each day, but Bea's true role is as the clinic's official meeter, greeter, and eater. With her natural Pug exuberance, she greets dogs as they arrive, distracting worried minds from why they are there. And as our resident eater, she is our canine role model, showing owners that not all Pugs need to grow fat.

Black may have white markings.

The squashed face was exaggerated in the 20th century.

What to Expect

Personality
The Pug's catlike, self-confident independence is endearing to some but an acquired taste to others. The breed has the most wonderfully expressive face. You can see exactly what they're thinking.

Health
Problems include environmental allergies that cause itchy skin (atopy), and dry eye, or keratoconjunctivitis sicca. "Grumbling" Pugs with brachycephalic syndrome need surgical shortening of their soft palates.

Time taker
The eyes, ears, and nasal fold need daily attention. Basic training is easy because Pugs are so food-oriented, but difficult to maintain without routine reinforcement. Expect to spend time at the vet's.

A wolf in disguise?
Can you believe, when you look at this face, that genetically the Pug is closer to the wolf than is the German Shepherd Dog (*see* pages 22–3)? This is a truly ancient breed; both the small size and the brachycephalic skull were developed millennia ago in China. This antiquity explains why it is so frustrating to train. This is a breed created to do nothing, just to be there, offering warmth and companionship. It is not a breed for hot climates, where compromised breathing, excess weight, and heat can be lethal.

Pugnacious survivors
The opinionated Pug has a surprisingly longer-than-average life expectancy. It may snuffle; many are now born with nostrils so tight they need to be surgically enlarged. It is prone to chronic infections of the ear canals and the skin fold over the nose. Caesarian births may be more common than in other breeds, because the pups' heads are so large, and Pugs may look old by the time they are five, but perhaps because of their delight in simply curling up and sleeping, and when not sleeping, eating, they are less prone to lethal illnesses than many other breeds. Minor problems are chronic, and health insurance is essential if you have a Pug.

Facts and Figures

Height:	25.5–28cm (10–11in)
Weight:	6–8kg (13–18lb)
Life expectancy:	13.3 years
First use:	Companion
Country of origin:	China
Colour:	Black, silver, fawn with black mask and markings
Excitable:	5
Trainable:	2
Vocal:	5
Playful:	6
Pushy puppy:	3

50cm (19¾in)

25cm (9¾in)

Puppy   Adult

0

Boston Terrier

Less of a couch potato than the Pug, although still up to Olympic standards in that category, the Boston Terrier's more energetic personality is a product of its ancient history. Its ancestors were 20kg (44lb) fighting dogs, and it was only at the beginning of the last century that the breed's size was reduced to the range that is seen today. This is a perky, entertaining canine companion, affable with people and other dogs, although some males revert to their origins when they think another male is challenging.

Face less flattened than a Pug's.

FACTS AND FIGURES

Height:	28–43cm (11–17in)
Weight:	4.5–11.5kg (10–25lb)
Life expectancy:	12 years
First use:	Companion
Country of origin:	USA
Colour:	Black and white, brindle and white, brindle and red
Excitable:	8
Trainable:	5
Vocal:	8
Playful:	8
Pushy puppy:	8

50cm (19½in)

25cm (9¾in)   Puppy   Adult

0

America's "first" dog

Surprisingly few breeds have developed in North America, and of all of them the Boston Terrier is the perennial favourite, as numerous as American Cocker Spaniels (*see* page 25) and always in the top 20 in canine-popularity lists. It is the nation's self-chosen "national dog". The size range is considerably greater than the Pug's. Most of those I see today in my city-centre veterinary clinic are under 6kg (13lb), but larger individuals are still intentionally bred and shown.

WHAT TO EXPECT

Personality
This is a playful breed, an excellent household companion, and a lively playmate for responsible children. It is also a supreme lounge lizard, making it an excellent apartment dog.

Health
As with Pugs, brachycephalic syndrome can cause breathing difficulties and is corrected by surgery to the nostrils, soft palate, and sometimes adenoid tissue. Atopy is a little less common than in Pugs, and dry eye much less frequent. More than 15 inherited problems are known.

Time taker
Daily facial cleaning is necessary, but coat care is minimal. The Boston can take its exercise in relatively small urban spaces.

Heads and tails
Boston Terriers' tails are not docked, they are naturally short, but in the USA and elsewhere, their ears are sometimes cropped. As far as I'm concerned, this is an extremely unpleasant mutilation, a vestige of their cultural past when ears were amputated to give fighting dogs less loose skin to hold on to. Like all brachycephalic breeds, the Boston is more susceptible to heatstroke, not only when left in cars but also outdoors on hot days. Responsible airlines will not transport these breeds when the ground temperature is higher than 27°C (80°F). With their flat faces, facial swelling from a bee or wasp sting can prove fatal; keep antihistamines handy.

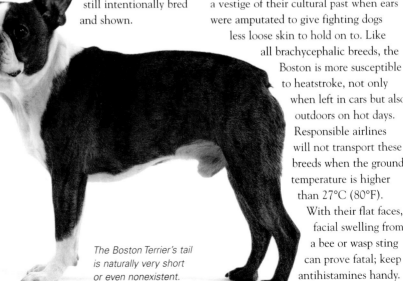

The Boston Terrier's tail is naturally very short or even nonexistent.

Dachshund

The ultimate urban sophisticate, the popular Dachshund comes in more sizes and coat types than any other breed. Variations in temperament within the breed are just as dramatic, and some individuals can be downright challenging. A number of years ago, a behaviourist conducting studies at Crufts Dog Show wrote that, of all breeds, the Shorthaired Miniature Dachshund was the one most likely to stare back and bark when it was just looked at.

Smooth coats only need rubbing. Wire coats need more extensive brushing and combing.

International urban success

Perennially one of the most popular breeds throughout Europe and North America, the Dachshund's smaller numbers in the UK belie its urban success. This is one of the most numerous breeds I see. Standard Dachshunds are less common, although they are more avuncular in their outlook on life. The Miniatures, as well as having the second-longest of all life expectancies, are more numerous because they fit well into city living, needing little open space for daily exercise. Smooth-haired ones need little body maintenance, Wirehairs need a little more, and Longhairs need daily brushing to prevent matts. Dogs bred to European standards have longer legs and more ground clearance – useful traits.

Coat length and personality

There is a direct link between coat length and personality. Wirehairs are by far the most relaxed of the three types. I can't recall ever meeting one that was troublesome to handle. Longhaired Dachsies tend to be shyer, and Smooth-hairs are the most excitable and irritable, with fearful behaviour and defensive aggression not at all uncommon.

FACTS AND FIGURES

Height:	Miniature 20cm (8in)
	Standard 25.5–28cm
	(10–11in)
Weight:	Miniature 4.5–5kg
	(10–11 lb)
	Standard 7–14.5kg
	(15–32lb)
Life expectancy:	Miniature 14.4 years
	Standard 12.2 years
First use:	Earth dogs
Country of origin:	Germany
Colour:	Extensive
Excitable:	4–7
Trainable:	3
Vocal:	7
Playful:	6
Pushy puppy:	4–7

50cm (19¼in)

25cm (9¾in) Adult

Puppy

0

Long hair softens the appearance.

WHAT TO EXPECT

Personality
There is enormous personality variation, but as a general rule, Wirehairs are the most relaxed, Longhairs sometimes slightly less so, and Smooth-hairs have the most varied temperaments.

Health
Slipped discs, causing anything from pain to life-threatening paralysis, are the hazard of all long-backed, short-legged breeds. Even so, the Miniatures live longer than all but Miniature Poodles (*see* page 44).

Time taker
House training and obedience training can both take considerable time, but once accomplished, exercise time is easy. And because these are healthy breeds, time at the vet's is average or less.

Miniature Schnauzer

I know two Miniature Schnauzers that, for years, sat obediently in the car while the family's working Labrador (*see* pages 20–1) was off retrieving shot birds. One year, the dogs left the car and, without any formal training, joined the shoot and diligently brought back eight killed pheasants between them. This is an underestimated breed – noisy, excitable, and playful, but with abilities that are often left untapped.

The coat is usually clipped over the body and tail but left long on the legs.

WHAT TO EXPECT

Personality
Energetic, but more even-tempered than many terriers of the same size, Miniature Schnauzers demand constant play and take matters into their own teeth and paws when they are bored.

Health
Conscientious breeders have potential parents' eyes checked for inherited disorders. Bladder stones occur more frequently than dog average, as do hormonal imbalances affecting the thyroid or adrenal glands.

Time taker
Expect to invest at least one to two hours daily in play time and physical activities, or face the displaced consequences of their natural playfulness. Grooming is time consuming; clipping is usually best left to professional groomers.

Regional variations in temperament

In many ways the Miniature Schnauzer is a more biddable German equivalent of the West Highland White Terrier (*see* page 30) but without the Westie's skin problems. Extreme popularity in North America brought indiscriminate breeding, leading to a problem with both noise and aggression in some dogs. This has not been the case in Europe, where, although the breed retains some of the territory-guarding characteristics of the larger Schnauzer from which it was developed, the Miniature Schnauzer remains an energetic but reliable, even equable, companion for families with responsible children.

A surgically modified breed

Like Poodles (*see* pages 44–5), Schnauzers don't moult but need trims every six to eight weeks to keep their fast-growing coats controlled. Many UK breeders are adamant that they would prefer to pay fines, even go to jail, than to stop docking their dogs' tails, as both UK and European law dictates. Some American breeders are equally adamant that a Miniature Schnauzer is not a Miniature Schnauzer unless its ears are cropped, a practice also prevalent in the new countries of the European Union. Neither of these procedures is of even the remotest value to the dog.

FACTS AND FIGURES

Height:	31–36cm (12–14in)
Weight:	6–8kg (13–18lb)
Life expectancy:	13.2 years
First use:	Ratting
Country of origin:	Germany
Colour:	Salt and pepper, black, silver and black
Excitable:	10
Trainable:	7
Vocal:	8
Playful:	9
Pushy puppy:	6

50cm (19½in)

25cm (9¾in) — Adult

Puppy

0

The ears are naturally semi-erect.

German Pointer

There are three types of German Pointer. The bearded, headstrong German Wirehaired Pointer is overwhelmingly the most popular in its native land but uncommon elsewhere, while the sleek, playful, and slightly smaller German Shorthaired Pointer is consistently among the top 20 most popular breeds in North America and the UK. The gentle, sometimes timid, but reliable German Longhaired Pointer is everywhere quite uncommon, even rare.

German pointers are commonly bred primarily for work.

Jack of all trades

German Pointers are multitasking dogs, bred to scent or sight game, then "point" in the direction of the hunter's quarry. On the hunter's command, they flush the game out of hiding and, once it is shot, retrieve it from land or water. That's quite a tall order, and although they are equally good at various aspects of their work, they are not as good at specific functions, such as retrieving, as are breeds like the Labrador (*see* pages 20–1) and Golden Retriever (*see* page 26), developed wholly for that one purpose. The result is that German Pointers aren't as easy to obedience train. Some lines of Wirehairs are downright fruitbaskets – addicts when it comes to joyful play.

Self-operating brains

That's not to say that training is difficult. It isn't. Shorthairs participate successfully in field trials in both North America and Europe. They are quite reliable with children and bark no more than other pointers. The Wirehairs are the most recently developed, and like Shorthairs, they simply must have routine, daily, vigorous exercise. Without it, they use their mental resourcefulness and create their own, often destructive entertainments.

WHAT TO EXPECT

Personality
Shorthairs are more placid than Wirehairs, and both are very playful. Neither is inherently aggressive, and females in particular make loving family companions for responsible children.

Health
Good breeders have their stock X-rayed for hip dysplasia. A form of self-mutilation called acral lick dermatitis affects this breed, as it does Labradors (*see* pages 20–1) and Dobermanns (*see* page 52).

Time taker
Plan for a minimum of two hours' daily exercise on open ground. Grooming is minimal.

Clean, easy-to-maintain coat.

FACTS AND FIGURES

Height:	Shorthair: 61–66cm (24–26in)
	Wirehair: 61–68cm (24–27in)
Weight:	Shorthair: 20–30kg (44–66lb)
	Wirehair: 27–32kg (59–70lb)
Life expectancy:	12.3 years
First use:	Gundog
Country of origin:	Germany
Colour:	Shorthair: chestnut and white, chestnut
	Wirehair: black or brown roan, white with black or roan
Excitable:	6–8
Trainable:	6
Vocal:	5
Playful:	9
Pushy puppy:	5

75cm (29¼in)

50cm (19½in)

25cm (9¾in)   Puppy   Adult

0

Weimaraner

What a handsome town-and-country dog this is. The Weimaraner's eyes range in colour from Baltic amber through gunmetal grey to winter blue. Its coat is often the colour of forest mushrooms. If you're looking for a dog with natural "presence", this is it. But if you're looking for a large breed that is easy to train, this graceful and athletic dog might not be the first choice. Males in particular can be opinionated and have a continuing need to assert their authority.

Pups often comfortably sit to one side.

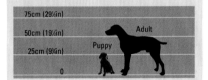

75cm (29½in)
50cm (19½in)   Adult
25cm (9¾in)   Puppy
0

An unusual ghostly colour

This breed's popularity increases year on year. In the UK it already numerically supersedes Pugs (*see* page 36) and is closing in on Dobermanns (*see* page 52). The Weimaraner is, in fact, quite an ancient breed, dating back to the 1600s, although its present conformation was set around 130 years ago. It was once a dual-purpose tracker and retriever, but now the vast majority are bred and raised solely for companionship, although some occasionally participate in obedience work and field trials. While some smaller breeds such as the Whippet (*see* page 53) can be the same colour, this is the only silver-grey-coloured large breed of dog.

Demanding and opinionated

Weimaraners love nothing more than quartering the ground, picking up scent, and tracking whatever is available, usually squirrels, rabbits, or foxes. Males can be headstrong and determined, making obedience training a test of wills. They can also be quite protective of their human families. Females are almost invariably more easy-going, more manageable, and the preferred sex if you are a relatively inexperienced dog owner and thinking of this elegant breed.

Long coat is elegant but still uncommon.

WHAT TO EXPECT

Personality
Males are relatively undemonstrative but naturally astute, capable guards. Training can be a challenge. Both sexes can be rather stubborn and are best in the hands of experienced dog owners.

Health
Weimaraners are 20 times more likely than the average dog to develop gastric torsion and bloat. One quarter of affected dogs die from the condition, and this is the greatest single reason for the breed's short median life expectancy.

Time taker
Grooming time is minimal, while training is more arduous. If they don't release their pent-up energy through at least two hours' daily exercise, Weimaraners can be incredibly destructive.

Rottweiler

Pup typically crosses paws.

If ever there was a breed that needs its tail, this is it. While some Rotties are gregarious personalities and great lickers, an undemonstrative Rottweiler needs all the help it can get to display its emotions – and that, of course, is exactly what tails were made for. Tails act as rudders and help maintain balance, especially when a dog is racing and weaving, but they also display a dog's feelings. Without one, a quiet dog can be difficult to read. Some Rottweilers are reserved, and with these dogs, it can be difficult to know exactly what they are thinking.

Displays of emotions

Many of us, by instinct or by learning, are reasonably adept at reading a dog's feelings, but I still have difficulty reading what a Rottweiler is going to do next. British breeders tell me it's quite simple: just watch their eyes. When they dilate, expect a mood change. Do you know how close you have to get to a Rottie's face to see its dark-brown eyes dilate? It's much better to monitor that perfect broadcaster of moods and emotions, the demonstrative tail. Rotties have retained their tails for almost two decades in some European countries, and in the UK since 2007, but in countries such as the USA, where docking remains popular, you will still have to look deeply into those dark eyes to see what's coming next.

Strong leadership needed?

This is a big bruiser of a breed, one of the strong, silent members of dogdom. It is, of course, an impressive watchdog, but it is more. Although neither particularly playful nor naturally destructive, the Rottweiler is quite easy to obedience train. It thrives when it has a natural leader in the household. This is virtually mandatory, because the Rottie has a natural inclination to dominate or even pick fights with other dogs. The most saddening fact about this teddy bear of a breed is its very short life expectancy, the consequence of the highest incidence of malignant bone cancer of all breeds.

WHAT TO EXPECT

Personality
With early training, an excitable, cuddly bear of a pup quickly grows into a calm, quiet presence in your home. Adolescents can be very bouncy and learn to use their weight to their advantage; adults are among the calmest of dogs. A reliable friend with the family, it can be naturally suspicious of strangers and other dogs.

Health
Hip and elbow dysplasias are very common. Owners have come to expect that their dogs will limp, starting sometimes as early as only a few years of age. Eyelid problems (entropion) also occur in the breed.

Time taker
Grooming is minimal. Training, necessary from an early age, is easy, but routine reinforcement of obedience training is needed, especially in intact males. Their calm, unexcitable demeanour means they can be exercised in moderate-sized open spaces.

Head is relatively large for body.

FACTS AND FIGURES

Height:	58–69cm (23–27in)
Weight:	41–50kg (90–110lb)
Life expectancy:	9.8 years
First use:	Droving/guarding
Country of origin:	Germany
Colour:	Black and tan
Excitable:	1–4
Trainable:	6–7
Vocal:	2
Playful:	2–5
Pushy puppy:	6

75cm (29½in)

50cm (19½in)

Adult

25cm (9¾in)

Puppy

0

Great Dane

This is the other popular heavyweight, by far the most noble and imposing of all popular breeds. Great Danes typically weigh as much as their human owners but are almost invariably much less active. The consequence is that although they are massive – 80 times larger than their Chihuahua relatives (*see* page 35) – once they are mature they are inclined to live at a leisurely pace and are surprisingly adept at city life.

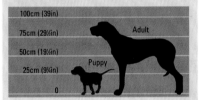

Harlequin colours are least common.

FACTS AND FIGURES

Height:	79–92cm (31–36in)
Weight:	50–80kg (110–176lb)
Life expectancy:	8.4 years
First use:	Guarding
Country of origin:	Germany
Colour:	Fawn, black, blue, brindle, harlequin
Excitable:	2
Trainable:	5
Vocal:	3
Playful:	3
Pushy puppy:	5

WHAT TO EXPECT

Personality
All pups are inquisitive, and Great Dane pups are generally more destructive than Rottweiler pups. Mature Danes are quiet, surprisingly affectionate, but ardent guards.

Health
Health problems are considerable. A dilated heart condition suddenly affects some, and an instability to the vertebrae at the top of the neck can cause wobbler syndrome. Most life threatening is sudden twisting of the stomach (gastric dilatation-volvulus, or bloat). Hip dysplasia is another inherited concern. As with all giant breeds, life expectancy is short.

Time taker
Large as they are, Great Danes are not time fillers. The coat is self-cleaning, training is uncomplicated, and exercise is taken at a leisurely pace.

Identity issues
Breeders say that the Great Dane descends from the fierce Alaunt, a fighting dog brought to Europe by the Alans on their conquests 1,000 years ago from what is now Asian Russia. Genetic studies show that the modern breed was developed within the last 300 years, probably by crossing descendants of the Alaunt mastiffs with greyhound stock. The Great Dane originates in provinces that passed back and forth between Denmark and Germany. It was given its Danish, English, and French names by the French naturalist the Comte de Buffon, but by the late 19th century the Germans knew it as the Deutsche Dogge, and it is now the national dog of Germany.

Size counts
A Great Dane grows faster than any other breed. Calcium supplements are never necessary when pups are fed well-balanced diets, but the vigour of daily exercise must be controlled to prevent unwitting damage to the growth plates of their fast-growing bones. Stairs are fine, relentless running is not. Great Danes are expensive to run. Food and medicines cost more, as does holiday kennelling.

The Great Dane is a breed of mature dignity but endearing gangliness in puppyhood.

Miniature and Toy Poodles

Fashion is surely fickle, and never more so than with the Poodles. In the UK they are in what seems to be permanent decline, and fewer than 1,000 pups of each variety are registered yearly. In North America and across regions of continental Europe, Poodles are still valued for what they are: highly trainable, wonderfully playful, non-moulting dogs that are ideal for families with allergy sufferers.

Coat can be cut like topiary.

Hair needs trimming every four to six weeks.

Size matters

Streamlined, athletic, small Poodles have existed for hundreds of years – bantam versions of tall, elegant Standard Poodles. Early in the 20th century, these small varieties were classified in the UK and North America as either Miniature Poodles or smaller Toy Poodles. This is a shame, because there is a wonderful dynamic spectrum of Poodle sizes, flowing from very small to lanky and tall. European registries are more flexible and recognize the range of individuals that are technically too small to be Standards yet too large to be Miniatures.

Poodles are nobody's "Poodle"

Small Poodles lost their popularity when they came to be portrayed by the media as helpless, feeble, dependent little lapdogs. The press still refers to someone who is a follower rather than a leader as a "Poodle". It is certainly true that, at the height of their popularity in the mid-20th century, there was much indiscriminate breeding and the breed's temperament deteriorated, but that is no longer the case. Virtually every single Miniature and Toy Poodle pup I see today has the potential to be a superb companion. They are less likely to trigger an allergic response in people than other breeds, because skin problems are few and they are bathed and clipped routinely.

WHAT TO EXPECT

Personality
Miniatures are active, alert, obedient, unlikely to try to run your household, and they live for affection. Toys are just a little less playful and perhaps a little more nippy.

Health
Both sizes can suffer from slipping kneecaps, while Miniatures occasionally inherit a predisposition to valvular heart disease. Early gum disease, by four years of age, is extremely common. Because of their good health, small Poodles have longer life expectancies than virtually all other breeds.

Time taker
Health is good, training is simple, and vigorous exercise, which they love, can be taken in small open areas. Clipping and grooming every four to six weeks is best left to professionals.

FACTS AND FIGURES

Height:	Toy 25.5–28cm (10–11in)
	Miniature 28–38cm (11–15cm)
Weight:	Toy 2.5–4kg (5½–9lb)
	Miniature 4.5–8kg (10–18lb)
Life expectancy:	Toy 14.4 years
	Miniature 14.8 years
First use:	Companion
Country of origin:	France
Colour:	Any solid colour
Excitable:	Toy 8, Miniature 7
Trainable:	Toy 7, Miniature 9
Vocal:	Toy 9, Miniature 9
Playful:	Toy 7, Miniature 8
Pushy puppy:	Toy 5, Miniature 4

50cm (19¾in)

25cm (9¾in)

Adult

Puppy

0

Standard Poodle

Those stupid haircuts give such a wrong image. I've come to admire the Standard Poodle more than any other breed. Beneath the often silly canine topiary is a good-tempered, relaxed, highly trainable, working individual. If left unclipped, the continuously growing coat becomes unkempt and may matt into cords and smell, and the risk of skin disease increase. Given a simple, all-over "lamb" cut, Standards look elegant and retain their dignity.

FACTS AND FIGURES

Height:	38cm (15in)
Weight:	20.5–32kg (45–70lb)
Life expectancy:	12 years
First use:	Water dog
Country of origin:	Germany/France
Colour:	Any solid colour
Excitable:	5
Trainable:	9
Vocal:	5
Playful:	9
Pushy puppy:	2

Working origins

Contrary to the image some canine hairdressers want to promote, this is anything but a frivolous breed. The odd haircuts – a popular style calls for shaved legs with puffs of hair left around all the joints – are stylized reminders of their origins as water dogs, bred to retrieve arrows or, later, birds from water. The first Poodles, the Pudeln, were probably developed in Germany and became the French "duck dog", or Caniche. The coat provides excellent insulation and should be left to grow longer on dogs that live where winters are cold.

The root of new breeds

All Poodles, but especially the Standards, are highly trainable, ranking with the best of all breeds. They enjoy interactive play, differentiated from their smaller cousins by their less excitable natures, their quieter character, and, curiously, their lesser need to try to push you around. That's quite a good combination. No wonder the Standard is at the heart of the creation of new breeds such as the Labradoodle and Goldendoodle, or that its smaller compatriots are the bedrock of new combinations such as the Cockapoo and Pekepoo.

WHAT TO EXPECT

Personality
While they are not at all aggressive – less so than many other breeds their size – Standards nevertheless make surprisingly good guards. Moderate in their ways, they are neither particularly destructive nor outrageously playful.

Health
One inherited disorder, sebaceous adenitis, causes chronic skin problems. The breed's very deep chest predisposes it more than almost any other breed to life-threatening stomach rotation, known as gastric dilatation-volvulus, or bloat.

Time taker
Immensely easy and satisfying to train, Standards thrive on vigorous exercise. Grooming is time consuming if you do it yourself; better to have them professionally clipped once a month.

This coat is simply clipped, like a sheep's coat, every six weeks. The face is shaved.

Lhasa Apso

I admit that I still have problems sometimes, when I can only look at them, in telling the difference between a large Shih Tzu and a small Lhasa Apso. But if I'm allowed to interact with them, the difference becomes more apparent. As popular as Shih Tzus in the UK, but less common in the rest of Europe and in North America, the Lhasa Apso is often more circumspect in its temperament, more thoughtful in its response to strangers.

Show dogs have hair over their eyes.

Alert guardians

Some of the ancestors of Lhasas and Shih Tzus were kept as companions and watch dogs by Buddhist monks in both Tibet and neighbouring Bhutan. The Tibetan name for similar dogs in that country is Apso Seng Kyi, which translates approximately as "bark lion sentinel dog". Lhasas certainly do bark, much more so than typical Shih Tzus. They are also pushier with their owners and can be opinionated when it comes to obedience training. The coat is profuse and dense, which is ideal for winter insulation but a challenge to keep clean and tidy, especially with a dog that convinces its owner that grooming really isn't high on his list of priorities.

Healthy and enduring

Lhasas share with Shih Tzus relative good health and a better-than-average median life expectancy. Breeders have told me that it's best to leave the thin puppy coat alone and not to clip it until the adult coat has fully appeared, which is usually by nine months of age. As with Shih Tzus and other similarly longhaired dogs, I feel it is vital to keep the hair away from the eyes. This will dramatically improve sight and, as a consequence, reduces the risk of a dog reacting fearfully to any unexpected handling or activity.

FACTS AND FIGURES

Height:	25.5–28cm (10–11in)
Weight:	6–7kg (13–15lb)
Life expectancy:	13.4 years
First use:	Sentinel
Country of origin:	Tibet
Colour:	Gold, sand, grizzle, slate, smoke grey, black, parti-colour
Excitable:	7
Trainable:	3–4
Vocal:	8
Playful:	4
Pushy puppy:	8

50cm (19½in)

25cm (9¾in)

Adult

Puppy

0

WHAT TO EXPECT

Personality
While almost as affection-demanding as the Shih Tzu, the Lhasa is more of a barker. Some can be quite pushy with their owners, and they get away with it because they look so cute.

Health
Dry eye (keratoconjunctivitis sicca) occurs more frequently than in the Shih Tzu, but otherwise there are few known inherited problems within the breed.

Time taker
Both grooming and training are routine time fillers. In hot weather many dogs have their tummies clipped out to keep them cool. All dogs thrive on exercise, but Lhasas can take theirs on relatively small areas of open ground.

Shih Tzu

This is a fine little urban housedog, happy trotting through mud in the park but even more content when ensconced on a sofa. It appears consistently in the top ten breeds in North America and is now more popular than the Yorkshire Terrier (*see* page 34) in the UK. While some of their ancestors probably came from Tibet, the modern Shih Tzu is a result of breeding in Peking in the late 19th century, in the kennels of the Dowager Empress Tz'u-Hsi.

FACTS AND FIGURES

Height:	25.5–28cm (10–11in)
Weight:	5–7kg (11–15lb)
Life expectancy:	13.4 years
First use:	Sentinel
Country of origin:	Tibet
Colour:	Any colour
Excitable:	9
Trainable:	6
Vocal:	6
Playful:	7
Pushy puppy:	4

50cm (19½in)
25cm (9¾in)   Puppy   Adult
0

Facial hair tied back improves vision.

WHAT TO EXPECT

Personality
Lap-loving affection-seekers, Shih Tzus are excellent dogs for families with children. They are quietly playful, lack the natural aggression of some breeds the same size, and are unlikely to demolish your home.

Health
The two most common inherited health problems are related to their anatomy: eye injuries (keratopathies) and breathing and heart difficulties (brachycephalic syndrome). Cataracts occur in some lines.

Time taker
Although they need only small areas of open ground for exercise and usually need to visit the vet no more than once or twice yearly, daily grooming is essential and takes time and patience.

A constellation of breeds
Small dogs similar to today's Shih Tzus first reached the UK early in the 20th century. Some of these dogs were selectively bred for small size and gregarious spirit, while others were bred for a slightly larger size and a more contained temperament. Eventually the former were recognized as Shih Tzus and the latter as Lhasa Apsos. A third branch of the family is the much less common Tibetan Terrier breed. Some of the Shih Tzus that I see are remarkably like the Pekingese in the drama of their squashed (brachycephalic) faces, but quite consistently, the Shih Tzu is a more trainable breed.

Beautiful but sensitive eyes
The dense, thick, and long coat needs considerable attention, otherwise it tends to knot and mat. While tying the hair on the head in a topknot keeps it out of the eyes and enhances vision, I prefer to see Shih Tzus with neat eyebrow cuts. They have wonderfully luminous, expressive eyes, and if you can't see them clearly, they can't see you either. These prominent eyes, like those of the Pekingese, are relatively less sensitive to touch than those of other breeds. An unfortunate consequence is that eye injuries are regrettably common, especially in the dogs with the flattest faces.

It looks like a cute toy, but this toy has feelings and emotions.

Pomeranian

It may look like a soft, warm powder-puff, but the feisty Pomeranian has a mind all of its own. It's one of the very smallest of all dog breeds but has inherited the strong, dominant, "follow me" character of the German Spitz, from which it was developed more than 100 years ago. At the time when Queen Victoria owned and popularized the breed in the English-speaking world, it was larger, and still known as the Dwarf Spitz or Loulou.

Like a baby fox but more trainable.

Nordic explorers
More than 600 years ago, small-eared, densely coated dogs accompanied the Nordic Vikings on their conquests and travels through the heart of Europe.

WHAT TO EXPECT

Personality
Owners think of Poms as small and frail. Small, yes. Frail, absolutely not. A Pom wants to be boss, and those I meet usually have owners willing to be bossed. My clue about the relationship is in the name. Beware of Poms called "Dynamite".

Health
Gum inflammation and the accumulation of plaque on the teeth, leading to classic canine "death breath", is very common. Poms should either have their teeth brushed routinely or, from an early age, learn how to chew safely on bones or dental chews.

Time taker
Poms need lots of body maintenance, especially daily brushing and combing of their long, straight coats, particularly the plumed, curled tail and the dense undercoat. They are heavy moulters.

The largest of these dogs, the Groß Spitz, were used in what is now Germany for herding livestock, while smaller ones (Mittel and Klein Spitzen) offered companionship. While these three breeds are in decline in Germany and elsewhere, the miniaturized version, named after the old German state of Pomerania, is increasing in popularity in Europe, North America, and Japan. It is surpassed by only two other micro-dogs: the Yorkshire Terrier (*see* page 34) and the Chihuahua (*see* page 35).

Compact thugs?
Although the Pom has acquired a reputation for being yappy and snappy, my experience is that if an individual is treated as a dog from the time it is a pup, rather than as a fragile, helpless ball of fur, and if it is properly obedience trained from the time it joins your family, not only will it not be snappy, it will be impressively responsive to obedience training, and even to agility training. What I can't guarantee is any easy way to reduce the breed's natural inclination to bark. Pomeranians are instinctive watchdog barkers, but they also bark for attention. Some individuals bark just because they like the sound of their own voices.

Breeds for apartment dwellers:
Greyhounds (no kidding!)
Italian Greyhound
French Bulldog
Basset Hound
Affenpinscher
Boston Terrier
Dachshunds
Pomeranian
Bulldog

FACTS AND FIGURES

Height:	22–28cm (8¾–11in)
Weight:	2–2.5kg (4½–5½lb)
Life expectancy:	13 years
First use:	Companion
Country of origin:	Germany
Colour:	White, cream, sable, grey, blue, brown, black, red-orange
Excitable:	8
Trainable:	5
Vocal:	8
Playful:	5
Pushy puppy:	6

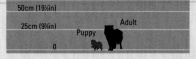

50cm (19¼in)
25cm (9¾in)
Adult
Puppy
0

Maltese

Of all small dogs, the Maltese is perhaps the most laconic. This is a surprisingly easy-going breed, and although the ancient Melita breed from Malta probably arrived on that island through trade with the Far East, the modern Maltese is the result of more recent breeding within the last 200 years, probably involving the Melita but also Miniature Poodles and spaniels. It is a particularly popular dog in Japan.

Ears are half-lopped.

FACTS AND FIGURES	
Height:	20–25.5cm (8–10in)
Weight:	2–3kg (4½–6½lb)
Life expectancy:	13.3 years
First use:	Companion
Country of origin:	Malta
Colour:	White
Excitable:	8
Trainable:	6
Vocal:	8
Playful:	5–7
Pushy puppy:	3

50cm (19¾in)

25cm (9¾in)

Adult

Puppy

0

A white spaniel

Pushiness, aggression, and a highly strung temperament are the job description for many small dogs, but the Maltese is the exception. Its temperament is more like a spaniel's than a terrier's, and I can't recall ever meeting an aggressive Maltese.

WHAT TO EXPECT

Personality
The Maltese is the least aggressive of all popular small breeds. It's also easily trained and not at all destructive – a good combination for a first-time dog owner.

Health
Gum disease is very common. An inherited and distressing liver condition called a liver shunt, or more accurately an extrahepatic portosystemic shunt, also occurs in some breeding lines.

Time taker
The necessary daily brushing and combing of a Maltese takes less time than that needed for a Pomeranian, but equal time needs to be devoted to oral hygiene.

While most of those I see lead rather sedentary lives, given the opportunity the Maltese enjoys typical canine physical activity. They thrive on attention. In fact, they demand affection from their owners.

Amenable and trainable
Like other "doglets", the male Maltese is an inveterate urine marker, desperate to leave his scent on any vertical surface, although he is not as driven in this as is

the Yorkshire Terrier (*see* page 34). The long, silky coat needs daily brushing, which the Maltese resents less than many other small breeds. While all breeds with white coats appear to have a slight predisposition to allergic skin irritation, this is a superb dog for those who want reduced size without the turbocharged temperament that often comes with it. I see one Maltese who was found uninjured after a plane crash, walking around the crash site. Small, but tough as old leather.

A show dog's coat is long, but pets are usually trimmed.

Beagle

Long tail whips with excitement when working.

If there were a canine Olympics, the Beagle would win gold medals in a wide variety of categories: most tolerant of other dogs, best all-round barker, most frustrating to house train, most deaf to obedience training. This is a truly curious breed, a combination of the best and the most exasperating of characteristics. The American variety, seen here, is considerably smaller than its British or French counterparts and is consistently in the five most popular breeds in North America.

Life support system for a nose

The Beagle's nose is absolutely brilliant, and although individual dogs take more perseverance to obedience train than do many other breeds, the contraband detecting "Beagle Brigades" of the Australian Quarantine Inspection Service and the US Department of Agriculture are proof that Beagles are trainable. Embarrassingly for me, I once had a Beagle scent out an illicit apple in my flight bag as I arrived at Logan Airport in Boston.

Lack of pigmentation on the nose is natural.

WHAT TO EXPECT

Personality
It may be the "Snoopy effect", but this is one of the breeds least intimidating to people frightened of dogs. Fortunately, it is also truly one of the most non-threatening.

Health
There are almost 20 known inherited conditions, of which pulmonic stenosis, a breathing problem, is the most common. Distressingly, Beagle epilepsy often responds poorly to anti-convulsant drugs.

Time taker
Beagles encourage their owners to take active exercise, because as far as they're concerned, your only use in the park is to get them there. Bred to work away from people, they then vanish over the horizon. Conversely, grooming time is minimal.

Beagles need good trainers

The Beagle's companionable and forbearing temperament is a logical extension of its evolution. They probably descend from small pack hounds, bred to be carried by mounted hunters. It is their pack temperament that makes them so patient, both with the demands of small children and with challenges laid down by other dogs. It will defend itself if need be, but the Beagle is less inclined than most other breeds to pick fights with other dogs. The word "merry" is often used by breeders to describe the Beagle. "Marching to their own tune" is equally appropriate. When in doubt, a Beagle uses its voice. The howl can be appealingly evocative, but a Beagle left alone is as likely to use a bark as a howl as its preferred method of making contact with the rest of its family. There is no off switch.

FACTS AND FIGURES

Height:	33–41cm (13–16in)
Weight:	8–14kg (18–31lb)
Life expectancy:	13.3 years
First use:	Small game hunter
Country of origin:	UK
Colour:	Tricolour, red and white, lemon and white, orange and white
Excitable:	8
Trainable:	3
Vocal:	10
Playful:	6–8
Pushy puppy:	3

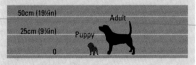

50cm (19¾in)

25cm (9¾in)

Adult

Puppy

0

Bulldog

Until relatively recently, a Bulldog was a walking medical disaster. Breed standards called for extremes such as a head "as large as possible". The result was an extremely bow-legged calamity with chronic skin-fold infections and great difficulty breathing, a dog that more often than not could be born only by Caesarian section, and with the second-shortest life of all breeds, half that of the longest life expectancy. Fortunately, breed standards have improved.

Symbolic breed
They snuffle, they snort, they fart, and when they clear their throats of phlegm even dog lovers leave the room, but this is a perennially popular breed in Anglo-Saxon North America, the UK, and Australia. It could be the Winston Churchill effect, the odd resemblance between Britain's pugnacious prime minister during World War II and a breed that had already gained a reputation for gladiatorial belligerence. Bulldogs look tough. But they're not. Few breeds are less aggressive or more laid back.

Improving health
Most of the bulldogs I've met have spent their lives concentrating on surviving! With a constellation of breathing, heart,

Exaggerated facial folds are related to skin problems.

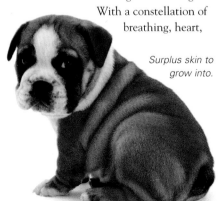

Surplus skin to grow into.

and mobility problems, there was little energy left in the breed for more normal canine pursuits, such as demarcation disputes with other dogs, listening to obedience training, or being playful with other dogs or family members. I'm now seeing a change. As sensible breeders breed their bulldogs back to how they looked 100 years ago, with straighter legs, smaller heads, and obvious necks, a newer, more doggy personality has emerged. These healthier dogs, which live considerably longer than the breed's present short expectancy, are more active and reactive than the Bulldogs of yesterday. It's as if the breed is undergoing a successful personality transplant.

FACTS AND FIGURES

Height:	31–36cm (12–14in)
Weight:	23–25kg (51–55lb)
Life expectancy:	6.7 years
First use:	Bull bating
Country of origin:	UK
Colour:	Fawn, red, brindle; solid or with a black mask or with white
Excitable:	3
Trainable:	3–5
Vocal:	3
Playful:	1–3
Pushy puppy:	3

50cm (19¾in)

25cm (9¾in) Adult

Puppy

0

WHAT TO EXPECT

Personality
Bulldogs are laconic. Just as their faces are compressed, so too are their emotions, unless the latent prey drive is activated and they become demonic. The breed is neither particularly playful nor demanding. They take perseverance to obedience train, but unlike other reluctant learners, they don't invest unused energy in destructiveness. They just lie there, snoring.

Health
Breathing and heart problems; dry eye; cherry eye; eyelid conditions; deafness; hip dysplasia; face, paw, and tail skin conditions…if you have a Bulldog, you soon become a medical expert – and poor if you don't have health insurance.

Time taker
While Bulldogs' daily exercise takes less time than average, time is needed for daily routine skin maintenance. Expect to spend a fair amount of time at the vet's.

Dobermann

The Dobermann should employ professional public-relations agents to overcome unwarranted bad press. Contrary to what you read, this is not a devil dog. Yes, the breed is a natural territory guarder and liberally uses its intimidating voice to state its commanding presence. Yes, it's naturally aggressive with other dogs. But the Dobermann is also one of the easiest breeds to train and is remarkably reliable with its own family.

Naturally lopped ears accentuate the true character of the breed.

The gold standard of hybrids

Today, mixing breeds to create new ones – for example, creating the Labradoodle from the Labrador (*see* pages 20–1) and the Standard Poodle (*see* page 45) – is frowned upon by kennel clubs. But this is exactly what the German tax collector Louis Dobermann did when he crossed Rottweilers (*see* page 42), Weimaraners (*see* page 41), and German Pinschers, adding dashes of Manchester Terrier and English Greyhound to produce this surprisingly affectionate, loyal, but, given the opportunity, amazingly destructive dog. Left with nothing to do, a Dobermann can destroy your home in a day!

Roller-coaster popularity

The Dobie is presently out of favour for two reasons. It's been tagged a dangerous dog, a biter, a threat. The male is certainly a dog biter, but the female is much, much less threatening to other dogs. Because the breed is so easy to obedience train, some owners, usually men, like to train them to be aggressive towards people, but this is learned aggression. It is just as easy, in fact far easier, to train them to enjoy the company of human strangers. Dobies also once had (and in many regions still do have) their ears amputated and their tails docked so that they looked threatening, increasing this bad reputation. The other reason they are out of favour is that poor breeding allowed the trait of nervousness to survive in some Dobies, producing potential fear-biters. Now that their popularity is waning, hopefully their breeding will return to the control of people who select carefully for only their best qualities.

WHAT TO EXPECT

Personality
Left with naturally lopped ears and a long, thin, wagging tail, the Dobie's true personality shows through. This breed thrives on being part of the human family.

Health
A common inherited heart condition called dilated cardiomyopathy is the main reason for this breed's short life expectancy. Other common genetic problems include cervical vertebral instability or wobbler syndrome, intervertebral disc disease, and a blood-clotting disorder, von Willebrand's disease.

Time taker
Grooming time is minimal, and the breed is easy to train, but Dobermanns need large dollops of mental and physical exercise – at the very least, two hours a day.

FACTS AND FIGURES

Height:	61–71cm (24–28in)
Weight:	30–40kg (66–88lb)
Life expectancy:	9.8 years
First use:	Guarding
Country of origin:	Germany
Colour:	Black, brown, fawn, or blue, with red markings
Excitable:	3–5
Trainable:	9
Vocal:	3
Playful:	5–7
Pushy puppy:	9

75cm (29½in)	
50cm (19½in)	Adult
25cm (9¾in)	Puppy
0	

Whippet

Breeds for the house proud:

Miniature and Toy Poodles
Miniature Dachshunds
Italian Greyhound
Bedlington Terrier
Yorkshire Terrier
Bichon Frise
Chihuahua
Whippet
Papillon

This is a breed that some men have difficulty with. They look so girly – the lithe, lean Barbie dolls of dogdom. But men soon learn that living with a Whippet is like having two totally different dogs residing in the same sleek body. Indoors, the whippet is the world's most successful couch potato. Outdoors, it becomes Vlad the Impaler, the shadow of death to squirrels and rabbits. Guys enjoy exercising their Whippets.

FACTS AND FIGURES

Height:	43–51cm (17–20in)
Weight:	12.5–13.5kg (28–30lb)
Life expectancy:	14.3 years
First use:	Rabbit hunting
Country of origin:	UK
Colour:	Any colour
Excitable:	6
Trainable:	6
Vocal:	3
Playful:	5–8
Pushy puppy:	1

75cm (29½in)
50cm (19½in)
25cm (9¾in)
0
Adult
Puppy

Calm, relaxed companionship

This, too, is a breed created by crossing other breeds – in this instance, small greyhounds and terriers. (The Bedlington Terrier, a breed with an equally long life expectancy and similar origins, is much like a curly-haired Whippet.) Whippets are wonderful children's companions, but their long limbs are fragile and can break easily. This is a breed that is virtually never aggressive with people, although, as with all dogs, it will bite if provoked.

Living hot-water bottles

Some breeds have a tendency to gain weight, but this is definitely not one of them. They lay down very little fat, and their skin is thin. With a very fine coat of guard hair and no insulating downy hair, Whippets easily suffer from the cold. As a consequence, they do something that many dog owners adore: they cuddle up to people for warmth, even creeping under the bed covers at night. Their owners call this behaviour "love". Few breeds need outdoor clothing, but in cold or inclement weather, the Whippet certainly does.

WHAT TO EXPECT

Personality
Whippets are calm, docile, and loving. They vividly express their emotions through the set of their extremely mobile ears, the position of their lips, and the look in their eyes.

Health
A typical Whippet has no more than an annual veterinary health check. There are no serious inherited health problems within the breed, but the thin skin is susceptible to tears, and the long, thin bones to fractures.

Time taker
Grooming time is minimal. Training time is average, and so is walking time. Whippets take their own speedy exercise as you walk, then yearn to return to the sofa.

Erect when alert, the ears are flat and the tail tucked when relaxed.

Border Collie

Obsessive? Compulsive? Disordered? The Border Collie may consistently win every single canine intelligence test, but this is a breed that lives on the edge. Where they are popular, animal behaviourists see more Border Collies with behaviour problems (obsessions such as chasing aeroplane shadows from the garden, or chasing their own tails) than any other breed, sometimes all other breeds. To stay sane, this breed needs to "do", and there's often little for city dogs to do.

Thoughtfulness is apparent at ten weeks.

Quizzical head tilting is common when watching or listening.

The best all-rounder

Registration figures belie this single-minded breed's popularity. In rural regions it is one of the most common of all breeds, the working companion of both livestock farmers and non-farming rural families. Invariably, it makes the best search-and-rescue dog, the best agility dog, the best obedience-trials dog, the best canine-athletics dog. It is so darn good at these things that in some activities events are divided, one section open only to Border Collies and another similar event open to all other dogs.

A canine challenge

This doesn't mean that Borders make good pets. Far from it. Breeders of show Borders selectively breed them for a reduced need for physical activity, as well as for show conformation, but even so this remains an amazingly focused breed with an enormous need for physical and well-defined mental stimulation. In the absence of outlets for their high levels of energy, they create their own games: chasing joggers or cyclists, rounding up other dogs in the park. So many people are surprised by the Border's demands on their lives that they are a common sight at rescue centres waiting to be rehomed.

FACTS AND FIGURES

Height:	46–54cm (18–21in)
Weight:	14–22kg (31–48lb)
Life expectancy:	13 years
First use:	Herding
Country of origin:	UK
Colour:	Black and white, tricolour, sable, blue merle, brown, black, red
Excitable:	8
Trainable:	10
Vocal:	3
Playful:	7
Pushy puppy:	5–7

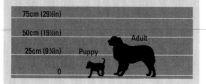

75cm (29½in)
50cm (19½in)
25cm (9¾in) Puppy
0 Adult

WHAT TO EXPECT

Personality

Just because they are so easily obedience trained doesn't mean Borders are reliable. They have a tendency to be fearful and are prone to nipping in pre-emptive defence. Any family with children and a Border Collie must be ever vigilant. Their herding instinct is powerful from puppyhood.

Health

As well as a constellation of eye conditions commonly called Collie eye, Borders are also genetically susceptible to hip dysplasia. Their high level of physical activity makes them more prone than average to physical injuries.

Time taker

All Borders shed profusely, but the long-coated ones need daily brushing and combing. Training is simple, as are different aspects of advanced training. Expect to spend time with dog trainers, discussing behaviour concerns.

Australian Shepherd

To capture the personality of this wonderful breed, think Labrador (*see* pages 20–1) with an IQ transplant. Increasingly popular in North America and becoming better known to dog owners in Europe after winning Crufts Dog Show in England in 2006, the Australian Shepherd exemplifies the transition of dogs from their old practical roles to their new function as affable, participating members of the extended human family. This breed is a harbinger of the future.

An ideal first-time choice

Developed in California around 100 years ago from collies and sheepdogs imported from Australia and New Zealand, this breed is very much like Californians once were: easy-going, laid back, and cool. Whether you want a relatively small dog or a large one, the Australian Shepherd fits the bill; its size range is greater than most other popular breeds. It may still be capable of sheep herding, and it's a winner at agility and obedience trials, but the Aussie's niche is that of an ever-more popular household companion.

Playful and trainable

Generally uninterested in being "top dog", less inclined than most other breeds to be snappy (although still responsive and alert as a watchdog), happy to mess around with kids, this is a superb modern companion dog, in the same category as the Golden Retriever (*see* page 26), Cavalier King Charles Spaniel (*see* page 28), and Shetland Sheepdog (*see* page 29). A potential problem is the tendency among some breeders to breed down in size, which can bring increased nervousness.

This breed shares an intensity of expression with the Border Collie.

(*see* pages 20–1); (*see* page 26); (*see* page 28); (*see* page 29)

WHAT TO EXPECT

Personality
Australian Shepherds are contented extroverts who want to be playful, active kids, with the bonus that they're more trainable than most kids, less aggressive or destructive, and will never, ever experiment with alcohol or drugs.

Health
While hip dysplasia is the only common inherited disorder, deafness may also occur in merles, because it can be associated with the merle colour gene in all breeds.

Time taker
The dense coat sheds copiously and needs daily attention. Obedience training is usually short and easy, but this breed thrives on advanced training, in both games and agility.

FACTS AND FIGURES

Height:	46–58cm (18–23in)
Weight:	16–32kg (35–70lb)
Life expectancy:	13 years
First use:	Herding
Country of origin:	USA
Colour:	Black, blue merle, red merle, red; either solid or with white
Excitable:	7–9
Trainable:	10
Vocal:	4
Playful:	8
Pushy puppy:	2–4

50cm (19½in) 25cm (9¾in) 0 Adult Puppy

Siberian Husky

Look into the light-blue eyes of an alert, intent Siberian Husky and you can see him thinking. This is a haughty, almost imperious breed, but the Siberian Husky is suffering from a surfeit of fashion. I've seen them in Tokyo and Rome, as well as in New York and London. Their numbers are ever increasing, but this is not a city dog. It's a breed that thrives best in the outdoors, the rural outdoors, and especially in crisp, cool weather, pulling something.

Baby blue eyes can persist into adulthood in Huskies.

A supreme athlete, the Siberian husky has phenomenal natural endurance.

Living on the edge

For centuries, the native peoples of the north survived in the harsh Arctic climate only with the help of their dogs. The draught-pulling husky dogs in Alaska, Canada, and Greenland were invariably large, but those used by the Chukchi people of Siberia were smaller and lighter. Just under 100 years ago, fur traders first brought these dogs to Alaska, where they excelled in local sled-pulling dog races. Within 50 years, the Siberian Husky was popular across North America, and in the last 50 years it spread to Europe and Japan.

A primitive breed

Genetic studies suggest that this is a truly ancient breed, and like other ancient breeds, such as the Chow Chow and Akita, the Siberian Husky is naturally aloof and seldom shares its emotions with others. These are independent dogs, and it takes an experienced dog person to train them. However, their innate love of extreme sports makes them ideal companions for people who want to develop recreational winter pursuits with dogs. Small as they are, Siberian Huskies are excellent sled pullers, even better at skijoring or "ski-pulka" – wearing a special harness and pulling a skier.

FACTS AND FIGURES

Height:	51–61cm (20–24in)
Weight:	16–27.5kg (35–60lb)
Life expectancy:	13 years
First use:	Sled pulling
Country of origin:	Russia
Colour:	Any colour for both coat and eyes
Excitable:	8
Trainable:	2
Vocal:	5
Playful:	1
Pushy puppy:	9

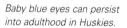

75cm (29½in)
50cm (19½in) — Adult
25cm (9¾in) — Puppy
0

WHAT TO EXPECT

Personality
Stubborn, aloof, predisposed to fighting with other dogs, hard to obedience train, unlikely to back down, this isn't a breed for the inexperienced. On the other hand, it is as handsome as dogs come, and with early experience it can learn to become part of the human household.

Health
With the exception of several eye conditions, the breed is free from serious health conditions.

Time taker
The dense coat needs constant attention. Training is time consuming, and behaviour off the lead unreliable. Hours of daily exercise are needed, as is time to find your delinquent dog after it has wandered off. These are award-winning time takers.

Jack Russell Terrier

These are the hard-muscled, resilient shock troops of the terrier world, feisty, sometimes a bit thuggish, and wonderfully doggy at the same time. Look into the eyes of a Jack Russell and you find them mutely saying, "I'm all right, Jack." Kennel Club registrations indicate that this is an uncommon breed, but that isn't so. Most Jack Russell litters simply aren't registered. These bounce-back bundles of high-octane energy are probably the most popular of all terriers in the UK.

Natural-born nippers

In the dog, some characteristics of wolf behaviour are diminished and others are enhanced. Jack Russell Terriers are tough little nuts. A wolf uses body language to avoid confrontations and fights, but a Jack Russell doesn't bother with such subtleties. "If in doubt, bite" is the breed motto. Fortunately, they're snappy rather than tenacious, but this is still a serious concern if you're contemplating living with a Jack Russell. Discipline training is vital. Males are more aggressive with other dogs than are females, who can be quite relaxed with other canines. Both sexes can be remarkably affectionate with people and thrive when part of household activities.

Hunting history

Take care when walking in the country. Their instinct to enter any animal's earth warren, without thinking about how to get back out, is overwhelming. Jack Russells come in smooth- or wirehaired coats. There is also the longer-legged Parson Russell Terrier, whose ebullient personality is somewhat more biddable than its more popular cousin.

WHAT TO EXPECT

Personality
These are rugged dogs. Although they are small enough to fit into a carryall, even soccer hooligans are happy to be seen in public with them. They make excellent twosomes, although it's best to have one of each sex, because fighting is common in same-sex households.

Health
Vets love Jack Russells. They have no serious inherited disorders, and although they can be a handful to examine and are more prone to physical injuries than many other breeds because of their attitude to life, they respond wonderfully to treatment and are uncomplicated healers.

Time taker
The breed's high energy demands at least two hours' daily mental and physical exercise – Jack Russells are always ready for another game. The wirehaired coat needs daily grooming.

FACTS AND FIGURES

Height:	25.5–31cm (10–12in)
Weight:	4–7kg (9–15lb)
Life expectancy:	13.6 years
First use:	Ratter
Country of origin:	UK
Colour:	Black and white, brown and white, tricolour
Excitable:	9
Trainable:	4–6
Vocal:	3
Playful:	7–9
Pushy puppy:	8 (bitches less)

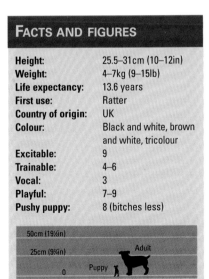

50cm (19¾in)

25cm (9¾in)　　　　Adult

0　　Puppy

The coat may be anything from smooth, to semi-smooth, as here, or wiry.

Cross-breeds and mutts

Mutts are experiencing a renaissance. Where I practice, both accidental and intentional mutts have become a prime choice of socially responsible families, people who believe in recycling. What was once a "cur" is now a "designer dog". Some clubs may still deny mutts a place in events, but from the UK Kennel Club's Scruffts Dog Show to the Mixed Breed Dog Clubs of America, mutts now participate in everything from agility to showmanship.

Cross-breeds and random-breds

The names used to describe dogs that aren't pure-breds can be confusing. Cross-breeds are the offspring of two different pure-bred dogs. Because a certain status is now associated with owning a cross-breed, journalists have coined the rather glib alternative description of "designer dogs". "Mixed-breed" dogs have more than two pure-breds in their heritage, although an individual may still show characteristics that are predominantly from a particular breed or type of dog, such as a terrier or a spaniel. Mixed-breed dogs are also called "random-breds" and have a variety of nicknames, some of which – mutt, bitser, sidewalk special, and Heinz 57 – are affectionate, while others, such as bastard and cur, are more derogatory. The word mongrel is evolving from a neutral term to a derogatory description.

Not yet breeds

A "breed" is a population of dogs with a common genetic heritage and consistent physical and behavioural characteristics. Intentionally cross-bred dogs may have "breed" names like "Maltepoo", but these are not true breeds because they don't yet "breed true". It takes seven or eight generations of selective breeding before there's real consistency in looks and behaviour in the progeny of a breeding programme. This has happened with only one new breed, the Australian Labradoodle, although Cockapoos have also been sufficiently developed to frequently breed true. Cross-bred dogs are sometimes called hybrids. A hybrid is a cross between two different species – for example, a bison and a domestic cow (zubronie), a lion and a tiger (tigon),

A few years ago, this Pug–Shih Tzu cross would have been deemed a mistake. Today, it has been bred for a ready market.

Rescue centres often house larger "mutts", the results of unplanned breeding. This pup's black-and-tan coat, as well as tan or tan and white, are common colours in mixed-breed dogs.

a horse and a donkey (mule). Cross-bred dogs aren't true hybrids, although that's a word that's routinely used for them.

Appearances can be misleading

What you see on the surface may not be what lies beneath. Some pups inherit the physical characteristics of one of their parent breeds but the mental traits of the other. It's impossible to predict what traits will be inherited in any cross. A mutt may look like a German Shepherd (*see* pages 22–3) but have little or no inclination to guard, or it may look like a Golden Retriever (*see* page 26) and defend its territory like a Rottweiler (*see* page 42).

Are mutts smarter?

There is a myth than mutts are more intelligent than pure-breds, and that myth is based on misinterpreted observation.

Pure-breds are usually born in privileged circumstances. They are socialized to people from birth and quickly learn to depend on us for food, safety, and shelter. Mutts, on the other hand, are often born into more deprived environments. As a

result, they learn early in life to protect themselves, to find their own food, and to be independent. They learn to think for themselves. That isn't fundamentally increased intelligence; it's just a different form of learning.

BRUCE'S TIPS ON MIXED-BREEDS

Mixed-breed dogs that come from working stock, especially the Collie and Shepherd mixes, need jobs to do. The simplest job is to make them work for their food. Invest in a rolling ball that drops food when it is nosed or pawed across the floor. Teaching "leave and come" is also vital (*see* pages 128–9). Teach them to use their brains constructively by creating search games (*see* pages 142–5). On the other hand, do absolutely nothing to encourage herding, chasing, or guarding, unless it is part of a structured programme of mental and physical activity. For a dog that has working breeds in its ancestry, don't create situations where he has the opportunity to think he's pack leader. Consider getting professional training advice, especially if you have kids. If you enjoy the outdoors, consider joining a working-dog club. It's far more fun than golf.

Spaniel–Poodle crosses vary dramatically in looks, even within a litter, and appear in a wide variety of mixed colours.

Labradoodles are often light in colour, but black and brown are also selectively bred for.

Authorized alliances

A first-generation cross of two breeds (breeders label these pups "F1") inherits exactly 50 per cent of its DNA from each of its parents. Most intentional cross-breeds you see advertised are F1 pups. Breeders who are interested in the long-

Are mutts better behaved?

Roger Mugford is an animal behaviourist with over 30 years of practical experience and data collecting. He says that mutts are less likely than most pure-breds to have dominance-related behaviour problems, both with their owners and with other dogs, but more likely to have separation anxiety-related problems, because they become more attached to their owners.

DO MUTTS LIVE LONGER?

Dog health-insurance statistics show that the median life expectancy of insured mutts is 13.2 years. This is less than some pure-breds, including Poodles (*see* pages 44–5), Dachshunds (*see* page 38), Chow Chows, Tibetan Terriers, Jack Russells (*see* page 57), and Beagles (*see* page 50).

Labradoodle and Australian Labradoodle

This is the grandparent of the intentional cross-breeds. A Labradoodle is any progeny of Labrador (*see* pages 20–1) to Standard Poodle (*see* page 45) matings; Australian Labradoodles are dogs selectively bred since the 1980s by a breed association well on its way to producing a consistent, standardized, and recognized breed.

Cockapoo/Cockerpoo and Spoodle

These crosses between Cocker Spaniels (*see* pages 24–5) and Poodles (*see* pages 44–5) have been bred for about 20 years. Some breeders aim to produce a breed that conforms to written standards, but these dogs remain more diverse than the Labradoodles, if only because four breeds may be used: American and English Cockers, and Miniature and Toy Poodles.

Pekepoo

Bred in Europe, North America, Japan, and Australia, this blend of Pekingese and Miniature or Toy Poodle (*see* page 44) produces fluffy dogs with dynamically varying temperaments. Many inherit the Poodles' trainability, playfulness, vitality, and pushiness; others inherit the Peke's ability to be a quiet observer, content to act and think on its own, in its own time.

FACTS AND FIGURES

Height:	43–66cm (17–26in)
Weight:	20–40kg (44–88lb)
Life expectancy:	Standard 12.3 years, Medium 13.3 years
Colour:	All Poodle colours, bleaching on maturity
Excitable:	2–9
Trainable:	8–9
Vocal:	Standard 4–5 Medium 4–9
Playful:	8–10
Pushy puppy:	Standard 2–3 Medium 2–4

FACTS AND FIGURES

Height:	Up to 48cm (19in)
Weight:	Up to 13.5kg (30lb)
Life expectancy:	13.6 years
Colour:	All solid colours and combinations
Excitable:	5–8
Trainable:	5–9
Vocal:	6–9
Playful:	5–8
Pushy puppy:	4–10

FACTS AND FIGURES

Height:	Very variable, up to 28cm (11in)
Weight:	2–9kg (4½–20lb)
Life expectancy:	14 years
Colour:	All Poodle and Pekingese colours
Excitable:	7–8
Trainable:	2–9
Vocal:	9
Playful:	2–8
Pushy puppy:	4–8

term potential of creating a new breed then breed from their first-generation crosses, and the offspring are called "F2" crosses. These and subsequent generations are much more variable in looks and temperament than F1 dogs, because they inherit varying proportions of their genes from the parent breeds. This is because an "F2" pup may inherit anywhere between 0 and 100 per cent of its genes from one of the founding parent breeds. By seven or eight generations, this variability has usually stabilized.

Unauthorized alliances

Fashionable cross-breeds are intentionally produced, but the vast proportion of surplus mutts – the dogs that are most likely to show up at dog shelters – are

The Pug's short face is elongated when it is crossed with a Beagle. Puggles are usually very well muscled.

Yorkiepoos rarely show the Yorkie's black-and-tan coat colour. Coats vary markedly, even in litters.

Maltepoo

Maltese (*see* page 49) to Miniature Poodle (*see* page 44) crosses produce mostly light-coloured offspring. Because both parent breeds have similar temperaments, they are more predictable than many other crosses. They are usually quite easy to obedience train and a joy to watch in activities such as agility. Coat care can be demanding and is often best left to professionals.

Puggle

Crossing a pack breed like the Beagle (*see* page 50) with the independent Pug (*see* page 36) results in offspring with unique looks, not unlike old etchings of the Pug's ancestors, and a self-centred spirit that can make them challenging to obedience train. Those that inherit the Beagle's inclination to use their voice can be melodic to some, exasperating to others.

Yorkiepoo

Crossing the Yorkshire Terrier (*see* page 34) with either the Miniature or the Toy Poodle (*see* page 44) produces progeny with dramatically variable coats. Their temperaments show a far greater degree of consistency, and these are almost invariably alert, energetic, playful, and vocal individuals. A large proportion of them also prove to be highly trainable.

FACTS AND FIGURES	
Height:	Variable, 18–28cm (8–10in)
Weight:	Proportional to height, 2.3–5.5kg (5–12lb)
Life expectancy:	14.1 years
Colour:	All colours, but white is most common
Excitable:	7–8
Trainable:	6–9
Vocal:	8
Playful:	5–8
Pushy puppy:	3–5

FACTS AND FIGURES	
Height:	33–38cm (13–15in)
Weight:	8–13.5kg (18–30lb)
Life expectancy:	13.3 years
Colour:	Lemon, fawn, tan, red or black with white markings, often a black mask
Excitable:	5–8
Trainable:	2–3
Vocal:	5–10
Playful:	6
Pushy puppy:	3

FACTS AND FIGURES	
Height:	Variable, 18–38cm (8–15in)
Weight:	Variable, 1.4–6.5kg (3–14lb)
Life expectancy:	13.8 years
Colour:	All colours and mixes
Excitable:	7–10
Trainable:	3–8
Vocal:	9–10
Playful:	7–8
Pushy puppy:	4–7

Maggi, on the right, one of my family's dogs, might look like a Labrador, but is in fact a Border Collie-Labrador cross.

the result of unplanned matings. These unplanned offspring are the "socially challenged" of the dog world – individuals from disadvantaged backgrounds, often poorly socialized to other dogs, sometimes poorly socialized to people too. Some are part guarding breed such as German Shepherd (*see* pages 22–3). Others are part "fighting dog". I've intentionally put that term in quotes, because virtually any dog is a potential fighter with other dogs. "Fighting dogs", such as Pit Bull Terriers, are trained and encouraged to fight, but fighting is part of canine culture.

Most dogs will use threatening body language to avoid a fight. Two factors differentiate "fighting dogs" from other dogs: they are less inclined to avoid fighting; and when they do fight, they are more inclined to bite the forequarters, especially the head and neck, and to hold on. It's the holding on that causes most damage. Those cross-breeds that are part "fighting dog" almost always have behavioural concerns.

MUTTS HAVE ANCESTRY TOO

What's your mutt's genetic make-up?
By 2005, the canine genome was defined enough for scientists to be able to identify a breed from DNA collected from a simple cheek (buccal) swab. In 2008, genetic testing of your mutt's ancestry became commercially available. A cheek swab is analysed, and from that, the breeds in your mutt's ancestry can now be determined.

Labrador crosses

Labrador looks appear to be dominant in crosses, except in crosses with German Shepherds (*see* pages 22–3), when the latter's looks and temper often dominate. Some dogs that look like Labrador crosses can be cases of mistaken identity: they have more hound in their ancestry and are likely to be less trainable and energetic but use their voices more.

German Shepherd crosses

It seems that both the morphological and the behavioural characteristics of the German Shepherd are perpetuated in crosses. They are likely to be both playful and trainable but can also be naturally dominant and prone to using their voice.

Border Collie crosses

Dogs bred to work find it incredibly hard to live quietly at home. Collie crosses usually inherit the Collie temperament and make intensely loving companions but are common in canine rescue centres. Behaviourists see more Collie crosses than any other mutts: behaviour problems, from soiling to barking and destruction, stem from their anxiety when left alone.

FACTS AND FIGURES

Height:	Variable, around 56–63cm (22–25in)
Weight:	Variable, around 25–36kg (55–80lb)
Life expectancy:	Around 12.5 years
Colour:	All colours, often solids
Excitable:	2–9
Trainable:	6–9
Vocal:	4–8
Playful:	5–8
Pushy puppy:	3–8

FACTS AND FIGURES

Height:	Variable, around 55–66cm (22–26in)
Weight:	Variable, around 28–44kg (62–97lb)
Life expectancy:	Around 12 years
Colour:	All colours, but black and tan is common
Excitable:	2–9
Trainable:	6–9
Vocal:	4–8
Playful:	5–8
Pushy puppy:	3–8

FACTS AND FIGURES

Height:	Variable, around 46–54cm (18–21in)
Weight:	Variable, around 14–22kg (31–48lb)
Life expectancy:	Around 13 years
Colour:	Often black or black and white
Excitable:	5–8
Trainable:	5–10
Vocal:	3–8
Playful:	5–8
Pushy puppy:	3–7

Long-term mutts

Continued random breeding within a mixed dog population eventually leads to a high degree of uniformity in the offspring. These dogs typically weigh 15–20kg (33–44lb), stand 40–60cm (15½–23½in) at their shoulders, and are light brown or black in colour. This is what many of the world's feral dogs look like, as do breeds such as the Canaan Dog, Carolina Dog, and Portuguese Podengo, all of which were developed from indigenous mutts – the local "feral" or "pariah" dogs.

Coat colour in dogs that breed on their own often reverts to tan, which is also common in terrier crosses.

POPULAR POODLE CROSSES

It's no accident that most popular new crosses include a Poodle breed. There was a time when Poodles were intensely popular, but they're no longer fashionable. I think this is partly because of the impression given by their demeaning haircuts. Modern dog owners didn't want to own a breed best known for canine topiary. The Poodle's fall from favour is a shame because, when bred for its brain, it's a brilliant breed: responsive, agile, and trainable. Breeders understand this, and although they (falsely) claim that Poodle crosses are "hypoallergenic" and therefore ideal for allergy sufferers, the Poodle is popular because its use guarantees vitality and trainability in the cross-bred pups.

Small terrier crosses

These crosses were once much more common than they are now, although Jack Russell Terrier (*see* page 57) crosses with other types of terrier, large or small, remain the most frequent. Expect any terrier crosses to have a strong prey drive. This makes them potentially troublesome dogs in homes that also have either cats or rabbits as pets.

FACTS AND FIGURES

Height:	Variable, up to 35cm (14in)
Weight:	Variable, usually 4–8kg (9–18lb)
Life expectancy:	Around 13.6 years
Colour:	All colours
Excitable:	7–9
Trainable:	4–6
Vocal:	3–8
Playful:	5–8
Pushy puppy:	5–8

Greyhound crosses

The pure-bred Greyhound is a breed commonly in need of a new home, and although large in size, it needs surprisingly little space in which to live. Greyhound crosses, often called Lurchers, are frequently seen at rescue centres. Lurchers have very variable temperaments, but expect them all to have a powerful prey drive.

FACTS AND FIGURES

Height:	Variable, 69–76cm (27–30in)
Weight:	27–32kg (59–70lb)
Life expectancy:	Around 13.2 years
Colour:	All colours
Excitable:	2–7
Trainable:	2–7
Vocal:	2–7
Playful:	2–7
Pushy puppy:	5–9

Bull Terrier crosses

Often lovable with people, these can be problematic with other dogs and should always be considered potentially dangerous to other small mammals, such as cats and rabbits. The Bull Terrier crosses almost invariably have high energy levels and will need to burn off their exuberant vitality in a controlled manner and environment.

FACTS AND FIGURES

Height:	Very variable, 35–51cm (14–20in)
Weight:	Very variable, 11–30kg (24–66lb)
Life expectancy:	Around 11 years
Colour:	All colours, but usually tan and white, black and white, or brindle
Excitable:	7–10
Trainable:	2–7
Vocal:	2–6
Playful:	5–10
Pushy puppy:	5–9

A new dog that's right for you

Pure-bred or mutt, hopefully you've now narrowed down what you're looking for. Your next decisions are whether to get a pup or an adult, and which sex you prefer. The final challenges are where to find your new dog and how to determine which of the many available is right for you. But before you commit, think again about the dog's needs. Ask yourself whether you are right for a dog. Will you be able to pay for it, provide time and space for it, and offer it mental and physical stimulation? For the next 15 years? Don't be selfish, be honest. Make sure that you're the type of person a dog would choose to live with.

Owners ideal for sensible dogs have:

Plenty of time
Good throwing arm
Great leadership qualities
Forgiving sense of smell
Raincoat for long walks
Patience of a rock
Comfortable lap
Faithfulness

Puppy or adult?

A young pup at eight weeks of age is like plastic, ready to be moulded as you want. It's right in the middle of the most impressionable period in its life, when it's most open to learning new behaviours, and when fears have not yet developed. Behaviourists sometimes use the term "socialization period" to describe this phase in a dog's life, and the advantage of getting a pup when it is young is that the socialization period continues until a pup is around three months old. This means that (provided it comes from a decent background) it's relatively easy to "socialize" a young pup to the activities and realities of its new home. For proper early socializing, pups should stay with their litter mates until they are eight weeks old. Singleton puppies and those who leave the nest too early are more likely to have behaviour problems later.

Acquiring an adult dog is more of a poker game. You get the hand that's dealt you – in this instance, a dog that has been socialized in circumstances you didn't control. Acquiring an adult dog is rewarding, because you know you're giving a home to an unwanted dog, but you're also inheriting the unknown. Inevitably there are behaviours that have to be "unlearned" before the behaviours you want your dog to have are learned.

Male or female

The male dog's brain is "masculinized" just before birth, when his testicles release the male hormone testosterone for a few days. As a result, male pups often grow faster than their female siblings and they are naturally more rambunctious than females.

Female pups are born hormonally neutral. Their hormones start to circulate at puberty, and this is when gender differences in temperament become obvious and apparent, and occasionally troublesome (*see* page 187).

Generally speaking, males are more dominant, active, and destructive, while females demand more affection and are easier to obedience and house train. Early neutering, before puberty, diminishes these differences and perpetuates many aspects of a pup's young temperament.

This eight-week-old Cavalier King Charles Spaniel pup might find me strange, but she is not fearful when I check her weight and eyes.

BRUCE'S TIPS ON VISITS

On your initial visits to possible sources of a new dog, don't take the kids along. They're likely to want either the first dog they see or the only pup that's left. Once you've settled on a breed and a breeder you're happy with, take the kids to help choose an individual from the litter.

Dog sources

While you can control the final third of the socialization period, it's up to the breeder to ensure that a pup has been raised in the best possible environment during its first eight weeks. Touch is perhaps the most important sense for all sociable species, including dogs and humans. An animal's personality is pitifully damaged by the absence of touch. Frequent gentle touching and handling of pups while very young is absolutely essential for good physical and emotional development. That's one reason why it's vital to choose carefully where you get your new dog. A mournful-eyed pet-shop puppy may tug at your heartstrings, but you should be aware of the potential problems you inherit when you acquire a dog from a dubious source, even if you're assured it has a spectacular pedigree.

Word of mouth

Low-tech, old-fashioned, highly reliable, personal recommendation is often (but not always) a good starting point.

Acquaintances sometimes breed from their own dog to perpetuate that line. They may be "amateurs", but often they produce well-loved litters, raised in their

Good rescue centres evaluate behaviour and go on offering advice after dogs are rehomed.

homes and well-socialized. For you, the advantage is that you probably already know the temperament of the mother and the likely size and nature of her pups when they reach maturity.

Internet breeders' websites

A few of these, especially those closely affiliated with individual breed clubs, are excellent, but many of them are very suspect. Beware of those that offer, "for your convenience", to deliver your pup to you. If you're told that, by e-mail or by phone, be extremely suspicious. It's very likely they are in the business of puppy production and don't want you to see the conditions they keep their dogs in.

Pet shops

Again, be very wary. Most pet shops, over 90 per cent according to animal welfare organization surveys, get their pups from commercial puppy farms or "mills". These pups are raised in medically and emotionally appalling circumstances.

Newspaper ads

Good breeders rely on reputation and word of mouth to sell their pups. The best breeders invariably have waiting lists and never need to advertise their stock. Be very wary of newspaper ads for new litters: these are often fronts for puppy mills. They are also the preferred method of "backyard" breeders – people who think they can earn a little extra income by breeding from their pure-bred bitch. Reliable amateur breeders usually have homes for their pups before their bitch is bred and, if they don't have enough, advertise on their vet's notice board.

Veterinary-clinic ads

This is almost invariably an excellent source. The staff will know the mother and sometimes the father too, because they may have acted as matchmakers. You'll be able to get a very accurate picture of any medical problems that might develop. The mother's worming during pregnancy, as well as the pups' parasite treatment, is guaranteed to be up to date. So too is the vaccination history of the breeding pair.

Dog shelters and pounds

The whole gamut of dogs – pure-breds, cross-breds, random-breds, pups, dogs in their physical prime, golden oldies – are available from shelters. You should not set foot in one until you have a firm idea of what you want. I know that sounds harsh, but in choosing a dog, if you don't let your mind rule over your

BRUCE'S TIPS ON BREEDERS

Good breeders will give you the third degree. They want assurance that you will provide a good home for their "babies". There's a Labrador breeder who explains to potential buyers that pups don't come ready trained, that it takes time and effort to produce a fine family pet, a dog that fits into your routines rather than having you fit into his. He then introduces people to a rambunctious male Lab (*see* pages 20–1) who jumps up on them and slobbers on their faces. Then he introduces them to another big male with good manners that sits politely for petting. He explains that this is what a properly trained dog will be like. He lets them ponder this for a minute before he explains that the first dog and this dog are one and the same. He's a responsible dog breeder.

heart, it's so easy to make a mistake. And let's face it, we all become hopelessly sentimental pushovers when we look at dogs behind bars. It's those eyes!

Breed-rescue associations

All breed clubs appoint individual members to be responsible for rehoming members of their breed that have fallen on hard times. A pure-bred may need to be rehomed because it has developed an unexpected behaviour problem, such as "avalanche of rage" syndrome in blond Cocker Spaniels (*see* pages 24–5). But just as common, probably more so, is the dog that needs to find a new home because of changed circumstances in the previous home, such as a death, an illness, or a move into accommodation that prohibits keeping dogs. The breed club's website or your local vet will have the e-mail address or telephone number of the nearest breed-rescue secretary.

Professional breeders

Some might be a bit quirky, single-issue people who think only of their breed, but professional breeders are, by far, the best sources of pure-bred dogs.

But it's not that simple. While some are terrific, others breed only for profit, not for the wellbeing of their dogs or of you. Tread carefully. When visiting a breeder, look for evidence of their "breedism". A door knocker in the form of their breed, dogs on all sofas and chairs, and show ribbons on all walls are excellent signs. Be wary of older pups kept as "potential show dogs". Many spent their formative weeks in a kennel and may find it hard to adjust to family life. The best breeders aren't there to make money, but rather because they truly, madly – let me repeat, *madly* – deeply, love their breed.

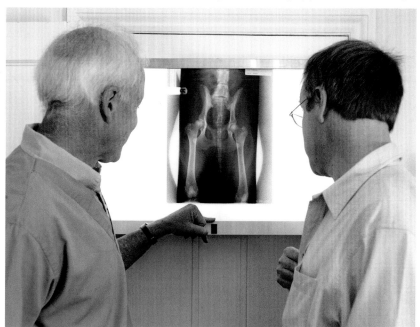

Careful breeders assess potential inherited problems, like hip dysplasia, before breeding.

QUESTIONS TO ASK

- **How long have you been breeding this breed?**
  The longer the better.
- **What's bad about the breed?**
  The more bad things they tell you, the more honest they are.
- **May I see the father?**
  He may be a professional stud dog from another breeder, but the breeder should at least have a picture of him and put you in contact with his owner so you can find out more about his personality.
- **Where do the dogs live?**
  Happy dogs live indoors in a home environment. They make the most sociable companions.
- **May I look around?**
  Conscientious breeders don't mind snoopers seeing how their dogs live.
- **May I see your other dogs?**
  They should all be friendly and approachable.
- **May I return the pup if there's an unexpected problem?**
  The best breeders demand that their pup is returned if there's any problem.
- **May I speak to others you've sold pups to?**
  Good breeders are confident about the success of their dogs.
- **Has your vet examined the litter?**
  The breeder should be willing to give you the name and telephone number of their vet.
- **Do you register health survey results on your breeding stock with the kennel club?**
  Good breeders are proud of the quality of their breeding stock and register the results. In more efficient countries such as Sweden, the registration of results is a condition of breed registration.
- **How often do you breed from the mother?**
  Good breeders, and kennel clubs, limit the number of litters a mother can have.

Assessing a puppy

Pedigrees mean nothing. A pedigree only indicates who the ancestors were. What you want to know about is the health and temperaments of the ancestors, and whether the pup you are considering was raised in a physically and emotionally healthy environment.

Registration with a kennel club means that paperwork has been completed, but it doesn't mean that facts have been checked. Most kennel clubs operate an honour system for registration. Once DNA fingerprinting is routinely used, breeding records will be more accurate (and honest).

Check that the mother and father have both been cleared by schemes to monitor inherited conditions such as hip or elbow dysplasia and eye problems.

Check how many breeds the breeder has; if more than one, the other breeds should have attributes you'd expect the breeder to be interested in. For example, you shouldn't be surprised if a breeder has working Labradors (*see* pages 20–1) and

working Cocker Spaniels (*see* pages 24–5), but you should be if she has Chihuahuas (*see* page 35) and Akitas.

Good breeders know their litters: they can tell you which pup is shy, which is active. Rely on their advice in choosing.

These Labrador pups are being raised in an "anything goes" home as potential "fur people." Watch how they react to each other. Dominant pups tend to make dominant adults.

Assessing a puppy's personality

With only one visit to see a litter, it's almost impossible to assess what type of personality a pup will develop. Besides, much of an adult's behaviour is based on learning and experience.

There is one exception, however, and that is testing a pup for innate, natural dominance. Pups that are dominant as youngsters are likely to grow into dominant adults. Alert pups that don't wriggle, squirm, and threaten when gently picked up may or may not develop into dominant characters, but youngsters who do are very likely to grow into challenging adults.

Experienced breeders know the personalities of individual pups and can keep written records. If you do a few simple tests (*see* box, left) weekly from six weeks of age, you can more accurately assess dominance.

TESTING FOR DOMINANCE

Carry out the following tests in a quiet place, away from the mother and littermates. You will usually, but not always, get similar scores on the different tests.

Pick up the dog.

1 Shivering	**2** Tentative	**3** Relaxed	**4** Resistant	**5** Aggressive

Place the pup on the ground in a new, quiet area and watch.

1 Shivering	**2** Tentative	**3** Relaxed	**4** Inquisitive	**5** Exuberantly curious

Roll the pup on its back for a minute.

1 Shivering	**2** Tentative	**3** Relaxed	**4** Wriggly	**5** Aggressive

Place the pup, facing you, 2m (6½ft) in front of you, kneel down, and call.

1 Doesn't move	**2** Tentative	**3** Slow walk	**4** Runs	**5** Mows you down

Pups that are insecure or nervous score lowest, while confident, potentially dominant dogs score highest. Both extremes are best with experienced dog owners. If you are a new dog owner, dogs with middle scores are likely to be the easiest for you to manage.

Assessing an adult dog

Efficient rescue centres assess both the health and the behaviour of their canine guests and should have written records of these assessments. Once more, if you have kids, don't take them with you on the first visit.

Check out the quality of the rescue centre as well as the staff. Both should be clean, organized, and efficient. Don't be too distracted by barking. Traditional dog kennels, with rows of housing units, actually promote dogs barking; however, more modern ones, where the units are built in the round so that dogs can easily see each other, reduce the amount of barking. Barking can be a behaviour problem that has unwittingly been created during a dog's stay at an old-fashioned kennel.

A dog's health

All dogs at rescue centres should be microchipped. Check that all have been fully vaccinated against the diseases that are common in your area, as well as treated for external and internal parasites.

Find out what they do to prevent infectious forms of canine cough. All the common forms of infectious cough are highly transmissible in crowded places, so much so they are often called "kennel cough". In the best kennels, new arrivals are housed separately for a week, to ensure they aren't bringing any of the forms of canine cough into the kennels.

When you see a dog that appeals to you, ask whether it is a stray or it has been handed in. If a dog has been handed in, a medical and behavioural history

Ensure adult dogs are assessed for inherited or acquired health problems. I am checking this rescue Labrador for vision problems.

CHIPS

A microchip is a device the size of a grain of rice, which emits electromagnetic energy. It's easily injected under the skin, and when an electromagnetic "reader" is passed over it, the reader receives a unique sequence of numbers. This accurately identifies individual dogs. Microchips don't move if the site is left untouched for 24 hours after injection. All readers can read all microchips, except some old American models that read only American-made chips. Pet travel schemes allow you to take your dog to rabies-free regions such as Hawaii, the UK, Ireland, Sweden, or Norway without going through quarantine. All such schemes insist on microchip identification.

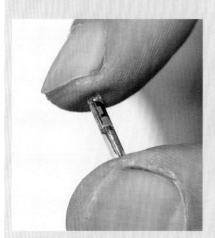

Microchips have an extremely low failure rate but should be scanned at least yearly to ensure they still emit their unique code.

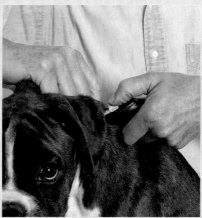

Chips are injected either midline on the top of the neck, just in front of the shoulder blades, or, in most European countries, just to the left.

The chips I use have a thermometer to give a dog's temperature, as well as its number. This is almost identical to rectal temperature.

Don't count on any dog being reliable off the lead when they see other animals.

might be available. In either instance, all good centres have their dogs' health status checked by a vet.

Expect the unexpected

All recycled adult dogs will come with unexpected baggage. Some might be wary of children or try to dominate them.

Some might lack sociability with strangers but be great with strange dogs, or be terrific with unknown people and try to kill any dog they see. All good rescue centres evaluate the behaviour of their guests. You should be told about an individual's sociability with people or other dogs, his energy level, the strength of his personality, his need for affection, his degree of independence, and both his training and trainability.

Expect separation issues

A rescued dog abruptly moves into a new cultural climate when it joins your family. After fending for itself, making its own decisions, after "doing" for all of its life, a rescued dog is expected to "do nothing". That's tough – really tough – especially for a dog that's become street smart.

The statistics from dog trainers are compelling. Overwhelmingly, the most common problems you should expect from a rescued adult mutt are those that are related to not being given stuff to do, and this is at its worst when they are left at home alone with lots of space to run around, from room to room, window to window. Whenever possible, condition your new adult dog to an indoor kennel,

---

Many medical conditions have a genetic component to them, and the best way to reduce their incidence is by breeding from dogs free of these conditions. Screening tests for inherited eye or joint problems, such as progressive retinal atrophy and hip dysplasia, are routinely used by all conscientious breeders. The most honest breeders will include the results of these tests in the registration documents for their pups. If you are buying a pure-bred dog, check with your vet or on the Internet to see what specific screening tests are available for that breed. Temperament problems are also genetic, and families of dogs with known problems should not be used in breeding. In the next few years, more DNA tests for inherited conditions will become available. Good breeders will use these in breeding programmes.

Response to training test?

1 Kneel in front of your dog, and while making gentle eye contact, offer a treat. A responsive dog should not react worryingly to your eye contact and should be happy to take the treat.

2 Without staring directly at the dog or looming over it, lean forward, reach out with your hand and touch the side of its ear. A responsive dog is comfortable with your doing so.

its own personal space; under a table can be a good location for a dog crate (*see* pages 80–1). Once your dog considers this as a secure place, its personal home, it becomes so much easier for you to maintain equilibrium at home, to quietly remove your dog from stimuli such as the doorbell until it is calm and controlled. This is especially important for Collie crosses (*see* page 62) with exaggerated herding drives, German Shepherd crosses (*see* page 62) with intense guarding instincts, and terrier crosses (*see* page 63) with powerful prey drives.

Assess personality outside kennels

A dog's behaviour outside the rescue centre can be radically different from that in the kennels. You can assess a dog's potential obedience by visiting a neutral territory – for example, a local park, where it can meet other dogs and other animals, play with toys, and see joggers, prams, or skateboarders. This is also the ideal place to learn how a dog responds to grooming. Even the mildest-looking dog can have a strong prey drive – an instinct to chase anything on two or four legs – even if it shows no interest when on the lead.

Adoption procedures

When adopting a dog, do check out the centre's adoption procedures.

I don't just mean warranties on health and "sale or return" policy. Good rescue centres want to continue rehoming new dogs, not just recycling dogs they have previously homed. These centres will give you written instructions on training, feeding, and preventive health care. The best provide continuing advice on basic obedience training and overcoming behaviour problems; some even offer continuing help with health problems.

You're a mere human so you won't see what a dog sees: really scary monsters lurking in the most unimaginable places. With any adult dog, but especially one you don't yet know, expect the unexpected. Something as innocuous as a plastic bag blowing along the ground might spook even the biggest, proudest, and seemingly most thuggish of dogs. I've known dogs that are frightened by:

- Babies
- Children
- Adults
- Elderly people
- People wearing uniforms, especially with hats or helmets
- People wearing backpacks or baby carriers, or pulling wheeled luggage
- People exercising, especially joggers and rollerbladers
- People who are shouting or drunk
- Other animals, small or large, even friendly puppies
- Vehicles, especially if they make unusual noises
- Natural noises, such as thunder, and manmade noises, such as fireworks
- Construction sites, including sounds, equipment, and the sight of workers
- Remote-control toys
- Surfaces they aren't familiar with, such as decking or stone floors
- Household items, such as vacuum cleaners and hairdryers
- Stairs with open treads
- Car washes
- Public transport.

Just about anything can spook a dog. When choosing an adult dog, the fewer scary monsters it sees, the easier your life will be.

All dogs, young or old, have varying degrees of curiosity and potential fear. Always let your new dog, under supervision, inspect the new and unfamiliar.

Chapter 2
A new dog in the family

Be prepared

Every day at the clinic, I meet caring, considerate, giving people, the most nurturing individuals, willing to invest time, money, and emotions in looking after companion animals. Yet there's no denying that many, in fact most, of these fine, intelligent people are dramatically – sometimes hopelessly – ill prepared for what happens when a new dog, pup or adult, arrives in their home. Preparation doesn't just mean having the right equipment – it also means having a consistent plan, the right attitude, ensuring that your mind overrules your pup's "big brown eyes" routine.

QUESTIONS AND ANSWERS

What does a new dog want from me?

The answer is extraordinarily simple. Dogs are motivated by food, mental and physical activity, a feeling of security, and a consistency in life. To feel safe and to know where they stand in the social order of living with us, dogs need and want your instant feedback.

Are you really prepared?

The right time to get a new dog is after you've completed your canine parenting education (*see* pages 12–17). If you've done that successfully, you've chosen wisely (*see* pages 64–71). You've chosen a pup that was raised inside someone's home, not in social isolation, and that has been accustomed to all types of noises – from vacuum cleaners to clothes dryers to screaming kids – has met other animals and all sorts of people, has been given chewy toys to play with, and has started housetraining and obedience training. If that's not what you've chosen, you've already given yourself a handicap and need to play catch-up. If that's the case, this book is not enough. If you're bringing a new dog into your home that needs not just training but rehabilitation as well, get involved with a good trainer now (*see* page 125). If you don't, problems may worsen day by day. A local dog club can often help put you in touch with an owner who has already "road-tested" your breed.

Time is short

The most impressionable period in your new dog's life is its first three months, and by five months of age this open learning period is closing down. The origins of most behaviour problems and temperament quirks can be traced to this time, which is why training a newly acquired adult dog is more challenging (*see* pages 86–91).

The day you get your puppy, the clock is running. And time flies. There is so much to teach, and nearly everything needs to start within a period of just 12 weeks, when your puppy is between eight and twenty weeks of age. It is

This may have bars but it's not a jail. A crate is a safe, secure, and comfortable den.

paramount that you know what you need to teach, and how to teach it, *before* your puppy comes home.

Good socialization

Good socialization means carefully and systematically exposing your new puppy to what its future life will involve. That means all aspects of life – other dogs and other species of animals, different types of people, new environments with varying surfaces to walk on, being touched not just by you but by strangers too. Good socialization means introducing each new situation in such a way that it's attractive, interesting, and fun, not

frightening. Good socialization produces confident, "bombproof" dogs, ready for virtually any challenge that life provides. Dogs raised in a noisy, crowded, urban environment are invariably better socialized than dogs raised in a sheltered rural setting. When introducing your new dog to the sights and sounds of life, it's vital for you to be on the lookout for signs of stress and fear: panting, shivering, trepidation, submissive urinating. If you don't recognize these obvious signs, you

may be pressing the dog into a situation that it can't yet deal with and, in doing so, creating potential fear, aggression, or anxiety problems for the future.

Train your family to train your dog

Before your new dog comes home, decide who is to take primary responsibility for your new canine companion. In a nuclear family, this is usually whoever takes care of the kids. In other family

Play games frequently with your new dog. The crate is used only when you can't give your dog your full attention.

units, an individual should take charge and be responsible for ensuring that all the other members of the family have a consistent approach. WARNING: men are invariably the weak link in the system. They are the ones who let the puppy roam rather than play in its pen, who feed the puppy excessively without having the pup do something in return, and who play games that create future problems rather than form a biddable personality. Be consistent. Write down your house rules, starting with "Nobody spoils the dog". Designate who's in charge when the primary carer is absent. Post lists of rules in appropriate places and stick to them.

Dogs should be safely secured when travelling. If your car is not suitable for a travel crate, use a seatbelt harness.

The essential shopping list

Shopping is fun, and later on you can indulge yourself (*see* pages 106–11), but right now keep it simple. Your new dog needs only a few essential items: a lightweight nylon collar (with identity tag) and lead, non-slipping food and water bowls, food, enticing treats such as freeze-dried liver, three hollow chew toys, a crate (with bedding and a cover) large enough for your pup to grow into, an exercise pen, a grooming brush, comb, or glove, and its own towel.

Puppy-proofing your home

A pup's ingenuity can be stunning. Given the opportunity, an innocent-looking, doe-eyed, cuddly pup can open cabinets and cupboards, yank cloths off tables, find items you didn't know you'd

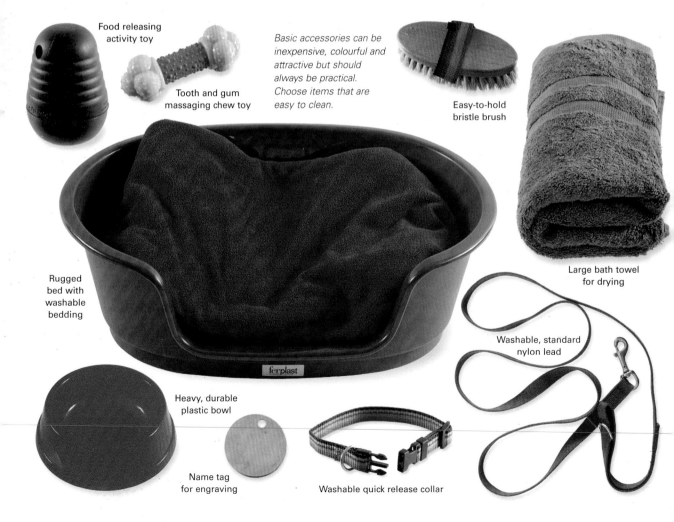

Food releasing activity toy

Tooth and gum massaging chew toy

Basic accessories can be inexpensive, colourful and attractive but should always be practical. Choose items that are easy to clean.

Easy-to-hold bristle brush

Large bath towel for drying

Rugged bed with washable bedding

ferplast

Washable, standard nylon lead

Heavy, durable plastic bowl

Name tag for engraving

Washable quick release collar

Growth hormone is released when a puppy is asleep. Pups need to rest, not just because they're tired, but to grow.

lost or didn't know you had, deflower your houseplants, and chew to China. Initially your pup will be restricted to a single room when outside the playpen, but before bringing it home, do a "safety audit" of all the places it can find. Dogs taste life. Chewable items include electrical and telephone cords, curtain cords, rugs, houseplants, or, in the case of my own last dog, one-of-a-kind antique Swedish furniture that had survived for over 200 years in their original paint until Macy came alone.

Handling your new puppy

Most of us dog owners innately know we feel better – more relaxed – when we stroke our dogs. And it's now over 30 years since scientists confirmed those beneficial physiological effects, the lowering of your blood pressure and your heart rate. If you want a cuddly dog that enjoys your touch, you must pick up,

stroke, cuddle, and groom your new dog regularly. If it struggles when picked up, hold it gently while talking soothingly and stroking its ears, chest, or even between its eyes. Give a titbit when it calms down. Your dog needs to feel safe in your arms. Temperaments vary, but touch is a vital sensation for all dogs too, and usually, very quickly, they calm down.

The ride home

Take your new pup's crate (*see* pages 80–1), some bedding for the crate, and someone responsible with you when you collect your new dog. If the breeder has a small towel with the litter's scent on it, put this in the crate to give a feeling of familiarity. Before embarking on your drive back home, let the puppy play vigorously for a time. If you're lucky, it will then sleep for part or all of the journey, but if it's awake, keep any activity to a minimum.

BRUCE'S TIPS ON TRAVEL

A car journey may be a new experience for the pup, so don't be surprised if it suffers from motion sickness during the ride home. Bring wet wipes with you, and ask the breeder not to feed or water the pup for three hours before travel.

Travel during a cool time of day, ensure plenty of fresh air, and during the journey have the puppy minder distract the pup if necessary with fingers through the crate.

Break the journey home if it takes longer than 90 minutes; make sure your puppy has a collar on and you have total control if you let it out of the car. Don't try to walk the puppy on a leash unless it has already learned how to do so. That will come later. Attach a leash to the collar, simply for security when you let your pup out of the car, and apply as little pressure as possible.

The first day and night

Believe me, if you start by giving your new dog a personal den and playroom (*see* page 87) and at first introduce it to other areas only under vigilant supervision, the behaviour of your kids and spouse will give you more problems than your dog ever will. It's amazingly easy to introduce a pup into your home if you do it properly; it's jaw-clenchingly frustrating if you start wrong. The rules are really simple. You want your dog to feel relaxed in its own space, to play there without wreaking havoc, to chew, and to empty both tanks where both of you are happy for it to do so.

A radio playing soft music often helps to calm an agitated dog.

Naming your dog

Some dogs inherit a name, like Sparkie III, others earn one by their looks or nature. I know a scruffy Yorkie (*see* page 34) named Shmatta, the Polish or Yiddish for "rag", a Golden Retriever (*see* page 26) named Cheeseburger, because it's what he loves and the colour he is, and an uncomplicated Jack Russell Terrier (*see* page 57) named Wysiwyg, the acronym for "What you see is what you get". However you name your new dog, aim for something simple, with few syllables and sharp consonants. Rex is an excellent name for a dog: distinctive, short, and easy to learn and understand. If you already have another dog, choose a very different name for your new dog so they don't get confused when called.

Grooming and feeding

Grooming isn't just about keeping skin healthy and hair clean and odour-free: it is also a powerful component of training. From day one, start grooming your pup.

Your dog might think that eating is something done to satisfy hunger. You may think that the most important aspect of feeding your dog is getting the right nutritional balance. A healthy diet is certainly essential for the dog's mind and body (*see* pages 98–105), but feeding is much more than nutrition. Feeding is at the very core of training your dog. It's really quite simple. You are in control of your dog's food. From the hour your new dog arrives in your home, use that fact to shape and mould behaviour.

Get your pup used to brushing and towelling early.

Watch for chewing

Chewing is as normal a canine activity as eating and sleeping. It's at the contented core of a dog's dogginess. Your dog needs to chew, and by controlling where it spends its time and what food and toys you provide, it's not difficult to train it to chew what you want it to chew. A free-range dog will try just about anything. I know a home where doors, table legs, skirting boards, carpets, walls, and furniture all bear the distinctive signs of puppy chewing. That's my home, where, for reasons of domestic harmony, we didn't restrict Macy to her own personal space when she was a growing pup.

A very personal place

Call it what you will – crate, carrier, cage, or den – a dog's personal space is not a jail! It's home. As soon as you get your new dog to your home, introduce its own home (*see* pages 80–1). A space for play is needed as well, whether you call it a playpen, playroom, or exercise pen. It can be a purpose-built pen or a small room in your home, perhaps the kitchen or, less attractively, a bathroom with baby gates on the exit doors. Remove all carpets and chewable articles if you're using a room. Your pup's playroom will include the den (*see* page 87), with comfortable bedding in it, in one corner, a toilet area in another corner, a bowl of fresh water in a third corner, and three hollow chew toys, stuffed with yummies.

Plan toileting

When it comes to housetraining, think about where your dog will eventually relieve itself and integrate that into the toileting area in the playpen. If it will be grass, lay down part of a roll of turf in the pen. If it will be the gutter, get a paving slab for it to relieve itself on. Your aim is to get it used to the feel under foot that it will experience later in life. Prepare the toileting area by laying down a remnant of flooring vinyl covered by a plastic sheet, then the "substrate" your dog will learn to toilet on.

Decide on a sleeping place

There's no right and wrong about where your pup should sleep at night other than it should be in its den. If the playpen will also be the sleeping place, and if you're not going to get up at night to let it out (*see* pages 92–7), leave the door to the den open so the toileting area is accessible. If, on the other hand, your dog will sleep in your bedroom, keep the den's door shut and get up to take it out to relieve itself.

QUESTIONS AND ANSWERS

My vet says I shouldn't let my pup out until 14 days after his last inoculation. But then he'll be 14 weeks old before he meets other dogs. What can I do?

Most vets follow advice given to them by vaccine manufacturers; a dog may not be protected until 14 days after the final inoculation, depending on the vaccine, at 10 or 12 weeks of age. Following this advice reduces risk from infectious disease but can compromise proper early socialization and lead to behaviour problems. Where I practise, I'm lucky. The most dangerous infectious diseases are extremely rare, and even parvovirus occurs at a relatively low incidence. In weighing the risks, I advise clients to exercise their dogs where I know conscientious owners – who have had their dogs vaccinated – exercise theirs. I also suggest taking new pups to friends who have inoculated dogs and vice versa. Discuss with your vet the risks of infectious disease in your area. For legal liability reasons, you will be given the vaccine manufacturer's advice, but it should be possible to read between the lines and discover whether there are serious health risks in letting your dog learn about life sooner.

Dogs have physical and mental needs.

BRUCE'S TIPS ON COMMUNICATION

The fastest, most efficient way to get your dog's attention, to communicate, and to bond is not through formal training but through well-thought-out, day-to-day living.

Pups raised in outdoor kennels or adults "institutionalized" in rescue kennels have not had the chance to focus on people, to learn to be responsive, and as a result their training doesn't go as smoothly as if they had been raised in a home with a family. Start your puppy off in a limited space and, day by day, week by week, let it earn more; supervise your pup vigilantly when it has "free" time.

Puppies are curious and will eat almost anything. Save the tastiest parts of daily meals for when it is in its den.

Crying, shivering, and cowering are clear signs of tension or distress, but more subtle signs, such as turning the gaze away from a stressful individual or situation, yawning, unexpected lip-licking or panting, or freezing on the spot are easy to misinterpret. More dramatic signs include submissive urinating, whining, howling, barking, or aggression. Innocuous events can trigger stress: when introducing a pup to a new home, take care not to unwittingly cause anxiety. It's surprisingly easy to create future problems.

Crate and playpen training

Fold-up, relatively lightweight crates are practical. A portable crate permits you to safely visit friends with your new dog.

These first days are as important for your training as they are for your new pup. From the second it enters your home, your new dog wants to please you, to make you happy, but it needs to learn how to do that. It can't unless you and your family have set house rules for yourself as well as for your new dog.

Why you should use a crate

As a vet, I expect to be told about any changes in the demeanour, activity level, mobility, gastrointestinal or urinary functions, odours, or looks of your dog. What I hadn't expected was to be told about your frustrations with your dog's housetraining, or pulling on the lead, or destructiveness, or mouthing people, or barking. I'm asked for as much advice about behaviour as I am about health, and I learned pretty fast that it's far, far easier to prevent problems than to overcome them once they've developed. At the root of prevention is giving your new pup its own den and play area.

Training your pup to think of the crate as a safe sanctuary is dead easy. Training your partner, kids, parent, or whoever, that a crate isn't a jail is tough, so let's look at the facts dispassionately. By providing a den and a playpen (*see* page 87), you're really confining your puppy to a small space for short periods of time, or

Use food treats to attract your new dog so that it willingly enters its den.

to a larger space for longer periods, but in either case to a limited environment where it's hard to make mistakes. In a nutshell, the fewer mistakes your pup makes early in life, the easier and more enjoyable both your lives will be.

Restricting your pup to a crate or playpen allows it to teach itself to use a toileting area, to chew on appropriate objects, to be comfortable in its own company. It protects your puppy from harm, including accidental injuries from kids or adults. It is preparation for the inevitable reality of virtually all pet dogs: to be left at home alone occasionally.

Training your dog to love the den
Don't push your pup into a crate, shut the door, and expect it to be happy. You need to train a pup to love its crate, and that's fast and simple when you use treat-filled chew toys. Most pups find freeze-dried liver intensely attractive, so offer a piece. Assuming this is wolfed down, put more just inside the closed door of the crate (which is inside the playpen) with your pup outside the closed door. Almost invariably, your pup will want to get in. Let it into the crate to eat the treat. Now, put the liver treat in a chew toy and let it work to get at it. Once this new dog-job is understood, repeat the

closed-door routine with the treat-filled chew toy inside the crate, again letting it in to work on the chew toy to get at the treat. Whenever you leave your puppy in the playpen, leave treat-filled chew toys inside the crate. This gives the options of either staying in the pen or willingly entering the crate to find the delectable chew toys. Cheese spread or peanut butter inside the chew toy will keep a dog busy. Your pup should be in the den at all these times:

- When you eat
- When your pup eats
- When you sleep
- When your pup sleeps
- When the phone rings
- When the doorbell rings
- When you go out
- When you need to take a break from puppy surveillance.

Feeding your new dog
When feeding, you have two options. In either case, measure out the daily food intake and set it aside. Option one is to feed most, but not all of that, in four equal portions during the day, with the feeding bowl inside the crate, saving the tastiest bits to stuff in the hollow toys for sucking and chewing on between meals. A more powerful, and in a curious way a more natural, option is to make a pup work for all its food by giving everything stuffed in chew toys. Bury the most succulent bits, such as liver treats, deepest in hollow bones or Kongs; soften the meal into a gruel, pack it in, and stick dry kibbles or biscuits in it.

Visiting the vet
Within 48 hours of acquiring a new dog, take it to your vet. Serious congenital conditions are fortunately rare, but less serious, nuisance conditions, especially internal and external parasites, are common. Your vet will certify the pup's health and discuss preventive care.

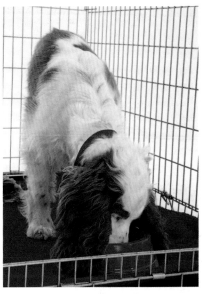

During these first few days, give your new puppy all his food inside the crate. This will help it to feel happy and at ease there.

HOUSE RULES

House rules vary from home to home but here's an example:

- (Insert name) is responsible for Rex. Get her permission before doing anything different with Rex.
- Always use Rex's name when you want his attention.
- Don't use Rex's name when he's within earshot and you're not talking to him.
- Rex may only be taken from his playpen immediately after using his toilet.
- Play with Rex only on the floor or on the lawn, not on furniture. No rough play.
- Don't give Rex any toys other than his chew toys.
- Don't give Rex any treats other than those in his chew toys unless he does something for you, such as sitting.
- Make sure Rex has frequent quiet time.
- Puppy classes are on Tuesday evening. Everyone should make time to attend.
- Rex is part of the family. Remember him when making your own plans.

Meeting the rest of the family

PUPPY PLAYSCHOOL

Play is at the heart of dogs' appeal. Dogs need routine play, with both people and other dogs. Puppy playschools are the perfect place for you and your pup to learn the rules of play. Find out from your vet where local puppy classes (*see* pages 122–5) take place.

Yes, it's all exciting, and you want everyone, including your new dog, to have as much fun as possible – but please remember that someone has to be in charge, and if you're reading this, I bet that's you! As far as I'm concerned, you're the leader of the pack, the health-and-safety manager, the problem preventer. Problems can arise when your new dog meets boisterous kids or the other pets in the family, or even the neighbours, so ensure that these encounters take place in circumstances where you're in control.

Meeting the kids

Before your kids meet your new dog, explain to them that it isn't a new toy, that it's a living being with the same emotions that they have.

Write down the house rules and post them by your puppy's den. I'd suggest these rules:

- Puppy pick-up and holding only takes place when parents say so. That also means no fights over who holds the puppy. No yanking or pulling.
- Be calm and quiet around the puppy. Don't scream, shriek, or yell at each other or at the pup. No running around the puppy.
- Only give food in the chew toys and in the crate.
- Don't wake the pup or disturb it while it's sleeping.
- No teasing, and don't encourage it to jump up.

Meeting the family dog

I've been a practising vet for so long, I've now met almost 10,000 new dogs during their first weeks in their new homes. Many of these have joined families that already have another dog, and yet the frequency of demarcation disputes between the new dog and the resident

dog has been amazingly low. Even so, it's best to assume that, at least initially, your resident won't be too happy either with the rambunctiousness of the new arrival or with the invasion of its own personal space by another canine. For that reason, it's best for them to first meet on neutral territory – for example, in someone

Introducing a new pup to your child

1 It's only natural for children to want to touch, stroke, hold, and lift up a new dog. However, for some dogs these activities can be frightening. Explain to your children the importance of keeping quiet and still when they meet your new dog. For the first meeting, have them kneel quietly in front of your dog on the floor. Your dog, in turn, should be kept under gentle but firm control with a collar and a short lead.

BRUCE'S TIPS ON CHILDPROOFING

Some pups are timid and fearful. Others get overexcited with rough-and-tumble play. Older pups can be unsure of themselves in new surroundings and act defensively. In all these situations, a dog might bite. It may be a playful bite or it may be a fearful one, but what's most important is you don't want it to happen to your kids or to others. Reduce the risk of dog bites by conditioning your new dog to childlike behaviours and activities.

Behave like a child and gently prod your pup, then instantly give a food reward. Poke and prod some more, instantly rewarding again with treats.

Once your pup considers poking and prodding as positive experiences, gently grab it and reward calm acceptance with more food rewards.

With this simple training, if your pup is now poked, prodded, or grabbed by a child, it is much less likely to be frightened or annoyed by the event.

else's home or garden. You should also thoroughly exercise your resident before they meet each other.

On neutral territory, your resident will be interested in investigating the space, and your new pup is just one of the sights and sounds it encounters. Let them investigate each other, and don't interfere unless either looks stressed or agitated. Leave the puppy on a house line (this is like an extremely long shoelace) so you can gain control if you need to. Back at home, let them meet again, in the garden if you have one, having removed all items the pup might find and play with that could provoke a jealous reaction from your resident. Let your pup in first, and don't let it get too excited. Expect your older resident to be irritated by the roadrunner antics of your puppy. If you

2 When your new dog calmly and willingly approaches your child, tell her to open her hand containing a concealed treat and offer it on the palm of her hand as a reward.

3 As the dog takes the treat, tell your child that she can now gently and quietly touch the dog's chest or neck but not the top of the head. Touching the top of the head is intimidating.

4 Once your new dog is assuredly comfortable with your child at its own eye level, tell her that she can stand up and reward calm behaviour in your dog with another food treat.

think there might be a snarl or snap from your resident dog, avoid staging the first meeting in the garden and take your new dog directly to the crate.

Don't be surprised if your dog has not yet learned to inhibit investigating by mouth.

Meeting the family cat

Cats rule. They're naturally superior to dogs, and they know it. If your cat is accustomed to dogs, it'll hiss, spit, and bat at your newcomer, and their lifelong relationship will be established. If, on the other hand, the cat runs away and triggers your new pup's instinct to chase, you've got problems on your hands. Some breeds, including most terriers, are more inclined to chase than others.

Never leave your resident cat and your new dog together. When you can't supervise them, put your puppy in the playpen. Problems can develop a few months down the line, when your pup is fully housetrained and is no longer restricted to his playpen. A boisterous pup, such as a Boxer (*see* page 33), might create its own amusement by ambushing the cat and inducing it to run away, giving the opportunity to chase. If this happens, attach a houseline to your dog's collar. If it looks like your dog is setting up a game, stand on the line. You want it to learn that games are played with people or dogs, but not with cats.

Pups naturally bite

I just love the look of a young adult dog's brand-new, shiny, perfect, snow-white teeth. Incisors for nibbling. Canines for grabbing and holding. Molars for slicing and chewing. In evolutionary terms, a dog's teeth and jaws are at the heart of

Introducing a new dog to the resident dog

1 The ideal location for your resident dog and your new dog to first meet one another is on neutral territory, in a space that neither of them feels it "owns". If weather permits, this should be a location outdoors rather than indoors. The first meeting needs two people, one to handle each dog. Initially, walk the new and resident dogs on their respective leads at a considerable distance from each other. Both of them should be primarily interested, as these dogs are, in investigating the various smells and sights of this fresh and new location. Reward both of the dogs with praise and food treats for behaving "normally".

its survival, adapted not only to capture, hold, kill, and consume prey, but also to protect, defend, or assert itself.

Yet we expect dogs to forget they have teeth, to inhibit their use, certainly never to use them as weapons. What we're asking of them is almost unnatural. Dogs need to use their teeth, and through training we can channel that need in a constructive way, by directing their need to chew toward chewing toys. This makes it so much simpler for them to learn to inhibit their natural instinct to bite, to learn to be gentle with all other animals including us (*see* pages 140–1). A pup needs to learn to be "soft-mouthed" while it still has its baby teeth. By the time its adult teeth have erupted, at about five months of age, its almost too late. Puppy classes are the perfect venue for learning bite inhibition.

BRUCE'S TIPS FOR TWO-DOG HOUSEHOLDS

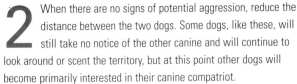

Don't give your new puppy any privileges "because it's a puppy" that are not given to your resident dog, and never, ever give the new dog any of the resident dog's toys. Avoid carrying out any training of one dog when the other can hear. If the other dog can hear, you may unwittingly be training it to disregard your commands in the future.

Keep to your established routines with your resident dog, but make sure that you provide satisfying individual time for both dogs.

Don't feed the two dogs close together. The best way is tail facing tail, so they can't watch each other.

If the new puppy gets too rambunctious and your resident dog tells it off, remember that this is natural. Allow it to happen under your supervision.

Preparing for the future

If you're like me, you want your dog to be fun to have around, to be active when you want activity and calm when you're busy, to enjoy the company of people of all ages, to be obedient not frightened, to walk well on the lead, to have a soft mouth and an inhibited bite, and to have a sense of humour. All of this is made easier if you include your pup in as many activities as possible. Take it in the car with you on the school run, let it meet the regulars at your local coffee shop, let it experience life. The more your dog learns now, the more enjoyable your relationship will be.

2 When there are no signs of potential aggression, reduce the distance between the two dogs. Some dogs, like these, will still take no notice of the other canine and will continue to look around or scent the territory, but at this point other dogs will become primarily interested in their canine compatriot.

3 Speak calmly to the family member who is walking the other dog, because this helps calm potentially nervous dogs. Once the dogs have met equally on neutral territory, it is much less likely that the resident dog will deeply resent the subsequent arrival of the new dog on its home turf.

A new adult dog

There are some wonderful advantages to a new adult dog, especially one known to you or to the person rehoming it. An adult dog can come with known manners and habits. Whether from relatives, neighbours, or a good rehoming centre, you should get a personality assessment of behaviour quirks, foibles, and needs. With so many unwanted dogs available – and killed if they can't be rehomed – getting a recycled adult dog is deeply soul-satisfying. There can, however, be unknown baggage.

Chew toy

Predictably unpredictable

A dog's ability to be sociable with people is acquired before 12 weeks of age. How to get along with other dogs is learned by 18 weeks, and so is learning how to inhibit biting. It's always easier to prevent problems than to treat them.

A new adult dog may pass its initial "test drive" at the rescue centre (where, all being well, you test drove a number of dogs and selected this one because it was quiet and calm) but then turn into an exuberant, jumping, pulling-on-the-lead, high-energy vagrant just as soon as you arrive home. Unexpected fears, with associated aggression, or seemingly irrational phobias may surface.

A common phobia is a fear of confinement, including being shut in a crate or pen. While unwanted behaviours may seem irrational, the range of these potential behaviours is entirely predictable. They are the result of poor early socializing, lack of house- and obedience training, or, in the case of entire adults (those that have not been neutered), hormones.

Adult dogs are rewarding, but it's the rare one that doesn't need some form of rehabilitation. Rehabilitating a dog can be difficult, frustrating, and very time-consuming. Although good shelters have told you what to expect, its only when

If your new adult dog is not housetrained or is liable to chew your belongings, prepare for its arrival with a suitably sized and equipped play area and attached den.

you get home that you come to see your dog's whole personality and how that personality interacts with yours.

Dogs crates, pens, and chew toys

If your new adult dog is housetrained and only chews its own toys, there's no need for a crate or a pen. If it's housetrained but you don't know how destructive it is, you'll still need a pen. In any instance, you'll want to provide a selection of chew toys; for a new dog with powerful jaw muscles, make sure these are the most indestructible on the market. Kong makes a heavy-duty range. Toys that drop food when rolled around can be destroyed if a dog learns how to get its teeth in the right places. As with pups, liver treats are the most rewarding. Use trial and error to find out what your new dog prefers stuffed in its chew toys. Dog biscuits in cheese spread or peanut butter are popular and nutritious for most dogs.

Dogproofing your home

All dogs are inquisitive, but a new adult dog can be big and inquisitive. Until you know otherwise, assume it'll stand on its hind legs to investigate all nooks and crannies. Kitchen counters laden with deliciously smelly food are no problem at all for amazing jumping dogs. Remove your fragiles, your valuables, your delectables (such as shoes, underwear, and socks) – anything that may be attractive or dangerous to your new dog.

Assume every rescue dog is an escape artist. Never leave a new adult dog alone in the garden until you're sure it's settled with something to do and that the garden is safe. In particular, check that your fencing is dogproof and secure, especially if you have a digger or a jumper. For small dogs, gates often need additional security at the bottom. Make sure the latches work properly and the gate is always latched. Fence off the compost heap, recycling and rubbish bins, and, if you're lucky enough to have one, the vegetable garden. Move plant pots out of harm's way, and never let your dog near the barbecue when you're cooking. Provide a specific toileting area (*see* page 96). If your dog has access to a terrace or balcony, think like a dog when you do your security check. Remember

QUESTIONS AND ANSWERS

Who do I ask for advice?

Just as you asked breeders for their advice about their breed and your vet for advice about your dog's health, ask dog trainers for advice about dog training. But not just any dog trainers. Seek out dog trainers who are members of a respected national organization – groups such as the Association of Pet Dog Trainers, the British Institute of Professional Dog Trainers, the UK Registry of Canine Behaviourists, or the Association of Pet Behaviour Counsellors. All of these have formal codes of ethics and complaints procedures. Whoever you're getting advice from, if it sounds sensible to you, go with it. If it sounds draconian, cultish, preachy, or freaky, discuss that advice with your vet or the veterinary staff. They are excellent when you need a quick second opinion on dog housing, living, or training methods.

that dogs can be superdogs. They will inevitably try to slide under or through bars or jump over them

One step at a time

The honeymoon with your new adult dog inevitably ends as soon as you arrive home, if only because it's now up to you to work hard to ensure that the potential of your new relationship is fulfilled. That means having a rational, systematic approach to what happens during these first weeks. As well as establishing a new hierarchy for your dog, in which it comes to respect you and your family, you'll also be introducing it to your other family pets, a new home and garden, the neighbours, and the neighbourhood.

The likeliest behaviour problem you should be on the lookout for is separation anxiety (*see* pages 156–7), which is extreme distress and anxiety when left alone for even a short period of time. The individuals most prone to separation anxiety tend to be those that are extraordinarily affectionate with you but perhaps somewhat shy with strangers. If your new adult dog magnetically follows you around, is rather submissive, or has a history of abuse, neglect, or having been in many different homes, assume that it will experience separation anxiety, and start desensitizing it now.

Getting used to handling

Even some pups resent your touching all parts of their bodies, but be especially careful during the first weeks with your adult dog. During the first days at home, discover what it is comfortable with. A few times each day, gently touch

Use non-threatening body language when you first meet a new adult dog. Touching under the chin is least threatening.

QUESTIONS AND ANSWERS

What if my dog cries or barks when left alone at night?

Play with your new dog, feed it, and let it relieve itself before putting it in its room or playpen. Don't make a fuss. Say as little as possible, avoid eye contact, stick ear plugs in your ears and disregard howls, cries, or whimpers. (Visit your neighbours beforehand, armed with boxes of chocolates, to explain there's a new dog and there might be a little separation anxiety noise during the first few nights.) Adult dogs can control their bowels and bladder overnight. Young pups can't, so if you're getting up to take your youngster to an outdoor toileting area, do so quickly and quietly, putting it back in its den. Your pup will want to play, but be resolute. It will take only a few days, perhaps a week at most, for your new dog to learn that howling just doesn't work.

the head, back, and sides. Take care when touching the mouth, ears, legs, and paws. Some dogs resent that. Most are sensitive to you touching their tails, but touching all over reinforces that you are in charge. So does grooming, the activity that eventually follows touching.

Once your new dog is comfortable with touching, add in lifting each paw for a second or two. Give frequent food treats as rewards for relaxed obedience. Gently but firmly hold on if your dog struggles, until it stops fidgeting. You don't want to teach unwittingly that wriggling is permitted. Keep these sessions short, just a few minutes at a time, and never grab. Slowly build up to paw lifting, so that your dog doesn't even

All dogs are inquisitive. Make sure that your dog is on its lead when it investigates any other family pets.

think about moving. Properly desensitizing your new adult dog to all sorts of handling takes a little effort.

When you know your dog is reliable with you, repeating the same activity with confident strangers enhances reliability, and makes it so much easier for me if I'm called upon to cut its nails!

The perfect new adult dog

Is your new adult dog a calm, outgoing individual, who is friendly to everyone but not overly clingy or frantic for your attention? Does it greet you but soon wander off because there's an interesting odour or sound that has caught its attention? If that's your dog, you're a really lucky person. You've acquired a well-rounded, uncomplicated new adult. Most recycled dogs aren't so emotionally sound. Expect there to be complications during the first days at home, especially if your new dog has been abandoned or abused. Your vet can provide you with the name of a good dog trainer who can help with any rehabilitation needs.

Meeting other dogs

Even if you're told that your new adult dog is well socialized with other dogs, be vigilant for unexpected idiosyncrasies.

For example, my sister inherited Bill, my late mother-in-law's dog. I'd known this neutered male, five-year-old Lhasa Apso-Staffordshire Bull Terrier cross (*see* pages 46 and 32) since he was first rescued at a year of age, and knew him to be a dog lover, an individual who sought out other dogs to joyfully play with them. So it was a surprise when my sister told me that Bill turned into Vlad the Impaler each time he saw another dog. Bill seriously wanted to attack and destroy. Bill's aggression turned out to be highly specific, because it was only directed at Staffies or dogs that looked like Staffies,

Cats rule, if given the opportunity to intimidate dogs by a hiss or a swipe, but always take care at first.

a breed he didn't meet when he lived with my mother-in-law but a popular breed where my sister lives. His behaviour was triggered by some experience he had before my mother-in-law first rescued him, and my sister's successful treatment of his behaviour is simply to exercise him in a park that is not frequented by Staffies.

BRUCE'S GATE TIP

Baby gates are excellent for restricting your new dog to a single room or floor of your house. When you have visitors, most importantly when visitors include small children, it can see them without being a nuisance. Having a baby gate on a doorway also means that, even in the heat of the moment, you aren't tempted to use the puppy crate or playpen for discipline.

If she'd had the time, my sister would have "desensitized" Bill by gradually introducing him to a reliable Staffie.

When introducing your new adult to your resident dogs or to other dogs, do so on neutral territory and initially keep moving, so the dogs don't have a chance to "face off" with each other. Let them sniff, but don't let the leads get tight (*see* pages 164–7). Their hackles may rise just from excitement, but if this reaction is accompanied by other signs of aggression, turn their heads away from each other and move away.

Meeting the family cat

Cats and dogs usually settle well together, provided the cat always has a place of safety. Unlike a new pup, however, a new adult dog may already be an experienced cat chaser. In their initial meetings, which should take place in a calm and quiet environment, keep your new dog on its lead so your cat isn't put at risk.

QUESTIONS AND ANSWERS

How long can I leave my new adult dog at home alone?

That depends on your new adult dog's previous experience but also, to some extent, on the breed. Active herding and working breeds such as Border Collies (see page 54) and Labrador Retrievers (see pages 20–1) tend to go stir crazy more rapidly when left alone, even if given chew toys for distraction. Less active breeds such as Rottweilers (see page 42) fare much better. In general, the calmer and more stable the dog, the happier it will be to curl up and sleep while you're gone. The more excess energy they have, the harder it is to keep themselves entertained only with toys. Initially, don't leave your new dog at home alone for more than an hour. Eventually, this can be increased with many dogs up to five or six hours.

If your dog gets overstimulated, you may need two people at these initial meetings. Find the critical distance at which your dog is not provoked to chase the cat, and work on gradually reducing it.

Meeting other small pets

Make sure your new dog doesn't consider free-ranging, small household pets, such as rabbits or guinea pigs, to be an exciting new form of lunch. Keep the first meetings quiet and calm. Don't make a fuss. With its lead on, give your new dog something else to think about: a chew toy, a carry toy, food, or a play activity with you. Always supervise these

encounters, never leave your new dog with other household pets until you are firmly convinced there will be no problems, and always ensure that smaller pets have a ready escape route.

Meeting the neighbours

You want your new dog to be as friendly with the neighbours as it is with you. Visit your neighbours before you bring your new dog home; explain what's happening (gifts are an excellent idea at this point), that there might be a little noise for the first nights while you train your dog to sleep alone, and that you'd like to introduce your dog to

Walking away from trouble

1 Shows of aggression are not particularly uncommon in rescued dogs whose backgrounds are unknown.

Typically, one dog tries to intimidate the other. This type of behaviour occurs most frequently when dogs are on their leads.

your neighbour under controlled circumstances so that the relationship works well. Provide your neighbour with food treats, such as freeze-dried liver bits. When they meet, have your dog on its lead while your neighbour, avoiding eye contact with your new dog, offers the treats. This conditions your dog to look forward to seeing your neighbours, and not bark protectively when they appear.

Expect the unexpected

A serious unexpected problem with a new dog is fighting. Be prepared for this by knowing the "ladder" of body language that signals potential aggression: the dog standing tall and

BRUCE'S TIPS ON HEALTH CHECKS

Whenever possible, get the vaccination and health records of your new dog. Ideally, contact the dog's previous vet in case there are any problems you should be aware of. That's not always possible with a rescued dog. Have your own vet carry out a full health check and insert a microchip (*see* page 69) if necessary; an existing chip number can be transferred to your address. Your vet will advise on a vaccine and anti-parasite programme, nutrition, and neutering if your new dog is entire (*see* pages 186–7) and put you in touch with a good local trainer who uses positive reinforcement methods.

still, the hackles raised, the tail stiff and high, the unblinking stare, the ears flattened onto the head, the growling, snapping, lunging, and finally, the biting. When you see any of these signs, you should walk away from the situation. Later, you will be able to counter-condition your new dog, so that it is no longer likely to pick a fight with others (*see* pages 164–7).

2 Watch your new dog to see if it shows any signs of impending aggression. These range from standing still and staring, or raising the tail, to raising the hackles. If you do see any of these threatening behaviours, inhibit a further escalation in your dog's body language by immediately leading it away from the presence and sight of the other dog.

Housetraining

Dogs are naturally tidy. That's at the core of their success as our most ancient companions. They are not hard to housetrain. Using confinement to prevent unwanted habits, never punishing mistakes, and making frequent visits to the toilet area, combined with food, praise, and play rewards for using it, is uncomplicated. It simply depends on timing, predicting when your puppy needs to eliminate, and efficiently taking it to the chosen spot. You're training your dog to do a swap: in return for dumping urine and faeces on command, you provide tasty treats and play.

QUESTIONS AND ANSWERS

What if I use turf or paving slabs, and he eats the turf or sleeps on the slabs?

No system works for all dogs. If you can't set up an indoor toilet similar to what he'll use outdoors, or if your dog plays with it rather than pees on it, confine your pup to his den and follow the "take dog out, bring dog in" instructions (see opposite).

The basic rules

Housetraining rules are simple. When you're around, keep your pup confined to the crate and take it out to the toilet area every hour. Also, visit the toilet area after your pup eats, drinks, or plays, and immediately after it wakes up. If you're not there, keep the crate door open to allow access to the well-considered indoor toilet area you've prepared, using the feel underfoot that will be normal outdoors (see page 79). Take your pup on the lead

A puppy is unlikely to mess in its bed, as long as it has frequent access to its toilet area.

Whether your new dog is initially using newspaper or a litter tray, quietly stay with it while it investigates its toilet.

to the chosen toilet area, and as it eliminates, use the trigger word or catchphrase you've chosen. Reward liberally, with every item in your armoury: lavish praise, tasty treats, squeaky toys, and satisfying touch. If it doesn't eliminate after three minutes, take it back to the crate, but be prepared for another garden visit in half an hour. When both systems have been emptied, play with your pup outdoors or indoors.

Take dog out. Bring dog in.
Take dog out. Bring dog in.
It's a bore, but this is what housetraining is all about. When your dog wakes up, immediately take it out. Within 20 minutes after it eats or drinks, take it out. Within five minutes after calm play and immediately after vigorous play, take it out. Activity makes urine. Also take a dog out frequently according to its age: the younger the pup is, the more often you need to take it to the toilet area.

Signs to watch for
Your dog is about to perform when it starts sniffing the ground, increases its

speed while it's walking, starts walking in circles, starts pawing the ground, or begins to crouch down. If you see any of these activities, you've only got seconds to get your pup to the toilet area. If you haven't done so already, take it to the

place where you want it to eliminate, and be as boring as possible. Pups are easily distracted – by spiders, flies, flowers, leaves. Life is thrilling! Don't accentuate any distractions. Stay quiet, in one place, and don't keep pointing

Taking the dog out			
Set up and post a routine so everyone in the family knows what to do. Don't *let* a pup out, *take* it out. Be there with it, regardless of the weather.	**Age**	**How long a pup can hold it**	**Minimum toilet breaks**
	8 weeks	2 hours	12 in every 24 hours
	12 weeks	3–4 hours	6–8 in every 24 hours
	16 weeks	4–5 hours	5–6 in every 24 hours
	20 weeks	5–6 hours	4–5 in every 24 hours
	6 months	6–8 hours	3–4 in every 24 hours
	7 months	12 hours or more	3 in every 24 hours

Keep your pup on its lead while it prepares to toilet. This ensures safety, now and in the future.

Because this pup will later have a garden to toilet in, it is being trained while indoors to toilet on grass.

where you want the pup to go. If your puppy doesn't perform within three minutes, take it back inside and place it in the crate, then repeat the outdoor exercise within 30 minutes.

Give treats and chosen words

Guys can find this difficult, but the more you overreact with joy when your pup performs, the faster it learns what to do, where to do it, and eventually to do it on command. "Wow!" "Good boy!" "That's amazing!" "You're wonderful!" "That's the biggest turd a little dog ever passed!" "I'm entering you in the puppy-turd Olympics!" Be a clown. Use a happy voice. You want your pup to think it's incredible for eliminating outside. Give a treat and toss a ball, or play chase. You want to teach that first it urinates or defecates, then the fun begins. Don't overdo the food treats: a clever dog will learn to deposit just a thimbleful of urine for a food reward and keep a large reserve

in the tank, knowing that more food rewards are possible.

An overview of the basic rules

If you say the same specific word or words each time your dog urinates, it will come to associate those words not just with urinating, but with the need to urinate. Hearing that word will eventually speed up the performance.

Trainers call this "conditioning". Your dog develops a conditioned response to hearing certain words they call "trigger words". Learning to urinate or defecate on command when hearing your chosen catchphrases means that later, if your dog needs to be left at home for a period of time or you're taking it on an extended journey, you're assured all systems are preventively emptied.

Think about the words you plan to use, and choose different words for each function, not words you use in everyday conversation. Bear in mind that the whole family must use the same trigger words. You might be happy to say "Do poopies" to your dog when you're in the park, but will your family? People I know use "Hurry up" as the trigger words to

make their dog urinate and "Do it" to prompt defecating.

Exactly what to do

Both you and your new dog need to stay focused on what you're doing. Take your dog, puppy or adult, on the lead, under your control, to the designated toilet spot, ideally one that you've primed with a little of its urine scent (for example, from soiled newspaper). Let your dog sniff and investigate the area, and as it starts to eliminate, use your chosen trigger word. At the instant it finishes, act the clown. Give your dog treats, praise it, and play with it.

Questions and answers

My spouse refuses to let me use a crate or a playpen and says it's cruel. How can I train my dog without using them?

My wife refused to let me use a crate or playpen and then regretted it when Macy chewed the corners off her most valuable (and I mean really, really valuable) antique painted Swedish furniture. A crate is only ever for short-term use and is the best housetraining tool there is, because it helps you predict when your dog needs to relieve itself. If you've hit a brick wall and can't use either a crate or a playpen, convert the kitchen to a large playpen and set it up as you would the playpen, with the bed in one corner, the toilet area in another, and water in another. Food will be in the three food-stuffed chew toys. Within minutes of your pup awakening or playing, or within 20 minutes of eating or drinking, take it to its outdoor toilet area.

Always go to the same spot. The feel underfoot, the tactile experience your dog has, is significant. What it feels early in life becomes "substrate preference", a desire to toilet when standing on a specific surface – for example, grass or pavement. Your dog will associate that feeling underfoot with the good feeling it has when it relieves itself.

Accidents will happen

Ignore accidents in the house. If your puppy toilets where you don't want it to, it is due to your lack of observation or poor timing. It's not the puppy's fault. With practice your timing will get better. Remember, you're new at this too, so don't beat yourself up when accidents happen – but likewise, don't punish your dog. To your dog, punishment only means that you are irrationally unpredictable and shouldn't be trusted.

If you witness an accident, quickly and quietly pick your pup up and take it outside. If it continues to toilet outdoors, give praise. As soon as possible, clean the soiled area by blotting away the liquid then neutralizing the odour with a purpose-made product. Vinegar also works well, as does methylated spirit or vodka. Remember, if your pup messes in the crate, it's your fault. The space in the crate may be too large, or the time spent in it too long. Reduce the length of time spent in the crate before being taken out to the toilet area. You'll quickly learn what the limits are. The basic lesson is: reward behaviour you want repeated, ignore behaviour you don't want. You'll gradually be able to extend the time between eliminations. Watch your pup's needs. It's the bladder's holding time that controls the timing of visits to the toilet area, not your timetable. Be patient.

Always give bountiful, encouraging praise and treats after your new pup has successfully emptied either tank.

Typical housetraining problems

Some puppies, trained to go on paper inside, take time to understand using an outside toilet. Don't just put your pup outside and expect it to perform. Put on the collar and lead and take your dog out, even if you have a fenced garden. The lead is not for corrections or pulling your dog, but only to keep it close to you.

Stay with it until it does perform, then do your rewarding-clown routine. Some puppies hold on outside because they're unfamiliar with the feeling underfoot, or it's raining, or that leaf that just fell from the tree was really scary. These pups wait until they're inside, where they feel safe, to toilet on their preferred substrate – for example, newspaper. If this happens,

confine your pup to the den and take it out more frequently, having already taken some of the soiled newspaper to the chosen toilet area.

Discipline is pointless

If you rub your dog's nose in its mistake, I'll do it to you! What a dumb, pointless, idiotic, stupid thing to do. Where did the idea ever come from? This might satisfy a foolish need for retribution, but all it does to your dog is make it cower from you, run away when you approach, and think that you're a mixed-up, irrational person. If you see your dog making a mistake, say "No!" firmly and take it to the chosen toilet area.

If you find a mistake, forget about it. Dogs can't understand you're angry because of what they did, even if it's only minutes before. That cowering look isn't guilt; it's recognition that you're going to do something awful to them. They only know that you're angry. Don't rub your dog's nose in its mistake. If you do,

you're a jerk, and you just shouldn't have a dog.

Indoor cat litter, turf, and piddle pads

As far as I'm concerned, these are cop-outs for lazy dog owners; they are most often used by high-rise dwellers. Peeing and pooping aren't the only reasons to go outdoors. Dogs should go out several times each day for the fun of scenting life, meeting other dogs, visiting the rest of the world.

Indoor toilet training does have a place for small dogs that live with elderly or invalid people, who find it difficult to take their dogs out frequently. Cat litter works well, with solids and wetted clumps removed at least once daily. Turf is heavy and needs frequent changing. Piddle pads are expensive and get smelly very quickly.

Housetraining an adult dog

The significant difference between training an adult dog and a pup is the potential need for your adult to "unlearn" before it can learn. If your new rescued dog has never been housetrained, it has nevertheless developed its own satisfying habits of elimination, which may include urinating and defecating in places you don't want it to. This is not the dog's fault.

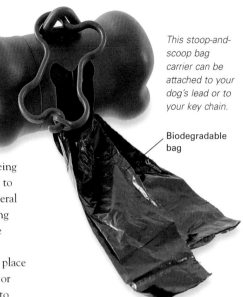

This stoop-and-scoop bag carrier can be attached to your dog's lead or to your key chain.

Biodegradable bag

Your new dog simply has to learn what you want from it, and to teach this you must start from scratch, as if your dog were still a puppy. Supervise it while it is in the house and restrict your dog's freedom to wander in the house until its habits are clean. You can, for example, leash your dog to you, and take it out hourly. This helps induce it to focus on you and on pleasing you. If your dog needs to urinate or defecate at inconvenient times during the day, take a look at its feeding schedule, which may need changing.

Unneutered male dogs mark their presence by urinating on vertical objects. Neutering drastically reduces the frequency of marking.

QUESTIONS AND ANSWERS

When I was young, we just put the dog in the garden and he learned to use it. Why do I have to go through all this?

There are three great advantages. First, your pup learns to eliminate on command. Time is more precious than it once was, so most of us are grateful to have dogs that operate when we want them to. Second, if you are there, you know when it's empty and can be safely left to wander around the house for a while. If you haven't watched, you don't know whether there's an accident waiting to happen as soon as it goes back inside. Third, you can report every single detail to me. You will instantly know when something is amiss, and it makes a vet's day to be given vivid details about the frequencies, textures, consistencies, and quantities of faeces and urine.

Housetraining more than one dog

Trying to carry out any form of training on two dogs within earshot of each other is fraught with problems. If you have two pups or adults, take each separately to the toilet area. Praise, reward, and train each of them to trigger words in the absence of the other dog.

Submissive urinating is not a housetraining problem

If your pup, or adult, urinates when it becomes excited or when you touch it, this isn't a housetraining issue. This is a form of abject, "I am not worthy", submissive behaviour.

Most pups outgrow submissive urinating, but if your dog behaves this way, tone down what triggers the response (*see* pages 158–63).

Multitasking body waste

Adult dogs urinate and defecate to discharge body waste, but of course they also use urine and faeces as visual and odour methods for communicating with other dogs. When housetraining an adult dog, it's important to differentiate between urinating to empty the bladder and urinating to mark the territory. Using urine to mark territory this way is strongly associated with sex hormone. Housetraining alone does not control this marking activity, but neutering almost always does.

Stoop and scoop waste

1 Various types of mechanical "poop scoops" are available. However, overwhelmingly the easiest equipment to use when cleaning up after your dog, and also the most inexpensive, is a simple, biodegradable plastic bag.

2 With your hand protected by the bag, pick up the dog's stool. The fringe benefit of your conscientious habits for me as a vet is that now you will be able to tell me quite vividly about the stool's texture, should you need to!

3 Invert the bag off your hand over the faeces, and tie it securely closed with a knot. Always dispose of the bag in a dog waste bin or in household waste, not into someone's garden or a hedge. There are enough anti-dog people out there already.

Good nourishment

What should I feed my dog? Don't pet food manufacturers add chemicals to make their food tasty? Is it bad if my dog eats cat food? How much should I feed my dog and how often? Will meat make my dog aggressive? I answer as many questions about a dog's diet as I do about any other facet of its life. We know how important nutrition is, so we're concerned about what we feed our dogs. Good nourishment isn't complex: dogs need just enough daily calories to maintain slim, healthy bodies, and extra when growing, pregnant, lactating, or recovering from illness. Puppies, in particular, have high energy needs.

QUESTIONS AND ANSWERS

What if my dog eats the cat's food?

You'll have a satisfied dog and a fuming cat. Cats have different nutritional requirements to dogs, and those needs may not be met by eating dog food alone. On the other hand, a dog's nutritional needs are more than met by any well-balanced cat food. Cat food is not dangerous for dogs. It contains much more protein than a dog needs, and as a consequence, it is tastier, especially to picky eaters. It is safe (though more expensive) for your dog.

Why dogs eat like dogs

Dogs are, like us, both predators and opportunist scavengers. They prefer meat and animal fat, but when these aren't available they'll eat what they can find, including berries and vegetable roots. A dog can survive on the most miserable of diets, but that's certainly not the fate of the dogs I see. The problems I see are those of excess; too much meat, too much fat, too many calories, not enough chewing.

Give all food – other than rewards – in your dog's food bowl.

This lean dog not only looks good for carrying no excess weight: research says lean dogs live much longer than fat ones.

Thin dogs live longer

In northern Europe and North America, one out of every three dogs is overweight. Many are clinically obese.

An American study published in 2006 reported on 48 Labrador Retrievers (*see* pages 20–1) from seven litters, all of which lived in the same location, were cared for by the same people, and treated by the same vets. It revealed that a group of 24 of these dogs that were fed an unrestricted diet showed X-ray signs of hip osteoarthritis at six years of age. The other 24 dogs were kept lean by feeding them 25 per cent less than their brothers and sisters. In this group, evidence of hip osteoarthritis first appeared at 12 years of age. The lean dogs also lived, on average, 18 months longer than their brothers and sisters fed ad-lib.

Good nourishment is more than just tasty food; balanced nutrition enhances the quality of a dog's life, as well as extending it.

Feeding your new dog

A puppy needs food to maintain all the normal bodily functions but also to grow. At the breeder's, puppies start being weaned off their mother's milk at three weeks of age, when they are introduced to solid food in the form of a soupy gruel. Some breeders pulverize dry puppy food and add water or goat's milk to it, while others feed tinned or other forms of wet puppy food or offer home cooking such as scrambled eggs, mince, and baby cereal. At six weeks of age, puppies are weaned off their mother (allowing her milk to start to dry up) and fed up to six times daily. When your puppy arrives in your home, it needs four meals a day, decreasing to three at three months, then two at six months.

Commercial puppy food, wet or dry, has more energy, vitamins, and minerals in it than the same manufacturer's adult food. Use heavy food and water bowls, ones that can't easily be tipped or pushed around on the floor. Ceramic bowls are excellent.

Refresh water bowl every day.

Types and brands of food

Commercial food may be wet (75–80 per cent moisture), semi-moist (15–30 per cent moisture), or dry (6–10 per cent moisture). Dry and semi-moist foods usually contain more energy-laden carbohydrates, while moist foods (in cans and sachets) contain higher levels of animal-derived protein and fat. The wetness of a food doesn't make it better or worse; it makes it more or less convenient for you, and often more or less tasty for your dog. Dog food comes in a great variety of price ranges, and as with most other things in life, the more you pay, the better the quality of the product you buy. The cheapest dog foods are those with the cheapest

QUESTIONS AND ANSWERS

What food treats are good for dogs?

The best treats are nutritious and tasty ones that you give as rewards because your dog has earned them. Remember: food isn't just to satisfy your dog's nutritional needs or something you use to tell your dog how much you love it. Food is your USP; it's what makes you different to all those other humans out there. Dried liver is the caviar of all dog treats, the Maserati, the Bugatti, the Rolls-Royce. There's something about dried liver that impresses dogs more than anything else. At my clinic we also stock dried chicken, lamb, and beef nuggets, as well as Pet-Tabs, a vitamin and mineral supplement that's particularly appealing to dogs – probably because there's liver in them.

ingredients and the smallest advertising budgets. The most expensive are those with the highest quality ingredients and/or the largest advertising budgets.

Ecologically well-sourced dog foods are now made not only by small, specialist manufacturers but also by the major, mainstream manufacturers.

What manufacturers add

All varieties of complete diets have vitamins and minerals added to ensure they contain all the dog's known nutritional requirements. Some of these substances – for example, vitamin E – act as antioxidants. Antioxidants prevent damage to nutrients in the food, and once they're consumed and in your dog's body, they may inhibit or quench the formation of damaging "free radicals" in your dog's body. Antioxidants are also called "free-radical scavengers".

CREATING A WELL-BALANCED DIET

An example of a homemade diet

Protein	70g (2½oz) chicken and 30g (1oz) chicken liver, cooked
Carbohydrate	140g (5oz) boiled rice
Fat	20g (¾oz) sunflower, rapeseed, or corn oil
Minerals	pinch of iodized salt and 10g (¼oz) sterilized bone meal

This recipe has around 880kcal of energy, enough for a day for an active 10kg (22lb) dog.

Feeding your new dog

1 Mealtimes are perfect occasions both to teach and to reinforce obedience training. Start by commanding your dog to sit while you prepare the meal.

2 Give the command "wait" before placing the food bowl on the floor in front of your dog. The lead ensures that you can reinforce compliance with your command.

Diets for large breeds sometimes contain nutrients that are thought to protect or help rebuild cartilage and joint tissue, such as glucosamine. The scientific case for these supplements is not yet convincing, but there are no known problems with them.

Nonfermentable fibres, such as wheat bran or cellulose, are added to "light" diets for overweight or inactive dogs or to breed-specific diets for breeds such as Labrador Retrievers (*see* pages 20–1), which are prone to obesity. Nonfermentable fibres contribute virtually no calories.

Flavours are usually derived from animal and plant sources, although curiously, synthetic artificial smoke or bacon flavours are added to some dog treats because the smell appeals to *our* preferences. Herbs and botanicals are sometimes added either for their flavours or because of perceived or real medicinal effects, while synthetic colours are used in some foods, especially the cheaper ones, to make them look brighter or meatier. Natural colours – for example, chlorophyll from green plants and carotene from carrots – are also used.

QUESTIONS AND ANSWERS

Can a dog live on a vegetarian diet?

Yes, although given a choice between obtaining essential amino acids and fatty acids from meat or vegetable sources, the vast majority of dogs will select meat over vegetables. A vegetarian diet usually must be supplemented with Vitamin D. The best commercial canine vegetarian diets are well supplemented, making them ideal for people who, for ethical or religious reasons do not want meat in their homes.

3 Give your chosen and consistently used release word, such as "OK". This releases your dog from the wait and allows it to start eating its meal.

4 Intervene during the meal with further commands. Being able to stop your dog while it is eating increases your control if it scavenges outdoors.

Energy sources

Dogs need energy, measured in calories, to live. Like us, they are omnivores (eating both meat and vegetables) and can get energy from any good source of protein, fat, or carbohydrate.

Dogs also need a range of organic compounds, loosely classified as vitamins, and 12 different minerals for their bodies to work efficiently. They need some minerals, such as sodium, in relatively large quantities, and others, such as iodine, in remarkably small quantities.

Vitamin and mineral deficiencies in pet dogs are, in my experience, very rare. Vitamin and mineral excesses are more likely, because owners feed well-balanced diets then sometimes add inordinate quantities of supplements. You can unwittingly create nutritional problems by oversupplementing a dog's balanced diet with excess vitamins and minerals.

Energy needs vary

From birth until it reaches half its adult size, your pup needs about twice the daily energy intake of an adult. During the rest of its growth, it needs around 50 per cent more than an adult dog. As soon as full size is reached, you'll need to cut back on energy intake. That means reducing the quantity of food you offer or switching

Carrots for fibre

from high-energy puppy food to lower-energy adult food. Serious illness can affect a dog's energy needs, and higher-energy food may be needed both during and after some illnesses.

Amino acids

Protein is made up of units called amino acids, which are the body's "building blocks". Dogs can synthesize some amino acids, but not others. The ones they can't synthesize but need to eat in their food are called "essential amino acids". High-quality protein, especially meat protein, contains a good balance of all ten essential amino acids. Amino acids are needed for all the body's biologically vital compounds and also donate carbon chains needed to make

QUESTIONS AND ANSWERS

Do dogs taste their food? Is variety important?

Of course! Even the vacuum cleaners of dogdom consume the tastiest morsels first. Consistently giving the same food maintains a stable balance of microflora in the digestive tract and results in well-formed stools, but it can be boring. If your dog tells you its food is tasteless, there's no harm in gradually switching to another food, as long as you don't unwittingly increase calories and your dog's weight.

glucose, a sugar that provides the body with energy. Given the choice, a dog will choose foods high in protein. That usually means meat.

Fats for concentrated energy

Dogs normally consume more fat than we do. Good fats come from animal fat or seed oils from plants such as sunflower.

Fats are made up of smaller units called fatty acids. Your dog can synthesize some of these but not others, which are called "essential fatty acids". These not only play a vital role in the structure and function of cells, they also carry the

DAILY ENERGY NEEDS IN KILOCALORIES

Technically, a calorie is the amount of energy needed to warm one gram of water by one degree Celsius (1.8°F). A kilocalorie, or "kcal" is 1,000 calories. It is also commonly called a Calorie, with a capital letter "C". Food labels usually list energy as "kcals".

Weight	Growing pup	Active adult	Working	Inactive	Senior
2–5kg (4½–11lb)	295–590	210–420	210–420	185–370	150–300
6–10kg (13–22lb)	675–990	480–705	675–990	420–620	345–505
11–20kg (24–44lb)	1065–1665	775–1180	1065–1665	665–1040	545–850
21–30kg (46–66lb)	1725–2255	1225–1600	1725–2255	1080–1410	885–1155
31–40kg (68–88lb)	2310–2800	1640–1990	2310–2800	1445–1750	1180–1430
41–50kg (90–110lb)	2850–3310	2025–2350	2850–3310	1780–2070	1460–1690

fat-soluble vitamins A, D, E, and K. Dogs love fat as much as we do. We fry food in it, smear it on bread, or spoon it over fruit. Pet-food manufacturers ensure that their foods have good quantities of fat because, as well as being necessary for the dog's body to function properly, fat smells and tastes good. Dogs are attracted to a food by the aroma of its fat.

The omega-3 family of essential fatty acids, such as DHA (docosahexaenoic acid) and EPA (eicosapentaenoic acid) reduce inflammation and may assist learning, while the omega-6 family, such as linoleic and arachidonic acid, are needed for good coat condition, blood clotting, and heart function.

Sugars, starches, and fibres

A final source of energy are the digestible carbohydrates, usually from cereals and legume vegetables. Some contain sugars, usually glucose or fructose, that are absorbed by the intestines, while others are broken down into sugars by enzymes in the intestines.

Undigestible carbohydrates don't break down but pass undigested through the small intestine into the large intestine or colon, where resident micro-organisms ferment the fibre, creating some fatty acids but also gases. If your puppy is bombing you out of your home, this is how and where puppy wind is made. Undigestible or fermentable carbohydrate is good for dogs. It may lead to gas production, but it also helps regulate blood glucose. There's evidence it also plays a positive role in immune function.

Excesses and deficiencies

Vets today rarely see dogs with clinical vitamin or mineral deficiencies, but we do see dogs suffering from excesses caused by the good intentions of their owners.

The most common conditions caused by owners feeding excess nutrients are the array of bone and joint problems that develop when pups are fed too much calcium while growing. It's over 30 years since the Swedish vet Ake Hedhammar explained what happens when pups are over-supplemented with calcium, but judging from what my clients tell me, breeders of large and giant breeds still tell new dog owners to add calcium to their pup's food. Don't! It's unnecessary and can be damaging, as can some breeder's advice about not letting a large pup go up or down stairs or run until fully grown. All moderate exercise is wonderful for growing pups, even the fastest growing.

SOME ILLNESSES CAUSED BY NUTRIENT EXCESSES	
Excess of:	**Medical conditions**
Vitamin A	Joint pain, dehydration, CNS depression
Vitamin D	Weakness, vomiting, diarrhoea, brittle hair, loss of appetite, calcium deposits in soft tissue
Vitamin B6	Muscle weakness and loss of balance
Niacin	Convulsions, bloody faeces
Iron	Constipation, bloody faeces
Iodine	Dry, dandruffy coat; eye and nasal discharges

Dog treats can be excellent for teeth and gums but high in calories.

Food chews

Mistakes can happen

I feed my dogs a variety of good-quality, tasty commercial foods, mixing wet with dry. Inca, a Labrador (*see* pages 20–1) prone to weight gain, is given "light" food, while Macy, a Golden Retriever (*see* page 26) who was not a food-obsessive, got the regular brand. I sometimes change brands (gradually over several days), and I only feed foods I know have been evaluated through feeding trials. Right now I'm feeding sachets of wet food with pasta, peas, carrots, and meat, added to dry food formulated for large-breed dogs. I feel

secure feeding commercial dog food, but I'm aware that the unexpected can happen. In 2001 in the UK, dog owners and vets were surprised by an epidemic of canine garlic breath. This was traced to inadvertent garlic contamination of a batch of vitamin and mineral supplement used by a variety of manufacturers. In 2007 in North America, melamine, a chemical found in plastic and fertilizer, found its way into commercial canned food. The contamination came from a large shipment of gluten, used as a binding agent in wet foods, from China, distributed to five pet-food manufacturers. Iams, Nestlé Purina, Hills Pet Nutrition, and others withdrew food from the marketplace. Canadian and New York State agriculture scientists also found the toxic chemical aminopterin in some contaminated supplies.

Dry food

Home cooking for your dog

I'm so old that I not only remember when milk and bread were delivered by horse-drawn wagons (Silverwood Dairies and Brown's Bread), I also remember when most dogs were fed on table scraps! Honest. That's when some dogs suffered from nutritional deficiencies. If you plan to cook for your dog, don't overdo the meat. Meat is low in vitamins A and D, but particularly in calcium. You can kill a dog by feeding it only meat. Avoid tofu and other bean products, especially for deep-chested dogs. These foods stimulate gas production and increase the risk of life-threatening bloat.

Prevent food guarding

Don't be surprised if your new pup, and especially your new adult dog, guards its food bowl. Food is very important to a dog, and it's normal for many to guard both their food and their food bowl. It's quite easy to prevent this from becoming

---

QUESTIONS AND ANSWERS

Do dogs need supplements?

There's a thriving business in nutritional supplements. Although the science remains in the most part tentative, I'm participating. I use free-radical scavenger supplements (containing selenium, zinc, vitamin A, and vitamin E) for older dogs, essential fatty acid supplements (such as fish oil or flax oil containing EPA and DHA) for dogs with joint, skin, or inflammatory conditions, and "chondroprotective" supplements (such as glucosamine or green-lipped mussel) for dogs predisposed to joint disease. I also use "brain food" supplements containing acetyl l-carnitine, DHA fatty acids, vitamins C and E, alpha lipoic acid, n-acetyl cysteine, coenzyme Q10, phosphotidylserine, and selenium for both growing pups and elderly dogs.

a serious problem, but harder to deal with it if the behaviour is already learned and has become ingrained.

Accustom your dog to taking food gently from your hand. This focuses its attention on you. Sit where you plan to feed your dog, offer small amounts of kibble in the palm of one hand, and stroke with your other hand. Offer only a few pieces at a time; too many and they might be scattered. The result is your dog doesn't mind either your presence or your touch when it eats.

Next, train your dog to accept you both touching it and removing the food bowl while it's eating. Do this by staying close while it's eating from the bowl, and adding a tasty treat – for example, liver treats – to the bowl. Use your hand to mix the treat into the food. Your dog will wonder how you did it, what magic you used to make the food so much tastier. Graduate to offering a liver treat by hand and, as you do so, lifting the food bowl, adding the treat, then giving it back. By doing so (daily at first and intermittently later in life), you train your dog to accept the temporary "loss" of food, and as an adult it will be less likely to guard food.

Wet food

QUESTIONS AND ANSWERS

Are raw bones good for pups?

Eating bones is the classic double-edged sword. Yes, of course raw bones are good for pups. Dogs evolved from a species that captured, killed, and ate other animals, including their bones. Bones are nutritious, and chewing on them keeps the teeth and gums healthy. On the other hand, I've had to operate on dogs to remove bones (especially chicken and lamb bones) stuck in their stomachs or intestines as often as to remove all other swallowed items put together. In my experience, chewing on bones is also the most common way a dog causes a "slab" fracture to molar teeth. If you plan to feed your new dog bones, start when it's a young pup and more likely to learn to eat and chew sensibly.

Raw bones go off; in warm weather, dispose of the remains on the day they're given. Raw bones are messy, for your dog and for your home. And raw bones are valuable commodities. If you have two dogs, one will always want the other's bone, even if it has its own. If there's aggression, don't give bones when two dogs are together.

BRUCE'S TIPS ON FEEDING

- Dark chocolate contains a chemical that's potentially toxic for some dogs.
- Raw onions, onion powder, avocados and raw potatoes are all potentially toxic.
- Train your dog to have food only from your hand or its food bowl, never from you at the table or off your plate.
- Raisins and grapes are toxic to some dogs. Give them in moderation or not at all.
- Avoid junk food. Avoid junk food for your dog too.

- If your picky eater seems to eat better from your hand or when the bowl is raised from the floor, have your vet check that there are no upper-neck problems.
- If you have two dogs, feed each one from its own bowl, preferably tail to tail so they don't watch each other eating.
- Check the water bowl several times each day and keep it filled with fresh water. If your dog is drinking more than normal, contact your vet immediately; this is often a sign of significant medical problems.

Shopping and travelling

Shopping, sociologists tell us, is our most popular pastime in the Western world, followed by walking outdoors – unless you're in Sweden where hunting (but still on foot) is the second most popular hobby. Wherever you live, dogs are the perfect intermediaries for combining these two popular leisure activities. The dog accessory market is burgeoning, with many international luxury names offering their logo-branded items to augment the extensive range of reasonably priced and practical articles available for you to choose from. Whatever you're purchasing, make sure it's designed with your dog in mind, not just fashion, and that it's useful when you travel with your dog.

An adult flat collar with clip fastening

A soft puppy collar with buckle fastening

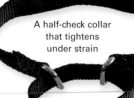

A half-check collar that tightens under strain

Collars, harnesses, leads, and ID

You already have a puppy collar and lead. As your dog grows, check that the collar still fits. It should be loose enough to get two fingers under, but not so loose it can slip over the head. When your dog gets an adult collar, it's up to you whether to use the same one all the time or, like one of my veterinary nurses and her Pug (*see* page 36), provide collars for different occasions, including a black collar with turquoise stones and silver conches for formal occasions. On dark evenings, I use a flashing-light, reflective collar so I can let my dog off the lead in the park and still see her. If you swap collars, remember to transfer tags. Head harnesses, such as the Gentle Leader or Halti, are ideal for powerful dogs, and body harnesses for small dogs or those with small heads.

A lead of 100cm (39in) is fine, but get a longer one, up to 10m (33ft), if you live where dogs are never allowed off their leads. Get an extendable lead only if you promise me you'll learn how to use it properly; my clients mostly use them to tie themselves and their dogs in knots. Some people like chain leads because they can't be chewed through. I don't: train your dog not to chew. Chain leads are much too heavy for young pups. Practical dog

Halti body harness

Body harness for use in a car

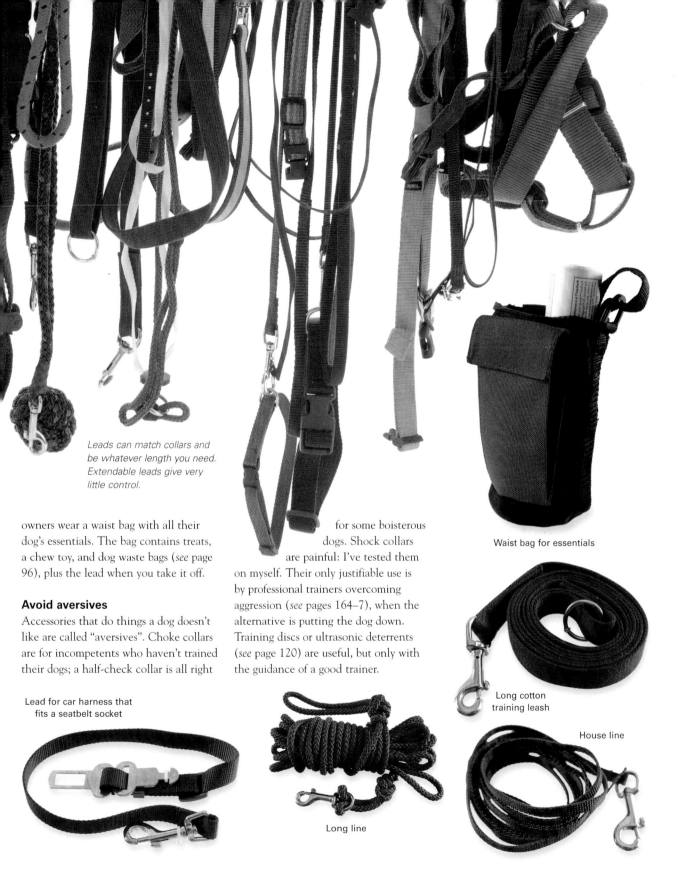

Leads can match collars and be whatever length you need. Extendable leads give very little control.

owners wear a waist bag with all their dog's essentials. The bag contains treats, a chew toy, and dog waste bags (*see* page 96), plus the lead when you take it off.

Avoid aversives

Accessories that do things a dog doesn't like are called "aversives". Choke collars are for incompetents who haven't trained their dogs; a half-check collar is all right for some boisterous dogs. Shock collars are painful: I've tested them on myself. Their only justifiable use is by professional trainers overcoming aggression (*see* pages 164–7), when the alternative is putting the dog down. Training discs or ultrasonic deterrents (*see* page 120) are useful, but only with the guidance of a good trainer.

Waist bag for essentials

Long cotton training leash

House line

Lead for car harness that fits a seatbelt socket

Long line

Good, bad, and ugly toys

Your selection of toys depends on your dog's size, activity level, and personal preferences. Find out what your dog likes by offering toys with a variety of uses: some to carry, some to manipulate for food (*see* pages 78–9), some to "kill", and some to "baby".

Kong

Avoid any toys that are similar to everyday household items you don't want your dog to play with.

Distraction toys

These are toys that provide food rewards when your dog plays with them alone. Some, such as activity balls, release food when moved around by nose or paw.

Textured bone

Others, such as hollow Kongs or hollow marrowbones, reward chewing. Other distraction toys include Nylabone-type and solid Kong-type toys that have been treated to give them appealing odours and are used for either chewing or carrying. Plastic empty water bottles are cheap and plentiful and can be carried by dogs or used as

Tug-of-war or
throwing toy

distraction toys, as the dog finds out
how to manipulate them to get water
out of the neck of the bottle. Take care,
however, if you have an inveterate
chewer in the house: plastic bottles
are easily shredded,
creating sharp edges.

Interactive toys

Use these toys when playing
games with your dog (*see* pages
142–5). They include Kongs on
ropes, tug-of-war toys, frisbees,
and of course tennis balls.
Dogs love tennis balls. My dog
collects abandoned ones from
the park. They're lightweight,
but potentially obstructive for
giant breeds with wide throats.

Playing with a toy with you is
important for your dog, because
if it focuses on a specific task,
like repeatedly returning a
tennis ball or Kong, or playing hide-and-
seek with treats or toys, your dog safely
releases any pent-up mental and physical
energy. That makes time alone, when
you can't interact with your dog because
you've got your own life to attend to,
much less stressful. For young, high-
energy, or untrained dogs,
interactive play offers an
opportunity for socialization
and helps them learn about
appropriate behaviour with
people and other animals
and – avoid inappropriate
behaviour like jumping
up (*see* pages 138–9)
or being mouthy
(*see* pages 140–1).

Comfort toys

Soft toys suitable for carrying around are
particularly good for breeds such as
spaniels and retrievers with a heightened
desire to carry. It's sad, but whenever any
of us go on holiday, we return with
comfort toys from wherever we've been –
a beaver in a canoe, a leprechaun – for
all seven retrievers in my immediate
family. Soft toys should be machine
washable and labelled safe for children
under three years old, although that only
means that the filling isn't toxic, not that
the toy is indestructible. Comfort toys

*Keep toys to a minimum and ensure they
are as unlike other articles in your home,
such as your shoes, as possible.*

aren't appropriate for all dogs. Terriers,
for example, often want to shake and
"kill" comfort toys and are inclined to
destroy them. Be particularly cautious
with any toy that has a squeaker
buried in it. Again, some terriers
have a compulsion to find and
destroy squeakers. Influenced by
female hormones, some bitches also
take to relentlessly squeaking their
squeaky toys. Take care
with discarded children's
toys, especially those with
plastic eyes or buttons.
Rotate your dog's toys
weekly, making only three
or four of them available at
a time. However, if
your dog develops
a particular
preference for a
soft comfort toy,
always leave
that one out
and available.

Soft cotton
rope

**Hollow activity
toy with food**

*Don't live in a toy store!
This dog has too many toys
and, as a result, may learn
to chew on anything.*

Blunt-tipped scissors

Double-sided dog brush

Grooming mitt

Slicker

Rubber curry comb

Grooming kit

Even if the coat may need only weekly attention, groom your new dog at least once a day so that it becomes accustomed to your doing so. Do this in a variety of locations, outdoors as well as at home.

Smooth- or short-coated dogs need only a chamois or soft-medium bristle brush. Dogs with longer coats need a comb and a slicker brush for removing tangles. Most dogs enjoy the feel of a curry comb or Zoom Groom, which removes dead undercoat and stimulates the skin. Use only blunt-tipped scissors when cutting any hair. If your dog needs heavy-duty grooming or even clipping, get expert advice from a professional dog groomer. Your vet's receptionist will be able to recommend one in your area.

Seasonal and fashion accessories

Yes, there are eye goggles, branded visors, sports-branded sweatshirts, faux-fur coats, and unending designer paraphernalia for your dog, but just who are these things for? Your dog has no say in the matter; are you absolutely sure it's happy to wear antler ears and sunglasses? There certainly are circumstances where clothing is necessary, such as rainwear for dogs with poor waterproofing, reflective coats for night-time walks or for hunting companions, cold-weather coats for poorly insulated dogs living in cold climates, and boots for dogs susceptible to paw damage from sharp, very hot, or very cold surfaces. On the fashion front, I stock a small range of thin but insulating T-shirts for dogs that state "I am ill", "Unwell", or "Please don't feed me. Vet's orders". Have fun buying accessories for your new dog, but bear in mind your dog's dignity as well as your fashion sense.

Thin-haired, thin-skinned individuals such as this Lurcher benefit from added protection against the elements.

Grooming not only cares for the skin and coat, it also reinforces your relationship with your dog.

Carry a first-aid kit. Carefree dogs are prone to minor problems you can manage yourself.

Travelling with your dog

Dogs are terrific travel companions. Some of you know I went travelling with my dog Macy, who romped in the Gulf of Bothnia in Scandinavia and the Gulf of Mexico in Mississippi, Lake Ontario in Canada and Lake Balaton in Hungary, the Yellowstone River in Montana and the Necker River in Lithuania, the Adriatic Sea in Italy and the North Sea in Germany. We stayed in campgrounds and motorhome and caravan parks.

If you plan to travel with your dog, even if only on short journeys, accustom it now to what you expect. Condition your dog to travelling in a crate, and if your

Identification tag

When travelling, carry clean, fresh water and a drinking bowl or bottle for your dog.

car is not large enough, purchase a pet harness that attaches to your car's rear seatbelt system (*see* pages 106–7). You'll need a seat cover to keep the back seat tidy and, of course, a car towel.

Car sickness

Car sickness is common in young pups. If yours suffers from it, condition it into not being sick by inviting it into the car, giving a food treat, then letting it jump out. Progress to putting it in the car, turning the engine on for a minute, then off, and rewarding it for not being sick. Next, turn on the engine, drive out of your parking space and back in, and give a reward for not vomiting.

Gradually increase the journey length until your dog is reliably conditioned. If you have an unavoidable journey before this, avoid a large meal before the trip, although curiously, a very small meal is helpful for some dogs. Your vet can supply you with anti-nausea medication, and naturally, take a towel and cleansing wipes with you.

Holidays with your dog

You'll need most of your dog's accessories, lead, food and water bowls, food and food treats, a large bottle of water for during the journey, bedding, a comfort toy, a brush or comb, a towel, scoop bags, and the vaccination certificate (which you might have to show at campsites).

For security, ensure that the name tag has your mobile telephone number on it. Of course, check ahead that wherever you plan to stay (including with your friends) accommodates dogs.

Dogs and heat

If you're travelling from one climate to another – for example, from northern to southern Europe or vice versa remember that your dog needs to adjust to climate changes just as much as you do.

Travel with your dog can be a pleasure, but do ensure that your vehicle is appropriate and properly adapted for your dog's safety and comfort.

Compared with humans, dogs are very inefficient in getting rid of excess heat. We sweat over our entire bodies, but dogs can only sweat through the pads of their feet. Instead, they rely on panting, a very inefficient way to prevent overheating. In direct sunshine, in a car with the air conditioning off and the windows closed, a dog can suffer from heatstroke within minutes. This happens fastest in hot weather, but I've seen dogs suffer from heatstroke even in winter when left in airtight cars on cold but brilliantly sunny days. Never, ever leave your dog alone in a car in sunshine, even if you've left the windows partly open. Find someone to look after it while you do whatever you have to do.

Taking your dog outside

SUPPORT NETWORKS

Make your dog contacts now
At first, you and your family are, of course, responsible for all of your new dog's activities, but do plan for the future from the start. If your lifestyle means you might need dog walkers, dog day-care centres, dog sitters, and dog boarders, ask your vet's staff for suggestions. Check their credentials and speak to people who have used their services.

Get down to your dog's level. This will encourage it to stay and play with you when it first ventures outdoors.

When epidemiologists found that dog owners have lower systolic blood pressure and triglyceride levels than similar people living without dogs, they thought these were the result of simply living with dogs. They were wrong. Further studies found that the health benefits occurred in dog-walking owners. Walking your dog is good for your health. Your dog should go outside as soon as possible, even before it's fully trained.

Outdoor safety, supervision, and socializing
Before your dog goes outside, take a few simple precautions. Make sure it's carrying two forms of ID, a name tag on the collar and an implanted microchip under the skin (*see* page 69). Your dog wants to get outside because it's exciting out there. You want it to venture outdoors because you know that the more positive and varied experiences it has now, the more laid back it will be when

Dogs are naturally waterproof, but the enjoyment of getting wet varies with the individual. Ensure your dog finds its first outdoor visits exciting, not frightening.

unexpected things happen later in life. Walk on varied surfaces, not just on grass, gravel, and pavement but also, for example, on shiny marble floors. Introduce different types of outdoor stairs and steps, park gates, and park visitors on bicycles or skateboards, pushing baby strollers, pulling wheeled luggage, or jogging by. Go on car rides and visit petrol stations and the car wash. Use public transport. Expose your dog to the cacophony of sights, smells, and sounds of a local construction site.

There's the odd curmudgeonly humbug out there, but the overwhelming majority of people have a knee-jerk response to puppies. They go soft, sloppy, and gooey. Even guys do. Capitalize on this. Take treats with you, and have strangers, who would otherwise never have spoken to you, give them to your new dog.

Control your new dog outdoors

It's great fun taking your pup out to meet life, but don't get carried away just talking to people you both meet. Yes,

your dog is gorgeous. Yes, your dog is adorable, but stay focused. Right now you're using a short lead and not an extending lead (*see* pages 106–7) for security. Lead training has yet to come (*see* pages 136–7), but when you meet other dogs, keep the lead loose and make sure it doesn't get tangled in the other dog's lead.

The outdoors is thrilling and exciting for your dog, and this will create challenges for you. You'll need to train it not to jump up on people (*see* pages 138–9). When a dog sees either urban wildlife, such as squirrels, or rural animals, such as rabbits or livestock, its instinct will be to chase. That's another dog behaviour you'll need to channel elsewhere (*see* pages 142–5). Confident dogs thrive outdoors, but for less confident ones, especially those that weren't well socialized when they were young, going outside the security of your home can be very frightening.

It can be scary out there

Puppies may be frightened by obvious things, such as big, growling dogs, or innocuous ones; an unexpected rustling of leaves can frighten an insecure dog. A frightened puppy may try to run away, cower with its tail tucked under its body, shiver with its ears back, hide behind your legs, or defensively snap, growl, or bite. Don't go motherly and protective and offer soothing words and warm arms.

Always keep your new dog on a secure, not tight, lead until it is reliably trained to wait and come on command from some distance.

If you do, unwittingly you're reinforcing your dog's behaviour. And don't try to drag your puppy toward what appears to frighten it. Instead, go all theatrical. Use a funny voice and offer toys, food treats, or games to get its mind on the positives outdoors, rather than the negatives.

If that's not enough to calm your new pup, then back away from whatever has frightened it until it calms down. From here, use treats, games, and activity to start rebuilding its confidence. When its possible and practical, gradually get closer to what's frightened it, praising and rewarding when your pup is more relaxed, but never when it's frightened.

"Trade you" training

It's only when you have a dog that you fully realize how much dangerous stuff is lying around on streets and in parks. "Trade you" is an important form of training, used when you want your dog to leave something interesting but potentially dangerous (takeaway chicken bones, dead rodents, used hypodermic syringes) that might be chewed or swallowed. Practise "trade you" routinely, indoors and outdoors, from the time you get your pup.

1. Give your pup its chew toy, but with no food in it.

2. Offer a liver treat, and as your pup drops the empty chew toy for the more powerful food treat, say "Drop".

3. Repeat this exercise several times in a row, several times a day, and once your pup responds well, graduate to having it relinquish a more valued item – for example, the chew toy with a biscuit in it, for the liver treat.

4. Once your pup consistently and willingly trades, graduate to items you don't want it to eat, such as sticks in the park or rubbish on the street. These exercises should be practised by everyone in the family, including responsible children, so your dog

Always have a distracting treat handy to trade with your dog when it has something you don't want it to have.

QUESTIONS AND ANSWERS

Is it OK if my dog chews sticks?

The right answer is no. Sticks are surefire income-earners for vets. They can pierce the throat, leading to infections and maybe to extremely complicated surgery. Bits can be swallowed, leading to pain or surgery to remove them from the stomach or intestines. Less dangerously, they catch in the roof of the mouth, causing discomfort and, if not removed quickly, infection. Dogs should be given chew toys, such as Kongs or hollow bones. That's my answer as a vet. But as a dog owner, I've let my dog chew sticks. My retriever's greatest thrill was to find a heavy branch and then parade it, her head and tail held high. When her neck was about to break, she put it down and chewed on the end of it. I let her do so under supervision, just as I let her chew on bones. Others will disagree with this, but there are risks in all aspects of life; in this, I found the value to my dog (and to me) outweighed the risks to her.

will trade with anyone. If you don't have any kids, rent some – the one caveat is if you have a new adult dog. Some adult dogs are protective of what they have and may guard viciously. Don't involve either your own kids or borrowed ones until you're sure that they aren't at risk from a possible bite.

Joining puppy classes

As far as I'm concerned, there's no better investment of your time and money than in joining well-run weekly puppy classes. These are usually restricted to pups under 16 weeks old and are worth the price of admission simply for the enjoyment of seeing other new dog owners with their sometimes bizarre range of new dogs.

Puppy classes, also called puppy parties or puppy kindergarten, can be chaotic if run poorly, but when run well they

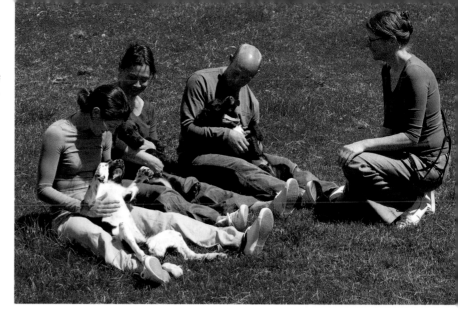

Playing "pass the puppy" accustoms pups to being handled by strangers.

let your pup meet other dogs and other people under well-controlled circumstances. What's really happening is that you're being trained in how to train your dog. Choose a puppy party run by a member of a recognized dog-training association (*see* page 191).

Be a good neighbour

Before even venturing outdoors with your new dog, know your local community's rules and regulations and stick to them. If you think your local rules are irrationally, unthinkingly anti-dog (and many are), use effective lobbying and the law to fight them. Anti-dog lobbyists are often vocal and active. Responsible dog owners frequently remain uninvolved until they find their freedoms have been compromised. Don't forget, dog ownership is one of our most popular recreational activities. There are lots of other dog owners who will join with you if you and your dog's right to exercise locally is being restricted. Most importantly, always carry plastic bags with you and always clean up your dog's

A well-behaved dog that remains calm and controlled around strangers – even those holding toys – is an ambassador for all dogs.

mess. If you've forgotten the plastic bag and only have paper money in your pocket, use that! Most "anti-dog" people aren't really anti-dog – they're anti-dog poop. Don't let your dog run riot either. Remove the causes of their concern, and you remove the problem.

The outdoors is messy

The hairier your new dog, the messier it will get outdoors. Your dog needs its own towel, for removing rain and snow. Use a water-filled washing-up bowl to remove murky water or mud from feet, and shower off sea salt or salt from winter roads. If your dog rolls in fox droppings (the most alluring perfume to many dogs), shampoo and rinse, not just to remove the sickly sweet stink: your dog has been where foxes are, and they are a common source of scabies mites.

Alone in the garden

Not now but eventually, if you're lucky enough to have a garden, you'll be able to leave your dog alone in it with suitable activity toys, water, and a shady place to relax in. My Macy spent her evenings in

ours, I'd like to say simply rolling on her back kicking her legs in the air, listening to birdsong, contemplating nature, all of which she did. But I know she was also on the alert for the unexpected, and if there was something exciting beyond the fence, she'd be out there to investigate. Before you leave your new dog alone in the garden for the first time, check the security of the perimeter to ensure your dog can't go over, under, or through it. Remove all potential edibles – and that includes inedibles, such as any garden or pool chemicals.

SETTING LIMITS

Wireless fencing

This works by training your dog to go no further when it hears a warning signal through the wireless collar it's wearing, or the collar will deliver an electric shock. If your dog is wet from rain the shock can be substantial. "Invisible" fencing leaves your dog unprotected against animals that can cross the invisible fence with impunity, unprotected against dog thieves, and unable to escape from possible danger without having pain inflicted. A physical fence is more humane and more effective.

Chapter 3
Simple obedience training

Encouraging acceptable behaviour

Your new dog has arrived home. You've provided personal space, and you're using food and chew toys effectively. Your family is brilliant, and everyone's singing the same song when it comes to playing and housetraining. I wish! Basic training is logical and simple, but family life sure isn't. It's easy for anyone in the family, including you, to get things wrong, to unwittingly train your dog to do exactly the opposite of what you want. This is quite normal, but if you understand the basics of training, you can minimize and correct mistakes.

Dogs are always learning

A dog's behaviour is moulded through experience, and whenever your dog experiences something that it likes, that reinforces its specific behaviour. Throughout their lives, dogs learn through active and passive experiences.

Passive experiences just happen and take place all day, every day. Your new dog is always learning from them, and you control these passive experiences by controlling your dog's environment. Don't break down and go sloppy in that control: continue using the playpen when someone's not there to monitor your new dog.

Active experiences are those that you create during the short periods you set aside each day for simple obedience training. This is when you show your dog how much fun it is not just to come, sit, and stay, or walk on a lead, but also how rewarding it is not to jump up on people or to mouth them or eat furniture.

Reinforce good, not bad, behaviours

A "reinforcer" is anything your dog likes. Some behaviour reinforcers, specifically tasty food treats, are more powerful than others, such as kind words and attention. Food, toys, access to people a dog enjoys being with, petting and stroking, your tone of voice, certain words you use, your facial expressions, access to the outdoors – all of these are day-to-day reinforcers of your dog's behaviour. There's another powerful behaviour reinforcer that's easy to forget about, and that's escaping from

Be aware that you are physically much larger than your dog. Standing over your dog can be quite threatening from its point of view.

"Old school" trainers used punishment to train dogs. Clever trainers use rewards. Their greatest reward for most dogs is a piece of dried liver.

It may be fun to be licked by a little pup, but unwittingly this pup is actively being trained to jump up at faces.

something unpleasant. If, for example, your dog is frightened by seeing someone on a skateboard and runs away, running away makes it feel better. This reinforces running-away behaviour.

When training your dog, use powerful positive reinforcers, especially food and toys, and couple them with less powerful reinforcers, such as your touch and voice. Eventually, once a behaviour is learned and entrenched, you'll graduate to using voice alone.

Always be on the lookout for negative reinforcers. Every one of us unwittingly reinforces something in our dog's behaviour that we later come to regret. Behaviours aren't forged in steel. They can be changed, but it's always easier to create a behaviour than it is to eliminate a formed one and then create a new one in its place.

A warm relationship is vital

At the core of enjoyable, productive, and successful dog training is the trusting relationship your new dog has with you.

If the relationship is positive, training is as logical and easy as 1-2-3. If you get exasperated and vent your anger on your dog, resorting to using discipline and

AVERSIVES

It's easy to be a negative trainer, to tell your dog what you don't want it to do rather than what you do want it to do. Then you get angry and discipline your dog when it doesn't understand what's happened. The Internet and even some pet shops are filled with aversives such as electric-shock or bark collars that guarantee quick training fixes. These are technological discipline machines for negative trainers. They don't deal with a behaviour problem; they deal with the consequence of the problem. They

guarantee physical or mental punishment when your dog does something you don't want it to do, and may make a problem even worse. Instead, look for the cause of the dog's behaviour. For example, work out why it's not coming back when you call it. What's the reward that it's found that's better than you are? Very mild aversives such as discs and water pistols are useful as simple means for breaking your dog's attention from what's distracting it, for giving you a split second to tell it what you want it to do. When you use

mild aversives, make sure it can't realize the "correction" is coming from you. You're after surprise, not retribution. A good trainer can show you how to use discs (or a water pistol) effectively.

Attention-getting training disc

punishment, all you'll ever have is a dog that obeys out of fear, not because it wants to please you. Your dog should not just trust your approach, your hands, and your touch, it should actively look forward to all of them.

Right now, with a new dog, you're at the very beginning of that relationship. If it's an adult, it's still not sure exactly how wonderful you are and might need time to forget former bad

relationships. This is particularly important with rescued dogs. Don't be confrontational; but at the same time, don't babble at your dog like a ditsy lamb. Never force your dog to have intense eye contact with you. It's needlessly frightening, pointless, and counterproductive. If you're in a bad mood, skip a training session. Don't take it out on your dog.

Understand your dog's body language

It's easy to make mistakes when training your dog if you misinterpret its body language. Most of us will recognize the overt signs that mean fear, worry, and submission: the desperate look in the eyes and the turned-back position of the ears, the tucked tail, rolling over showing

the belly, submissive urinating. But less overt signs such as panting, yawning, or simply looking away are just as important to watch for. Even a wagging tail that in some instances means happy alertness,

BRUCE'S TIPS ON TIMING

Dogs weren't born to sit around counting their paws. They need to be stimulated. They appreciate challenges. Your new dog is an unpainted canvas, waiting for you to start working on it. Be encouraging, and it will love short, frequent training sessions. Train whenever an opportunity arises. Sitting on command before a meal counts as a training session. Be sensible where you have other sessions. Start in quiet places where you have most control for example, a hallway with few distractions. Be realistic. Let me repeat that: be realistic. You're training a dog – a vibrant, sociable, and very trainable species, but it's not a human. Ask your vet to show you an MRI scan of a dog's head. You'll see lots of protective skull, honeycombed with extensive concussion-diminishing air sinuses. The brain? When you see its size, you will understand why some people tell me their dogs are peabrained.

Touch is a potent reward for pups like this one. Carrying also reinforces your authority.

in others means worry and trepidation. During a training session, if your dog shows any of these body-language signs, it is stressed; you should stop the training and give your dog something else to do. Stress interferes with learning. Work out what element of the training or the situation was causing the stress, and either avoid or don't repeat whatever stimulus triggered it.

Always use appropriate rewards

Find out what rewards your dog likes best, but don't just dole them out willy-nilly. Have your dog do something to earn each one.

Food is usually, but not always, the most powerful reward for a dog. Keep a selection of treats with ascending palatability to hand, so that you have a scale of rewards appropriate for the degrees of difficulty of whatever you're training your dog to do. Dehydrated liver pieces are usually the most rewarding treats, while small cubes of cheese and fresh or dehydrated pieces of chicken, lamb, or beef are also very appealing.

For non-foody dogs, a tennis ball or a squeaky toy will make an excellent reward. They work especially well for some terriers. Playing tug-of-war with you can also be a superb reward for some individuals. However, don't overestimate how rewarding your affection is, because it's the rare dog that will strive for nothing more than your godlike approval. That's a secondary reward. Start with food and toys.

The left hand on the collar helps stabilize movement, while the treat in the right hand lures the dog into position.

Simple training equipment

You have, of course, already acquired a selection of simple training items (*see* pages 108–9), but each time you visit the Internet or a pet shop you're tempted by more sophisticated ones offering instant success if you use them. Well, there's no such thing as instant success in dog training! Most of these dog-training aids use either pain or fear to control dogs, neither of which is necessary. In the extraordinary (often life-or-death) circumstances where some of these items might be needed, they should be used only by experienced dog trainers, who understand exactly when and how to use them.

A simple piece of equipment you should invest in is a longline, the long "shoelace" that I've previously mentioned. This is simply a 10m (33ft) long piece of nylon cord, with a trigger clip at one end and a big knot at the other, which stops it from running out from under your foot. Until your dog reliably comes when called, or waits on command, pop a longline on the collar so that you can get your dog off furniture, stop it at the top of the stairs, or control it at doorways.

Getting help

We're a pretty inconsistent lot, humans. Our decision-makers won't let us drive cars without taking driving instruction, yet they let us raise our kids without any formal instruction in how to do it. Do you realize how much damage that causes? When I become king of the world, I will start compulsory child-parenting classes for prospective parents. I will also inaugurate compulsory dog-parenting classes, for prospective "dog parents". In the meantime, by all means use this book, and your previous dog experience, but don't be shy about getting help. Even just an hour with an efficient and pragmatic trainer can work wonders.

DON'T WASTE TIME

The first year of a dog's life, from infancy to sexual and physical maturity, is equivalent in many ways to the first 16 to 18 years of a child's life. Can you imagine trying to start your child's formal education in the late teens? The younger a dog is, the easier it is to train. Don't procrastinate. Waiting until it's six months old before joining a dog training club is possible, but you'll spend lots of time undoing unwanted behaviours and catching up.

QUESTIONS AND ANSWERS

Should a dog be sent away for training?

Almost never. Certainly never for standard obedience training, which is probably all you'll ever want. If you send your dog away, it comes back obedience trained to the professional trainer, not to you. Dogs are sometimes "sent away" for specialist training – for example, to retrieve to the gun. At Hearing Dogs for Deaf People, professional trainers train dogs to act as ears for deaf people, but then their new owners are invited to live at the training centre for a week, during which time the dog's training allegiance is transferred to the owner.

My dog walker has offered to train my dog. Should I take up her offer?

Check out her training credentials. If she's a qualified trainer who uses positive reinforcement methods, is happy to take you out too, so that your dog responds to both of you, and you can afford her, it's a good offer. As long as it's one-to-one. There's no realistic way that a dog walker can train one dog while walking others.

A three-way relationship

The aim of any form of dog training is to enhance the relationship your new dog and your family have with each other. The important side effect is that your neighbours benefit too, because you have a well-controlled, reliable dog they see as an asset, not as an evil.

Any good dog trainer forms a ready relationship with your dog – a relationship that quickly becomes reciprocal. The trickier partnership the trainer must make, and in fact the primary one, is with you. You two have to work in harmony.

If you have a new adult dog, you'll benefit from an obedience instructor or sometimes from a behaviour counsellor (*see* opposite). If money allows, an initial investment in one-to-one training is ideal. Potential problems can be quickly identified, and a plan can be made to cater to your specific needs. You're then ready for less expensive, but equally rewarding, group classes at a local dog-training club. Obedience training is almost always better taught in the real

Training with other dogs helps teach them to pay more attention to you.

world of the company of other dogs. If you have a new pup, however, my advice is simple. Join a six-to-eight week-long session of weekly puppy classes.

What puppy classes are

A family-oriented puppy class (or puppy playschool, or puppy party, or puppy kindergarten) is worth paying to visit just for its entertainment value. They're funny, they're fun, and, for your pup, the adventure of attending one is coupled with wonderful values. A puppy class creates a social environment where your pup has the opportunity to develop social skills – not just with other dogs but with people of all ages – in a non-threatening, controlled environment. It's amazing to see how fast pups learn. Shy and fearful ones gain confidence. Thugs-in-waiting learn to tone down and behave more gently. The best classes balance socialization with basic obedience. All pups, and the people who accompany them, learn how to listen and ignore distractions, as well as the basics of how to wait, come, sit, and lie down on call. You'll pick up tips on how problems develop and how to overcome them.

This squeaky toy instantly gets the dog's attention.

BEING POSITIVE

Positive reinforcement training uses rewards, not punishment, to mould or change behaviours.

How to choose your puppy class and instructor

Unfortunately, there is no requirement that instructors at puppy classes (or obedience schools) know how to train dogs to be well-mannered pets. Absolutely anyone can print up some business cards, rent a space, and claim to be a dog trainer. Each dog needs its own tailored approach to obedience training. Tenderness works with insecure dogs, while more confident or even thuggish dogs respond to a strong will and strength of character.

Decide whether a group class or private lessons are best for your situation and your personal challenges, and ask your veterinarian or the Kennel Club for referrals. Select a trainer affiliated to an organization that uses positive-reinforcement training methods and has both a code of ethics and a formal complaints procedure.

Good and bad puppy classes

Pups love attending good puppy classes, where you'll see them using toys and treats, settling down and learning, but also playing with other pups off their leads. Efficient trainers are confident in their methods, and it's obvious that pups are rapidly progressing.

Bad puppy classes teach you to use fear or pain to train your dog through domination techniques like jerking your pup's lead, shaking your pup to teach it you're the boss, or the "alpha-rollover", a dominance technique, thankfully now used only by dog trainers from hell.

Observing before committing

Whether you're seeking a trainer for a new pup or a new adult, get suggestions from your veterinarian or from other dog owners, visit the recommended class before signing up, and seek answers to these questions:

- Is the trainer accredited and insured?
- Does it look like the trainer actually likes dogs?
- Are positive reinforcement methods, not fear or punishment, taught?

- Does the class seem happy? Are the dogs under control?
- Are there enough trainers to students?
- Are advice and instructions given clearly? Are there written instructions to follow at home?
- Does the trainer have a flexible approach when training different canine personalities?
- Does the trainer mention the Kennel Club's Canine Good Citizen test and suggest your dog works towards it?

All the answers should be affirmative. Reliable instructors don't describe particular breeds or mixes as untrainable or aggressive. If a reliable instructor prefers not to work with certain breeds, they should direct you to another school that does.

Talk to users, and be wary of unrealistic promises. Don't sign up unless it feels right to you. If you don't like the methods used in the class, find another club or instructor.

How the trainer trains

1 At productive classes, both the dogs and the trainer obviously enjoy what they are doing. This trainer, teaching his dog to "hold", has his dog's full attention: the dog wants to please.

2 As learning progresses, the trainer does not loom intimidatingly over the dog. As the dog responds well to training, the trainer's body language remains rewardingly positive and relaxed.

Classes that use clickers

Many training classes teach you how to "clicker train" your dog. A clicker is simply an item that clicks when squeezed. That click noise is a "marker". To your dog, at first it's just a meaningless sound, but soon it becomes associated with rewards, such as food treats or toys to play with. Clicker training is a superb method to use when training your dog, but timing is extremely important – so much so that you should have a dog trainer show you how to do it rather than rely on either a DVD or my telling you how on these pages.

Timing is vital with clickers.

Ensure your dog trainer belongs to an accredited dog-training organization.

Private or group lessons?

The advantage of group lessons is that both your dog and you see how others are doing and realize that what you think are your own particular problems are no more than variations on a short list of themes. If you're new to living with a dog and have a zillion questions to ask, it's useful to have some one-to-one time with a dog trainer, but it's still advantageous for you and your dog to participate in group sessions. If and when behaviour problems arise, most of these should be tended to through private lessons. Similarly, if you have just acquired an adult dog, a private lesson is a useful way to ascertain where problems may lie and how they can be overcome. This is often then done through group lessons.

TRAINERS AND PROFESSIONAL ORGANIZATIONS

WHAT TRAINERS CALL THEMSELVES
Dog help comes in many different guises. Ensure you're getting the type of help you need. Someone may be superb at advanced obedience but not good with behaviour problems, or vice versa.
Dog trainers train you to train your dog to listen to you and obey your instructions. Of course, dog trainers also train dogs.
Dog obedience instructors are dog trainers under a slightly different name, probably specializing in "obedience" at both preliminary and advanced levels, such as those used in obedience competitions.

Dog behaviourists, ethologists, or psychologists are dog trainers equipped with advanced training or experience, who have additional skills for helping overcome canine behaviour problems.

HOW TRAINERS ARE CERTIFIED
Ensure trainers belong to a professional group.
The British Institute of Professional Dog Trainers (BIPDT) certifies its instructors at several levels of competence.
The Association of Pet Dog Trainers (APDT) certifies its members, who emphasize positive-reinforcement dog training.

The UK Registry of Canine Behaviourists (UKRCB) maintains a code of practice for its members, who see dogs referred to them by practising veterinarians, for behaviour problems.
Centre of Applied Pet Ethology (COAPE) members have completed either a correspondence or a lecture course in animal behaviour and follow a written code of conduct.
The Association of Pet Behaviour Counsellors (APBC) also sees dogs referred to them by practising veterinarians for behaviour problems.

Getting your dog's attention

Fresh diced chicken
for food rewards

I walk my dog in the park each morning, to the twitter of birds and the plaintive, distant cry "Tolstoy!" Tolstoy is a Siberian Husky, and every day, Tolstoy's owner practises her spectacularly efficient method of *not* getting Tolstoy's attention. He is superbly trained to understand that hearing his name means he should continue sticking his nose up other dogs' bums. It's easy to get such training wrong; even easier to perpetuate wrongness. Make sure you win over the other wonders of life.

How to use your dog's name

I can assure you, the sights, sounds, and smells of life are much more interesting and intriguing than you are. Your new dog wants to investigate them now – instantly – whatever it's doing. To gain your dog's attention you have to compete with the thrills and excitement of this new life with you. You've already chosen a crisp, short, and distinctive name, but please use this name only when you want your dog's attention. During simple obedience training you'll use the name to gain attention, then couple it with the command word – for example, "Tolstoy, sit." The words coupled with your reward are "Good sit."

Your voice and body language

Your dog should be positively thrilled when it hears you say its name. Use the name only to call for fun, games, and

BRUCE'S ATTENTION TIPS

Only use your pup's name to attract its attention. Discover what it values most – food, toys, or games – and develop a selection of rewards, so that when distractions occur you can increase the value of the reward you can offer. Only use tiny food treats during training sessions, something that is quickly chewed and swallowed.

The more often you practise, the more reliable you both become. Practise basic obedience exercises many times a day – 15 to 20 times is wonderful – but for only a minute at a time. Make doing something for you part of your puppy's routine. Train before meals, when it's hungry.

When rewarding your dog's attention, limit praise to the positive tone of your voice, smiles, and treats. You'll probably want to reward by petting and cuddling, but physical contact during an exercise such as "sit" may encourage your puppy to get up before the exercise is over.

Teaching your dog to pay attention

1 Old-fashioned dog trainers use punishment to train dogs. Enlightened ones use rewards. This dog is initially being trained to respond to a food reward.

2 Using rewards, the dog is "lured" into the position you want it to assume. At the same time, the verbal command is given. It is rewarded with food and praise.

rewards. Never call your dog to discipline it, and never call it when you can't enforce the recall. If a dog learns that response is optional, as Tolstoy has, you'll find it frustratingly hard in the future to get its attention for just about anything.

During these first days with your new dog, attempt to get its attention only when you know you can. Dogs respond to happy voices, smiles, non-threatening body language, and, when they're not too distracting, strokes and tickles.

For example, when calling your dog to "come", squat down to its level, throw your arms open wide and say "Tolstoy! Come!" enthusiastically. Women usually find it easier than men to behave this way, but guys, try it. Not only is it efficient and fun, any watching women will also intuitively mark you down as a potentially superb father. Don't ever act like a dominant male, because a harsh low voice is threatening, looming over your dog is intimidating, and grabbing triggers fear.

Use daily activities

A dog will quickly learn to associate the sound of its name with the positive feelings it experiences from toys, meals, treats, cuddles, or play activities that come linked with that name. Use these daily highlights to your advantage. During training sessions, it's easiest to get your dog's attention where there are the fewest distractions. Carry out the first sessions in the quietest and dullest part of your home. This is often a hallway. Once you easily get your dog's attention there, graduate to more stimulating locales where there are more distractions: first a larger, quiet room; then a room where there's more activity; the back garden; and, eventually, exciting public spaces.

3 The dog follows the reward with its nose, and as it lies down, the command "lie down" is given. When it complies, it is rewarded with a treat and praise.

4 This dog is learning to walk nicely on a loose lead beside its owner, who uses the food reward to lure the dog into position. The dog's head and shoulders are next to its owner's left leg. The owner will stop the moment the dog starts to move ahead of her.

Calling your dog

Once your dog comes to you on command, train it to come away from distractions. With a quiet, non-gesturing helper, show your dog the helper has a distraction – a toy or treat – and you have nothing. Have your treat-laden helper walk a few paces away. Your pup will naturally follow. Now, call your pup to you while your helper turns away and ignores your pup. Use the longline if necessary to help your pup tune into you. Praise it when it simply looks at you, and give praise with touch, with words, and with Olympic-quality games when it returns. Food rewards can also be used intermittently.

Training your dog to come on command is a life saver – one of the most important obedience commands it will learn. The foundation of a reliable recall is your relationship with your dog. With a new dog, use your most powerful reinforcers during recall training: the tastiest treats, the best toys, and, after you've finished and are playing, cuddles, strokes, and favourite games.

Look inviting

You want your dog to think that coming to you is worthwhile, more worthwhile than anything else. You want it to think that being with you is better than being away from you. That's why your rewards should be compelling and you should train your dog when it's hungry. Your new dog has no idea what the word "come" means, so at first, don't say "come" until your dog starts on its way to you. Pair what it's doing to the word you're saying. Be theatrical. Make it want to come to you rather than stay where it is.

Training your dog to come when called

1 For most dogs, the great outdoors is intensely exciting and full of distractions, some of them dangerous. For the safety of your dog, a vital command is to "come" when called. Get a friend to hold your dog while it watches you walk off.

2 Your dog is more likely to come to you when you are on the ground at its level with a potential object of play as well as a treat. With the food treat in hand, this trainer vividly encourages her dog to come and, as it does, issues the "come" command.

What if my dog doesn't respond to my first call to him to come?

Stand on his longline and say nothing. You're in control. When he looks at you, smile and show him the treat. Don't give up using a longline until your dog responds on the first call every time.

Use a longline or a houseline

A longline is a light lead, about 10m (33ft) in length, with a large knot in the end (*see* page 107). It is used outdoors to aid recall. A houseline is shorter than a longline and has no knots (*see* page 107). It is typically used to keep your dog under control in the house. For example, if you have your foot on one end of a houseline you always have your dog under control. Both types of lead are available from pet

shops and vets, or can easily be made out of lightweight nylon rope or cord.

Whatever exercise you're carrying out with your dog, be in a position to enforce your command gently, without grabbing. By using a longline during recall training, you ensure that you're always in charge.

It's not a fishing line

Don't reel your dog in like a fish struggling on a line. Coming to you should be a positive thing. The longline is there simply to ensure a dog doesn't run away. Use it to give yourself confidence that no matter how long it takes, you'll always get your dog back by using praise and treats. Don't go and get it physically unless it's in danger, and never tell it off for not coming back. If it doesn't willingly do so, consider using a different form of reward. No matter how exasperated you are, finish with fun and games so your dog looks forward to the next two-minute training session.

- Be consistent with your commands: always use the same word.
- Make sure your dog comes right up so you don't have to reach out to give rewards.
- Don't call your dog if it's running away or toward something more exciting than what you can offer it. Never give it a command that you can't implement. If you allow your dog to ignore a command, you teach it that it doesn't have to return to you.

The "release command"

Your dog needs to learn that a specific word means a command is over. I use the phrase "OK" as a "release command" for my dog, although something that your dog is less likely to routinely hear, like "free", is better.

3 Ensure compliance by attaching a lightweight longline to the dog's collar. At first, keep one end of the line with you so that your dog doesn't wander too far. Graduate to only wearing a shortened longline, then no longline.

4 Once your dog reliably comes to you on command in a quiet location, graduate to an area with more distractions. At first, keep distractions minimal, such as other people present, before training where there are other dogs.

Wait and stay

There's a subtle difference between the commands "wait" and "stay". "Wait" means "stop where you are". Use "wait" when you're on the move, through doorways or at kerbs, and when you see a danger but your dog is oblivious. Your dog learns to stop, regardless of what it's doing, where it is, or what position it's in. "Stay" is more of a contract with your dog; you are leaving it somewhere for a short while but will return. "Stay" training, like training to sit, lie down, and stand (*see* pages 134–5), needs good, repetitive reinforcement, because your dog needs to learn to stay for an extended time before it hears the release command.

Teaching your dog to wait

1 "Wait" means just that: "Stop what you're doing now." As the owner approaches the kerb he puts a slight amount of pressure on the dog's collar.

2 At the kerb, having gained his dog's attention, the owner hand signals the dog, in front of his face, to wait. As he does so, he issues the command "wait".

3 The owner maintains the "wait" hand signal with his right hand and places no tension on the lead, held in his left hand. His left hand is where it should be when walking his dog.

Wait training

Most training teaches your dog to be by your side and to come when called. The commands "wait" and "stay" are different; they ask your dog to wait with you or not to be with you at all.

Wait is simply that. It can be a life saver. At a kerb, it means your dog is less likely to bolt into danger. When the car door opens, wait stops it from jumping out into traffic. Train your dog to wait every time you remove its lead in the park. Obeying the command "wait" teaches your dog that you're in control. Having been asked to wait, a dog then needs either a specific release word or another command, even if it's only "go play".

4 When he is ready to proceed, he withdraws the "wait" hand signal and gives the release signal, such as "let's go". Dogs must wait for your release command.

5 Once the dog is released from the "wait" command, he continues to walk to heel (*see* pages 136–7). Calm breeds or individuals are easily trained either on the lead or off the lead to "wait" on command. More rambunctious dogs need lots of repetitive reinforcement of this command. It is vital to start "wait" training in a quiet location without distractions.

"Stay" training

To obey a "stay", a dog needs confidence that you'll come back. Learning to stay in one place can be difficult for a nervous dog who emotionally needs you close by, for a wild puppy who wants to be everywhere at the same time, and for dogs who try to do your thinking for you.

When you return, release your dog from the stay and get down to its level for a cuddle or play. Once your dog stays reliably in one spot, generalize training so it can stay wherever you ask it to.

Problems with greedy dogs

Food treats may be too powerful to use as rewards for this training when working with food-obsessed dogs. The reward is so appealing that the foodaholic just can't wait or stay to get it and is tempted forward by the aroma of the snack. If this happens, avoid the most highly valued food treats when training, and use ones that your dog values less.

For a minority of dogs, toys should be used as a reward during the initial stages of training, rather than food treats.

Remember, whatever the rewards you are using, and whatever the problems you encounter, keep your voice happy.

Use consistent words

Do you remember the last time you tried to learn a foreign language? How it all sounded like a stream of gibberish? At the beginning of training, everything you say to your new dog sounds like gibberish to it, so give your dog the advantage of hearing consistent gibberish. Decide on the exact words that you'll all use during

Teaching your dog to stay

1 Use an obvious hand signal when training your dog to "stay" on command. With the dog on its lead to ensure compliance, the owner signals and commands the dog to "stay".

2 Maintaining the hand signal, verbal command, and eye contact with his dog, the owner moves his farthest leg away. Sometimes a reminder, by holding the collar, is necessary.

training, make a list of the words you plan to use to teach your dog the basic obedience commands, post it at home, and – I'm not kidding – make small copies for everyone to carry around.

Your dog might get these exercises wrong, either through misunderstanding what you want or by having a giggle and turning it into a game. I save the word "no!" for serious misdemeanours and use the more neutral "wrong", spoken in a flat tone, when a pup rolls on its back or tries to play. If your dog does the same, say "wrong", take a step forward to stand it back up, then start again.

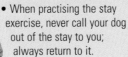
Chain of commands

These commands are followed by either another command such as "come", "sit", or "down", or a release word, such as "OK" or "free". Your dog is now starting to learn a sequence of commands. This is the basis of games that string together learned behaviours, such as waiting until you throw a toy, running after it, picking it up, carrying it back, and dropping it.

3 Having taken a first step away, the owner maintains the verbal and hand signals for another second. If the dog moves, quietly replace it in the original position.

4 Once the puppy has stayed, the owner returns to its side and gives quiet words of praise before releasing his puppy with the release command but no further praise.

Sitting and lying down

Your pup knew how to wait, stand, come, sit, lie down, and stay long before you met. Training is simply teaching it to do these very natural things at your request. Three lessons – sit, lie down, and stand – are variations on the same theme. Use your words of instruction carefully. Sit means sit. Stand means stand. Lie down means lie down. Asking a dog to "sit down" is confusing.

Training to sit

Start by getting your pup's attention: let it smell the treat you're holding between your thumb and forefinger and have a taste of it. With your pup's nose on your fingers, slowly move your hand up and over its head. The nose and eyes will follow the treat. As it naturally starts to sit to keep its eyes on the treat, say "sit", and when its butt hits the ground, reward with both the treat and specific words of praise: "good sit".

Teaching your dog to sit

1 Dogs should obey all reliable members of the family, regardless of size. With the treat in the right hand for attention, the left hand holds the harness to prevent unwanted forward movement.

2 The food treat is slowly moved above the dog's head, and as the dog spontaneously sits, to keep an eye on it, the trainer gives the command "sit" and rewards compliance.

Another way to teach your dog to lie is sitting on the floor with your knees raised. Lure it under with a treat until it lies, then reward it.

Don't hang around; give your release word, play with your dog a little, then repeat the exercise.

Training to lie down

With your pup in a sit, both of you facing the same way, and the treat in your hand, move your hand down between its paws and back towards you. Do this slowly so that it's easy for your dog to follow. As it

starts to lie down to maintain nose contact with the treat, give the command "lie down", and when its elbows are on the ground, reward with the treat and the specific words of praise, "good down". Then give your release word, play, and repeat the exercise. Gradually extend the length of time your dog sits or lies down. Some dogs need you sitting on the floor with them to increase their confidence.

Ask your dog to sit or lie down while you prepare its food or when it is near kids or frail or elderly people.

Training to stand

Your vet or groomer will appreciate this. With your pup in a sit and you by its side, treat in hand, draw the treat in a straight line away from its nose and forward. You

want your dog only to shift its weight forward and stand, not to walk, and you can place your left hand in front of its knees to block forward travel. As your dog starts to stand up, give the command "stand" and then food and praise rewards.

BRUCE'S TIPS ON POSITION

Dogs quickly tune into your body posture. Don't loom over it; your imposing presence may frighten it. Crouch down in an enticing way when you start training. That's not intimidating to a pup. As training progresses, move to an upright position.

Teaching your dog to lie down

1 In the "sit" position by its owner's side, both the dog and the owner are facing in the same direction, ready to start the exercise.

2 The owner moves his right hand with the treat down near the pup's front paws. Don't slide the treat forward. If you do, the pup's butt end will come up.

3 As the dog lies down, the owner issues the command "lie down" then rewards. If the pup's backside comes up, start again from "sit" with the treat closer.

Walking on a lead

Your new dog has to understand that, thrilling as life is, it's best to walk beside you, and that pulling gets it nowhere. A new pup or untrained adult naturally pulls. This is rewarding, especially for twice-a-day park visitors, because, next to boring old you, the park is exciting. Pulling you toward it, a dog meets interesting scents and objects, and then gets its greatest rewards, scampering around visiting park buddies. Each time you allow a pull, you add work for yourself. Train your pup to walk contentedly on a lead.

Hold the lead and any food reward in your right hand, the slack in your left.

Your objective

A walk starts before you leave the house, as soon as you pick up the lead. Your dog already sits on command and calmly lets you put the lead on. If not, go back to "sit" training (*see* pages 134–5). Your dog waits on command and lets you go out of the front door first. If not, go back to "wait" training (*see* pages 130–1). Your objective is for your dog to learn to walk quietly by your side, not in front of you. Don't expect a dog to learn instantly; take it a step at a time. This takes all of your attention, so train when you're alert.

What to wear

Never use an extending lead for this training; a short lead is best. Most dogs will be fine in a collar, but if you have a large or overenthusiastic dog, try a head halter. This is humane and effective. The lead attaches under the chin, and when

Teaching your dog to walk on a lead

1 Trainers train dogs to walk or "heel" to the left. Get the dog's attention with the command "let's go".

2 Start walking with your left foot, the one nearest your dog. The lead is slack and the dog's shoulder beside your leg.

3 The moment the dog moves in front of you, whether or not the lead is tight, stop.

MISTAKES TO AVOID

Don't always walk with food to follow. Your dog is a smart customer and will learn soon that it only needs to walk properly if you've got food in front of its nose.

Don't use low-value rewards. This exercise can take a little more time, and a dog should be amply rewarded when it performs well.

Don't stare at your dog with beady-eyes. It's very intimidating.

Don't let your dog decide what and where to sniff. Dogs need to sniff; every so often take a break from walking on the lead and give permission to sniff.

Don't let your pup greet everyone. If friendly people or other dogs appear, stop walking and command your pup to sit.

Don't pick up a dog that refuses to walk on the lead. This teaches that refusal is rewarded by your touch. Persevere until it finally volunteers to continue the exercise.

Don't let your dog become a yo-yo on the lead. Don't yank on it. Constantly yanking or pulling back – strangling your dog – teaches it nothing except to try to get away.

Don't have your dog on one side one day and the other side another. Be consistent. Dog trainers opt for the left.

---

the dog pulls forward, its own momentum pulls the head down. Ensure that the halter is fitted correctly, so that the noseband can't work up into the eyes, and release pressure as soon as possible.

Rewarding and releasing

When your dog has walked two or three steps, put it into a sit and reward it. Repeat this several times, but stop before your dog gets bored.

At the end of training, tell your dog that training is over. Your chosen release word is important, so use it each time you finish any training session. Have your dog sit, then say the release word. That release word means it can do whatever it wants, rather than concentrate on you.

Potential problems

If your pup is not paying attention or pulls ahead, keep your cool and just stop. Once the lead slackens and the dog looks at you, smile, praise, offer a food treat to bring it into position, and start again. But if your pup drops on the ground and refuses to walk, work out why. Is it not interested in the treat you're using? Is it so used to being carried that that's what it always expects? Is it frightened? Is it ill? Eliminate the cause of the behaviour before trying lead training again.

Before training is successful

I'm not about to suggest that you don't leave the house until your pup will obediently walk on a lead while out. By all means, visit the local park, but keep your requests and expectations fair.

4 Lure the dog back beside you into the correct position and give it a treat once it's in that position.

5 Start walking again. Repeat the start-stop until the pup realizes it is rewarded for being in the right place.

BRUCE'S TIPS ON WALKING

- Make sure your dog's collar fits well, so that there's no risk it will slip over the head, and that it carries an ID tag.
- Play with your dog to burn up energy before starting a lead-training session, and keep sessions short but frequent.
- Practise in the boring hallway before graduating to more stimulating places.
- Concentrate! Turn off your mobile. Pay attention to what you're doing.
- If you're tall and your pup is small, use peanut butter on a wooden spoon as a lure. This saves your back. Believe me.
- If you don't understand what you're doing, get help.
- Always praise your dog when it gets it right, and end on a positive even if it's been a pain in the butt.

Preventing jumping up

Jumping up on people is positively thrilling. A pup gets touched, spoken to affectionately, maybe even the odd treat. You know you don't want your pup to jump up when it's bigger and stronger, so every so often you say "no" or "get down" and reprimand it. Sometimes you just ignore it. You know what? By sheer chance, you've hit upon the most effective and efficient method of dog training: intermittent rewards. It's as if your new dog were playing a one-armed bandit and sometimes hits the jackpot. It's easy to *create* a jumping addiction. Here's how to *avoid* one.

Teaching your dog not to jump up

1 Using body language that encourages the dog to seek attention, the owner has inadvertently taught it to jump up.

2 When you see your dog, remain calm and still. If your dog jumps, turn away and disregard it.

Simple steps

Prevention is simple. It's based upon your pup having previously learned to "sit" before meals, "sit" before attention, "sit" before play. When your new dog is sitting, it can't be jumping.

When people come to the door, your pup is instructed to sit. While walking, if strangers want to meet your cuddly little thing, it's instructed to sit. Curiously, it's harder to train your family and strangers than it is your dog.

Train your family and strangers

Jumping up is more of a problem with enthusiastic, highly sociable dogs than it is with insecure ones. Enthusiasts thrive on attention, even if it's negative attention such as "Get off me!"

Because jumping up is so rewarding, you should seriously regard it as an addiction. It's far easier to prevent than it is to cure. People will say they don't mind your pup

jumping on them. Say "Bad person!" and explain that, yes, it's adorable, but many other people don't like dogs jumping up. If you're not consistent in your training, you'll end up with a dog that irritates some people, especially people who are already anti-dog.

Greet the dog at its level

It's much easier to get your dog to sit if everyone – you, your family, neighbours, and strangers – initially greets it from an upright position. Once it is sitting and calm, bend down to give the treat. Save cuddling and playing with your new pup until it has reliably sat and not jumped up. When you do play with your dog, get right down on the ground, which becomes your puppy's cue that it can act like a puppy and be petted and played with. If you've got an overenthusiastic pup, leave a short houseline on, and as it starts to jump up, put your foot on the

line so your pup checks itself back down. Praise it once all feet are back on the floor and it is in the "sit" position. With a new adult dog, keep it on a longline at home and in the park until you know it's not a jumper; and if it is, use the longline so that it checks itself.

3 If your dog has an unmitigated zest for life, commands may not be enough. Attach a houseline to its collar, and when it tries to jump up, stand on the line so it checks itself down.

4 Once you have your dog's attention, command it to "sit" and give a food reward for compliance. If it jumps again, give it no attention and turn your back.

Preventing mouthing

To a puppy, mouthing and biting your hand with pin-sharp teeth is as natural as eating and sleeping; so is growling while doing it. This is what pups do in their litter; puppy play can be rough. If it gets too rough, the bitten pup shrieks and stops play. Game over. Pups learns through trial and error how to limit the power of their bite. You want your dog to mouth or bite chew toys, not you.

Attention seeking

Puppies mouth to get attention. Some are also finding out how far they can go, how dominant they can be. If mouthing works in puppyhood, a dog continues with it as an adult, and the word for that is "BAD". A puppy that mouths is cute and funny.

Only weird people enjoy being mouthed by fully grown dogs. Pups easily learn to mouth for attention. As with jumping up (*see* pages 138–9), it is easier to overcome when a dog is young. Only reward good behaviour. Give your dog attention and praise if not mouthing, but none if it does.

Teaching your dog not to mouth

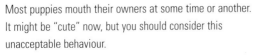

1 Most puppies mouth their owners at some time or another. It might be "cute" now, but you should consider this unacceptable behaviour.

2 The instant the puppy puts its teeth on any part of you, shriek loudly so the puppy is startled. He will naturally let go.

How to use the mouth is learned early, when a puppy is still with its littermates. Dogs learn from other dogs how to inhibit their bites. Orphans, lone pups, or those that leave the litter too early are the ones most likely to have biting and mouthing "issues". These dogs need additional help in their training.

The exercise

To overcome this problem, we simply do what dogs do. Pups "punish" others for mouthing them too hard by stopping any further play. That's the rule: play stops when puppy teeth touch human skin.

When your pup mouths any part of you, shriek like an injured pup. If you've got a wired-up toughie and a shriek makes it more excited, bellow like a wounded bull elephant. Men often find this easier than loudly yelping or shrilly crying out. Break off and leave the pup. If there's a door, walk out, shut it, and count to five. Return to the room the pup is in, and ignore it. After a minute, when you're assured it's calm, command it to sit, to reassert your authority, then give the release word and you can start playing again.

Puppy bites and children

Puppies and children almost inevitably wind each other up, and excitement leads to problems. Kids move unpredictably and scream or shriek in a way that can excite a pup. Waving arms and running away, in fear or fun, excites pups even more. Don't leave children and new dogs together. Teach your children to move slowly around your new dog and to turn to statues and avoid eye contact when it gets too excited. Always have a chew toy between a dog and a child. It reduces the risk of the dog mouthing the child.

Don't let children wave their hands around your new dog. Don't do so yourself either.
Don't grab your pup to pick it up. Grabbing with your hands is like a littermate grabbing with its jaws. Both can trigger a mouthing response.
Don't play "chase me" games until your pup has learned not to mouth you.
Don't play tug games of strength until your puppy learns to give up toys easily.
Don't pull toys from your dog's mouth. Teach it to come off toys at your command.
Don't leave toys all over the floor. When not in use, they should be in the toy box.
Don't let your dog growl during play. If it growls over possession of a toy, end the game instantly.
Don't pretend you're a dog and growl.
Don't deny your dog its normal need to mouth. Give ample play time with other dogs and a selection of suitable chew toys.
Don't share your kids' toys with your dog.

3 Immediately offer your hand to the pup again. It should remember your shriek and not mouth you.

4 Give quiet praise and a tasty treat for not mouthing you.

Playing with your dog

Dogs enjoy playing games for the same reasons we do. They feel good when they play, and neuroscientists have identified the feel-good factors, the actual chemicals their bodies release, that contribute to their enjoying play so much. Like us, dogs play for these physiological rewards, but play is also a natural outlet for their biological need to chase, capture, and chew. Your dog needs the physical and mental satisfaction of these activities and will create its own satisfying games, such as chasing vehicles or joggers, unless you intervene and control play. Playing games with your dog is a natural continuation of obedience training.

Games are educational
Use games to reinforce standard obedience and to reward your dog's good behaviour. For example, with hide-and-seek games, you hide yourself or a toy, and when your dog discovers either, it's rewarded for its efficient recall to you (*see* pages 128–9). A variation

Keep tug-of-war games low-key, short, and fun for both of you. If growling starts, the game is over.

is to lay a simple scent trail for your dog to follow to whatever is hidden. The games you play with your dog educate you about how your dog thinks. You learn how willing it is to interact with you.

Games give you control

Playing with your dog builds the trusting bond between the two of you. The better your dog trusts you, the easier it is both to train it further and to reinforce previous training.

Games are also the best way to mix the business of training with the pleasure of playing with you. Your dog won't differentiate between one and the other. It will keep its attention focused on you, concentrating on you because there's always the possibility that, out of nowhere, a chance to play may arise. Before getting to games themselves, there are two exercises that make life safer: "leave it" and "drop it".

Learning to leave it

"Leave it" is a potentially life-saving exercise, vital training to prevent your dog from scavenging. Mouthing, tasting, or swallowing things they shouldn't, in turn leading to vomiting, diarrhoea, poisoning, or obstructions, are among the most common reasons why dogs are brought to see me at the clinic.

With a treat visible in your hand, move it right in front of your pup's eyes. As it reaches for it, close your hand. Your dog will soon quizzically back off and may sit down. It has temporarily left it.

Repeat this, and as it leaves it again, say "leave it". Reward the good behaviour with the specific words of praise: "good leave". Repeat this sequence frequently,

Dogs love to play tug-of-war. This is a safe game to play with all but the most dominant dogs. Play after "drop it" has been learned.

QUESTIONS AND ANSWERS

What if my dog is not interested in playing with toys?

This can happen with a dog that has not played with toys during puppyhood. These dogs simply need time to learn how to play. It can also happen when a dog has too many toys, so remove all of them except for one chew toy and let your dog see you hide that away. Make the toy a real resource by showing that others want it but your dog can't have it. Play piggy in the middle. Two people throw the toy between them, encouraging the dog's interest. If you don't have a helper, tie a string or thin rope to the toy and throw it up in the air or swing it. Act excited, but still ignore your dog. Just like us, they like the forbidden and are interested in what you have and they haven't. Eventually, let the toy come almost in reach of your dog, in the air or on the ground, then take it away. Finally, let it make contact and "win" the toy.

A retrieve toy

BRUCE'S GAMES TIPS

- You're in control; you decide when, where, and what to play and when play ends. Start with short play periods, and stop while your pup is still interested.
- If your dog tries to instigate play and you want to play, have it obey an obedience command first, before starting any game.
- Choose game toys carefully (*see* pages 108–9). Puppies in particular find the weight, texture, and smell of some toys much more attractive than others. Maximize what your dog naturally likes to do – fetching, digging, rolling, using its nose – and integrate those activities into games.

- Keep all game toys out of your dog's reach and bring them out only at game times.
- Keep your body posture and voice exciting and appealing. Think theatrically, but stay in proportion to your dog's excitement. Don't wind it up too much.
- Keep toys low to the ground. This prevents your dog from feeling that it needs to jump up for them.
- If your dog jumps up, mouths you, or refuses to "drop it" once it has learned that command, stop play immediately. Game over until the next time.
- Know your dog's physical and mental limits and avoid possible dangers, such as torn ligaments from jumping games.

gradually lowering your hand from your dog's eye level down to floor level. This is the location of most of the items you'll want your dog to leave alone.

Drop it

This is another potentially life-saving exercise, but it is also an active component of retrieve training.

First, gain your pup's interest in an attractive toy by waving it or dragging it along the ground. Wiping your hands on it adds the satisfaction of your scent. Your pup will inevitably take hold of the toy in its mouth. When it does, say "Drop it", and as you speak, place a food treat right by its nose. As it scents the food, your pup should naturally let go of the toy. Try to catch this, so that it isn't a distraction as it hits the ground. Immediately after, tell your pup to "sit". As it sits, praise and give the food treat. The "sit" prevents it from jumping up to grab the toy or the treat. Eventually fade out the food treat.

You now have a pup trained in one of the core activities for retrieving. As drop

If your dog "play bows" like the dog on the right, it's asking to play.

training progresses, you will ask your pup to sit before dropping the article. The words "thank you" can be used as a drop command as your pup passes the article over to you.

Hide and seek

This game satisfies a dog's need to hunt or investigate. It is very useful. Because some toys are designed to drop food from them when moved, offer your dog a game in your absence.

With your dog out of sight, place a few dog treats (kibbles taken from the next meal) around the

Playing hide and seek is fun for both children and dogs.

room. Let your dog in, tap a finger on the floor by a treat, and as it finds each treat, say "find it". Repeat this with each treat.

Once your dog reliably responds to the command "find it" by searching and finding easy-to-find treats, advance to the next stage, where treats are more difficult to find. Put them behind furniture, in open paper bags, or in any of the food-dropping toys. Even you, hiding behind a tree, can be what your dog is trained to search for.

Keep quiet, and let your dog use its nose. Don't show it where treats are once it has got the idea. Allow it to find them on its own, and if it naturally brings back a toy to show you, give praise. Your dog is well on his way to retrieve training.

For "nose work" games, start by encouraging your dog to find its dinner. If you're the object that's hidden, hide behind a tree, keep quiet, and let your dog work out where you are. Finding you is a huge reward. Play this game often and you'll find that, more and more, your dog will keep checking to locate you when you go on walks.

Mistakes to avoid

Don't move outside until your dog reliably comes back, sits, and drops the ball.
Don't correct your dog for not doing one part of the exercise (for example, coming back) when it's correctly doing another (for example, holding).
Don't use chew toys, and avoid chewable wood. The best retrieve toys are made specifically for this purpose, like dumbbells.
Don't leave a retrieve toy lying around. Hide it away between retrieve games.

Retrieve it

In this much more complicated game, your dog finds the item to be retrieved – a ball, a frisbee, a squeaky toy, or a dead duck – picks it up, brings it back to you, and drops it in your hand. In doing so, it strings together a succession of several behaviours: "run after – pick up – recall – hold – sit – give/drop".

A dog can play either on its own or with your help with an intermittent rewarder toy that releases food treats.

"Retrieve it" is a great game for a dog because it satisfies a number of its natural desires: to find, to carry, and to work as a team. It gives your dog the chance to chase, but under circumstances where you are in control.

This is much easier for some dogs to learn than others; not surprisingly, the retrievers do very well. If you're no good at throwing, arm yourself with a tennis racket or a purpose-made ball thrower. First, develop your dog's interest in the object. Sitting on the floor inside with no distractions, roll a ball on a rope (so you can control it) toward your dog. When it picks it up, encourage it to come to you, and praise it for holding the ball in its mouth with the specific praise words

"good hold". Exchange for a piece of food with the drop command "thank you".

Repeat this exercise, gradually increasing the distance you ask your dog to come back from. Finally, introduce asking your dog to "sit" holding the object in its mouth for a second before giving the drop command "thank you" and offering the food reward.

A full retrieve is a sequence of exercises linked together like a chain. If there's a problem in a single link, the chain breaks down. The broken link in the chain should be repeated as a separate exercise until it has been reliably learned before continuing with the full retrieve.

Bruce's tips for retrieve training

You decide when to play retrieve, not your dog. Keep the retrieve toy (never a squeaky toy) out of sight and, if possible, out of scenting range, until playtime. If your dog chooses an item for you to throw, and you do so, it's just as likely to choose when it wants the game to end or to just run off and chew it.

Never try to pull the retrieve item from your dog's mouth. That only leads to tug-of-war. Instead, offer a tickle, a food treat, or something else, always accompanying the release with the words "drop it".
Don't let your dog turn retrieve training into "catch me if you can". Never chase your dog if it refuses to bring back or drop the toy. Walk in the opposite direction to the one its coaxing

you to take. Let it be proud and proprietorial for a few minutes before quietly returning to the "drop it" command. Never correct a dog while it has the retrieve item in its mouth either. That confuses it.

Typical simple retrieve toy

Chapter 4
Dogs are not angels

Why dogs do what dogs do

At this point, it's worth repeating that, no matter how much you think it is, your dog is *not* a furry person. When you say, "If you do that again, Tolstoy, I'll get really cross with you," your dog just hears its name and your tone of voice. That wonderfully understanding look in the eyes is at the core of a dog's enduring charm – but it is a look, no more. Your dog has the potential to do what canines evolved to do, no more.

NEUTERING YOUR DOG

Neutering influences behaviour
Puberty is reached at any time from five to 12 months. Males start lifting their legs to urinate, and urinate more often, to mark territory. Females come into season, announced by a discharge of blood from the vulva. Sex hormones affect a dog's behaviour as much as they affect ours. Early neutering (spaying or castrating) before puberty perpetuates a dog's existing personality. Depending a little on the breed but more on the individual, early neutering makes dog training easier. It does not eliminate a dog's teenage phase. Neutering or not, this is a hurdle you need to get over.

Genetics limit a dog's behaviour
Your dog inherited a mental flexibility from its wolf ancestors. It instinctively understands body language, and because we share a surprising variety of body language with dogs, it will understand some of your feelings and emotions.

Dogs learn from experience, and unless yours learns to trust people, it will be instinctively cautious, wary, or fearful of unfamiliar ones.

Your dog considers itself to be part of your family. Your territory is its territory, and it may bark to explain this to others, both dogs and people. All of these behaviours are canine. We like some, but not all, of them.

Learning from littermates
Learning about relationships started in the litter. During the first three weeks of your pup's life, its entire social structure was canine. It learned how to seek out comfort and began to develop

THE DEVELOPMENT OF THE DOG

Rapid growth and development
Physical maturity arrives quickly – in most breeds within a year of birth – but emotional maturity takes longer, often 18 to 24 months. The first year of a dog's life is equivalent to the first 15 years of a human life.

One day old

Ten days old

Seven weeks old

Four months old

We all want perfection from our dogs. I bet some of you even expect it, but be sensible: these are not angels in furry disguise.

relationships. As its senses developed further over the following five weeks, people became an integral part of its world. It became accustomed to being handled, at ease – at peace – in the presence, and even in the hands, of

a different and very large species. The potential for fearful behaviour didn't develop until your pup was over two months old.

Individuality

Your new dog has a distinct personality. That includes its own personal energy level and compulsion to do things that dogs need to do, such as investigating, marking territory, using its voice, and communicating with other dogs – as well as its individual ability to understand what you want it to do, like controlling its natural inclinations, listening to you, preferring to spend time with you.

Some experts call these latter qualities "communications intelligence", and some breeds – herders such as Border Collies (*see* page 54), workers such as German Shepherd Dogs (*see* pages 22–3), and gundogs such as Labradors (*see* pages 20–1) and Golden Retrievers (*see* page 26) – have developed, through selective breeding, excellent communication intelligence. They have longer attention spans than, say, terriers, and so are capable of concentrating better on you and what you're doing. But even if you have an individual who is a good listener, you should be prepared for some growing dog problems.

BRUCE'S TEENAGE DOG TIPS

Experiencing life is magnificent. Don't expect your teenage dog to respect your rules or understand your concerns.

- All teenagers, canine or human, want to experiment. If your dog experiments and finds something rewarding, it will repeat the behaviour. It's up to you to work out what the reward is, then find another reward that will distract your dog from doing what you don't want him to do.
- Don't lose your cool. Some teenage dogs can be a nightmare.
- Don't keep shouting "No!" Reinforce the "dos", not the "don'ts".
- Save "No!" for occasions where your dog is putting itself or others at risk.
- Teenagers have unlimited energy. Make sure you find extra time to help your dog vent surplus steam.

Teenage rebelliousness

Getting from fairly obedient puppyhood to affable adulthood means going through the teenage years. It's not just hormones that turn an obedient new pup into a boisterous teenager. Many pups are neutered before the hormonal onslaught of puberty, yet given the chance, they too may forget their housetraining, chew on table legs and carpets, inexplicably start to cower or hide, become tentative, reticent, or submissive, or (perhaps most commonly) one day decide simply to disregard you and your commands and do what they feel like doing.

Training problems are inevitable. When they happen, work back through what you've been doing. The problem is just as likely to be due to your inconsistency as to adolescent rebelliousness. New adult dogs almost invariably arrive with hidden challenges, and fearfulness and separation anxiety are particularly common in rescued dogs.

Six months old   One year old

Excitable new dogs

Dogs don't hide their feelings, so expect your new dog to be excitable. Over-the-top is dog normal, especially in adolescence. Excitable behaviours include nipping your clothes or you, jumping up to get nearer your face, barking, chasing anything that moves, not coming when called because something else more exciting has been found, or lunging forward on the lead, desperate to get where you're heading as fast as possible.

Life is thrilling. Young dogs don't hide their zeal for activity.

Avoid unintentional excitement

Let's say your dog turns into a ballistic missile and goes berserk with excitement the moment you put the lead on and take a step forward. If you take one more step now, you're unwittingly rewarding the excitable behaviour. You're refuelling the energy tank. It's amazingly easy to make simple mistakes. For all excitable behaviours, go back to basic obedience lessons. You haven't failed; your dog simply needs more reinforcement of early training. If your dog is a chaser, increase your "wait" training (*see* page 130). If it's a nipper, return to "mouthing" training (*see* pages 140–1). If it's jumping up at people, revisit "jumping up" training (*see* pages 138–9).

Pulling on the lead

The most common excitable behaviour my clients want to overcome is pulling on the lead. If you can concentrate and find a few spare hours of time, this problem can be overcome in pups or young adolescent dogs in a day. Believe me. What happens is that your dog learns, on its own, which of its activities leads to continuing to walk forward and which of its activities leads nowhere.

You need to be relaxed for this and equipped with a bag of food.

Preventing pulling

When your dog gets excited as you put its lead on or start to walk, do absolutely nothing. Just stand there and wait for it to unwind. Don't give any clues. No eye contact. Nothing! It may take a long time, at first a very long time, which is why you must have

patience, but eventually your dog will sit down, and when it does, give the praise "good sit" and a food reward. Your dog is now learning, on its own, without instruction, what you want it to do. It's also learning, on its own, what not to do. These starts and stops are initially very frequent. It may be quite some time before you can even leave your front door.

Let your new dog quietly investigate the unknown.

BRUCE'S CALMING TIPS

- Don't restrict training to a specific location, otherwise your dog will control its excitement just in that location.

- The advantage of dozens of five- to ten-second training sessions during a walk is that your dog is learning to respond in a wide variety of locales with an equally wide diversity of distractions.

- Don't restrict this "settle down" training just to walks. Practise obedience commands in your stationary car as well. A food-stuffed toy is an excellent car reward.

Initially, take a step at a time. One step. Stop. Wait until your dog sits on its own. "Good sit." Give a reward. Another step. Stop. Wait until excitement subsides and it sits on its own. "Good sit." Give another reward. After many repetitions, your dog will sit more rapidly. Gradually increase the number of steps you take before stopping and waiting for it to sit spontaneously, always rewarding with the same words and a food treat. The response will become ever more prompt.

Constantly repeat this exercise. Your dog learns to settle down on its own and you can now reintroduce, with high reliability, active obedience commands that it will actually hear and respond to.

Extend the training

Now you can interject short obedience-training sessions into your walk, and after your dog waits, sits, stays, stands, or lies down, introduce a new command. "Let's go" means start walking again.

Now you won't need food rewards. The command "let's go" – active walking under your control without lunging ahead of you – is the reward.

Problems will happen

Life is particularly exhilarating for naturally excitable dogs, so be prepared for the unexpected. Technically, we're supposed to be smarter than our dogs, so introduce an element of the unexpected when your dog pulls. For example, when you feel tension develop in the short lead, surprise your dog by turning immediately in the opposite direction. Always use a short lead, and whatever you do, avoid using extending leads. Your natural inclination to extend the lead in response to pulling is interpreted as "victory!" by your dog when it pulls.

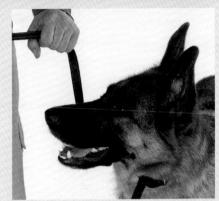

HELPFUL EQUIPMENT

Anti-pulling devices
Most of these devices, such as choke chains and "no pull" harnesses, use discomfort or pain to try to stop pulling, and some overexcited dogs dementedly learn to strangle themselves on them. A head halter, such as the Gentle Leader or Halti is an excellent device, especially for large, boisterous dogs. The lead is attached to a ring on the halter, just under the chin. If the dog pulls on its lead it pulls its own head back and to the side. When using a head halter, ensure that it fits properly and cannot slip off over the head. Head halters can be used in combination with regular flat collars.

Head halters are practical and efficient for controlling a strong dog that pulls on its lead.

Unless they are trained not to do so, all dogs naturally pull when excited. This is the most common canine behaviour "problem", controlled through simple training.

Frustration and boredom

Most dogs I see remain at home alone for hours at a time each day and cope quite well with this type of lifestyle. They learn early in life that, sometimes, there's not much to do other than play with chew toys or doze off for a few hours. With sensible early learning, the majority of dogs are content to amuse themselves safely, but your dog needs guidance from you. Without your help in channelling its natural energy, it will find its own exciting ways to cope with frustration and boredom. These diversions include chewing, digging, howling and barking, or escaping to where life is more exciting.

Use a secure playpen containing activity toys when leaving your new dog alone.

A predictable problem

Boredom is a common condition for "home alone" dogs. However, feelings of frustration and boredom can also be experienced by dogs that are at home with you but have little activity to occupy their minds.

New pups require time devoted to their becoming well socialized, to housetraining, and to obedience training. Adolescent dogs need the largest amounts of both mental and physical exercise. Older dogs often have learned that boredom is a natural and expected part of life and, when bored, go to sleep. Naturally energetic breeds such as Labrador Retrievers (*see* pages 20–1) and Border Collies (*see* page 54) are most likely to suffer from boredom, while less active breeds such as the Pekingese or Greyhound inherently cope better with boredom. If you have an exuberant, high-energy, new adult dog, it needs outlets for mental and physical activity. If your new dog is naturally calm and happy to be a watchful observer of life, it is less likely to develop problems associated with frustration and boredom.

BRUCE'S DISTRACTION TIP

Do you have a wild and woolly new dog that, after a little bit of activity, becomes an overwound toy and a frenetic ankle biter? This is excitable puppy behaviour that usually follows a period of boredom or inactivity. Shouting "ouch!" and leaving your pup for a symbolic minute of "time out" might work for some pups, but not for others. If your pup won't calm down to this ploy, induce it into a "sit" or "down", since that focuses its mind, then direct the excitement elsewhere – for example, to a delicious chew toy.

The results of boredom

Boredom doesn't just lead to complaints from your neighbours about your dog's barking or howling, or the excavation of your flower beds, the repositioning of your cushions and rugs, or the removal of your wallpaper.

There are no limits to a bored dog's creativity; as a vet, I often have to attend to the medical consequences. They can

be minor problems, such as torn nails from digging, more serious ones, such as mouth injuries from chewing, or devastating ones, such as broken bodies from road-traffic accidents.

Prevent boredom-related problems by understanding your dog's natural needs. If a problem does arise, think through how that happened and modify your dog's environment or lifestyle so that it won't happen again.

Preventing boredom
Start by getting down to your dog's level, in the house or in the garden, to get its view of your home's natural resources. You'll be amazed just how different it is down there.

Be neat! Tidy up. If there's nothing potentially chewable down there except the chew toy you've chosen, that's what your dog will chew.

This activity toy releases morsels of food when it is batted around – ideal rewards to alleviate boredom.

Only use the crate for short periods of being left alone while housetraining. When your dog is reliably housetrained, use the playpen when it is left alone and you are not yet sure whether it will be destructive. When you are happy to leave it alone in one or more rooms, use food-releasing cubes to prevent boredom.

Dogs are usually less active when their stomachs are full, so if your lifestyle means that your dog is home alone for several hours during the day, give the major meal just before you depart, rather than waiting to do so when you return. This increases the chance that your dog will rest for part of the time you are gone.

Finally, be reasonable about how much time your dog spends on its own.

Chew-toy training

If your dog is contentedly chewing on a toy, it's not barking, running around, trying to escape, or destroying your life. Chew toys are an absolute must for all dogs. Your objective is to turn chewing on a chew toy into a lifelong habit: good habits are just as hard to break as bad ones. Here are some basic chew-toy rules.

- A chew toy cannot be destroyed or completely eaten.
- Squeaky toys are training lures and rewards. They are edible. They are distortable. They are NOT chew toys.
- When stuffing a chew toy, start with the tastiest stuffing deepest and finish with moistened dry food.
- If your dog likes ice cubes or ice cream, place the chew toy in the freezer for a few hours.

Overcoming boredom

If your dog is bored, it's being neglected. This is your responsibility, and you need to spend a little time thinking about how to overcome the boredom.

OUT AND ABOUT

Canine cabin fever

In Canada, where I grew up, trappers out in the woods during the worst weather of winter, went stir crazy from being cooped up indoors. They suffered from "cabin fever". Well, I see dogs year round that suffer from cabin fever, simply because they're left at home alone so much. Dogs thrive on being part of our activities. If you're going on an errand, take your dog, even if it's only for the car journey (and it's not too hot and sunny). Are you taking a coffee break at a local outdoor cafe? Your dog would love the opportunity to inhale the latte and watch the world go by.

If you give a dog an unwanted shoe as a toy, be prepared for your favourite ones to get chewed too. Dogs don't discriminate, and shoes are just perfect for possessing and chewing.

If you have the time, increase either the number of excursions or the length of time spent in the park. If your local park doesn't allow dogs off their leads, find another one that does. If you haven't got the extra time, check with your vet for a reliable dog walker. A useful alternative is a neighbour with more time who might like to walk your dog.

If you live in a city, look into your local doggy daycare facilities. These can be expensive, but the best of them ensure satisfying social, mental, and physical activities for your dog.

Play more games with your dog at home. Send it searching for food treats, play tug-of-war, or, if it's safe enough, play catch. Teach your dog some tricks. Training it to give a "high five" is a simple way for both of you to have fun.

And, please, never punish your dog after the event when you find that it's

Good chew toys have a unique feel and smell different to other household articles.

done something destructive out of boredom or frustration. First of all, it's too late. It won't know why you're angry. Even more important, it's not your dog's fault. It really isn't. If your dog is destructive in your absence, work out why. There's always a lesson for you to learn when it reacts to being bored.

QUESTIONS AND ANSWERS

What if I live with an obsessive digger whose reason for living is to engineer massive excavations?

Some dogs dig to bury bones. Others dig to find cool places to lie in. A few dig to get under fences, to escape to the forbidden other world out there. And some dig because they think they're budding mechanical engineers and are interested in what two front feet are capable of doing. Regardless of why your dog digs, redirect this natural instinct to where you're happy to have digging by providing it with its own sandpit. If you have an "under the fence" digger, you may also need to lay chicken wire along the bottom of the fencing. This can be buried so that it is not unsightly, and it discourages digging by the fence.

Dogs may dig to search for rabbits or roots but also just because it's a deliciously satisfying activity.

Separation anxiety

Overexcited dogs can be destructive, and so can bored dogs, but there's a third reason why some canines bark, urinate, or destroy when they're on their own: anxiety because they're separated from you. While boredom, frustration, and excitability are all normal dog feelings or emotions, separation anxiety is a learned behaviour, and it's learned through your being inconsistent. This is a state of mind we sometimes unwittingly train our dogs to experience. Most books state that separation anxiety occurs most frequently in rescued dogs with a history of abuse, neglect, or having gone through a series of homes. Active research suggests this might not necessarily be so.

QUESTIONS AND ANSWERS

What do I look for to reduce the risk of separation anxiety developing?

In my experience, both frantic, over-the-top dogs and "clingers" that curl around your feet looking mournfully into your eyes are the extremes of personality most likely to develop separation anxiety. If you are rescuing a dog, look for an individual that is calm, outgoing, and friendly, and as happy to wander off to check out the surroundings as it is to check you out.

Signs of separation anxiety

Separation anxiety causes dogs extreme distress when left alone even for a short time. A dog may run rhythmically from room to room, turn into a statue staring at the door or out the window, bark, urinate, or destroy, and when you return, go berserk with joy. Dogs prone to this problem tend to be those that stick to their owners like glue or those that are deeply affectionate with their owners and somewhat shy with strangers.

What causes it?

University researchers monitored litters of Labrador Retrievers (*see* pages 20–1) and Border Collies (*see* page 54), two breeds known to be particularly susceptible to separation anxiety, from

In the absence of its owner, this Border Collie has found some clothing and taken it to its bed, where it may be chewed.

birth to 18 months of age. They noted that the dogs raised in socially diverse environments between six and twelve months of age didn't develop separation anxiety, while those raised in isolated environments were more likely to do so.

In an associated survey, male dogs were more likely to develop separation anxiety than females, and, interestingly, the condition was no more likely to develop in dogs from rescue organizations than it was in dogs obtained from breeders.

Their statistics revealed that up to half of all pet dogs showed signs of separation anxiety at one time or another, yet only 10 per cent of dog owners had sought help to overcome the problem.

Preventing separation anxiety

Raise your pup in a stimulating social environment. The more people it meets and plays with, the less likely it is to become emotionally dependant on your always being there. Accustom it from a young age to being separated from you.

Leave it at home alone for increasing periods of time. Occasionally leave it for an hour with willing neighbours. If you plan to put it in kennels when you travel, introduce that aspect of life when it is under a year of age. And perhaps most importantly, downplay emotion in goodbyes and hellos. These may be emotionally very satisfying to you, but they mix up your dog and increase its feeling of loneliness when you're away.

The lesson

Ignore your dog for at least 20 minutes before leaving home. That means no physical, voice, or eye contact. Your body language matters. A lot! Relax your body. Any agitation will transmit to your dog. If you want to take it a step further, walk around yawning. That's a calming signal dogs quickly pick up on.

Don't say, "I'm only going out for ten minutes". Pretend your dog isn't there.

Beatrice, my nurse's Pug, stares out the window until her owner returns. Others bark from anxiety.

Ensure your dog is well exercised, fed, and has something to do, like chew on a chew toy. Leave the radio on. Desensitize your dog to routines that say you're about to leave. Pick up your keys just to pick them up, but not to leave. Put on your coat and walk around, but don't leave.

Calmly limit your dog's access to the whole house, so it can't run from room to room. Use the crate if this is right for your dog, but not if it associates being crated with your leaving.

Practise mock exits, avoiding any form of goodbye, and avoid eye contact when you return. Give short and low-key praise only once your dog is calm.

BRUCE'S TIPS ON ANXIETY

- Never punish your dog for unwanted behaviour while you've been away. Simply clear up the damage without paying any attention to your dog.

- Each dog has his own personality. While many dogs feel secure in their den, being restricted to the crate may just frustrate others. Be flexible in how you use the crate to overcome separation anxiety.

- If you're at home all day, each day, accustom your new dog to being left at home alone by leaving it alone each day for varying periods of time. Don't let it follow you from room to room. Install a baby gate to break this routine.

- Leave a light and the radio or television on.

More puppy problems

Above and below Monitor your dog to prevent it scavenging on faeces. Before visiting new places, ensure your dog's tanks are both reading empty.

It's live and learn during the first months with a new dog, but there are three common problems that may become permanent if they're not nipped early. Many pups urinate when they're greeted. This is temporary if the only cause is excitement, but permanent if your dog's insecurities are not overcome. Car journeys are a common part of life, but for some dogs they occur so infrequently they cause either nausea or excitement. And finally, some individual dogs, given the chance, will eat stuff we don't want them to eat, such as their own or other animals' faeces. All of these conditions are preventable or treatable.

Wet greetings

Excitement urination occurs because the young sphincter muscles aren't strong enough to retain urine in the bladder if a pup becomes excited. Greeting you or playing with you triggers a flow of urine. This is a temporary problem that pups outgrow as their muscles gain strength.

Submissive urination falls into a completely different category. Dogs have evolved behaviours designed to reduce violence between them. To prevent a physical attack, a lower-status dog may grovel, roll over, urinate, or do all three. Submissive urination is a type of "I am not worthy" greeting, used by your pup to acknowledge your superiority.

Don't mistake submissive urinating for poor housetraining. This problem is caused by a lack of self-confidence.

Avoidance and prevention

Your family, guests, and strangers are invariably looming and "big" in your pup's eyes. All of you find your pup so appealing that you stare at it, especially at those beautiful eyes. You want to hold your pup close, so you reach down to touch it or pick it up. You might stroke it on its head or shoulders. An insecure puppy will interpret all of these activities as dominant challenges and will respond with an appropriate submissive gesture, the wet greeting.

Avoid the situations that trigger wet greetings. Disregard your pup when you arrive home. Avoid eye contact. Don't bend over it for any reason at all. If it controls its bladder, mutter a few words so it hears your voice, but still avoid eye contact. If it remains dry, give a food treat for not urinating. Physiologically, dogs find it difficult to eat and urinate at the same time; eating competes with urinating. When you have guests to the home, encourage them to pretend your puppy doesn't even exist, and if you have an excitable dog, put it in its playpen or behind a barrier gate.

Car journeys

Start your pup travelling in the car the week you get it, ideally in its crate in the back of the car. When obedience training starts, include sessions in the stationary car so that your dog sits or lies down in it on command.

If your puppy is sick when the car is in motion, sit it inside it with the engine off and the radio on, and give food rewards or a favourite toy for not panting with excitement or showing signs of nausea. Once your puppy is calm in the car, progress to starting the engine, then to pulling out of your parking space and right back in, then driving a short distance, and eventually driving longer distances. If car sickness is severe, discuss the problem with your vet, who can help with anti-nausea medicines.

QUESTIONS AND ANSWERS

What should I do if my puppy eats animal faeces?

It's "normal" (dogs are scavengers), but it's disgusting. It can cause digestive upsets and should be avoided. Poop-eating starts as an adventure and rapidly becomes a habit. Unless there's a nutritional deficiency, and these are extremely rare, treatments such as adding papain enzyme, pumpkin, or pineapple to the diet don't work. Nor does telling your dog off. Training your dog to "come" (see pages 128–9) and "leave it" (see page 143) works. So does aversion therapy. If, for example, your dog goes to the cat litter tray and thinks of it as dessert, with help from your vet, use a syringe to inject some of the faeces with a safe but unpleasant substance such as Tabasco sauce or Bitter Apple spray. Most dogs that eat the treated faeces teach themselves not to do so again.

A tempting cat litter tray

Fearful behaviour

Fear is a natural, potentially life-saving behaviour, at the core of an animal's survival. Young pups have virtually no fear, but the feeling starts to develop well at around two months of age. Fear is physiological. The chemical changes in the body trigger many of the signs of fear, such as dilated eyes or trembling. The feeling of fear leads to learned responses, and the most common of these is biting. Because fear is a core emotion we share with dogs, it is usually simple to recognize the signs of fear.

- Panting or shallow breathing
- Trembling
- Teeth chattering, sometimes with increased salivation
- Corners of the lips pulled back
- Tail tucked down and rump tucked low
- Dilated eyes
- Hiding behind your legs
- Cowering under furniture
- Freezing like a statue (behaviourists call this "conservation/withdrawal" or "learned hopelessness")
- Asking to be picked up or attempting to climb on your lap
- Trying to escape
- Barking or growling
- Biting
- Shedding hair (which is why so much hair is dropped on the examination table at the vet's)
- Increased touch sensitivity (which is why injections at the vet's are more painful for nervous dogs than for relaxed ones)
- Increased heart rate
- Increased sound sensitivity
- Loss of appetite (which is why nervous dogs refuse tasty treats from vets)

Every single dog will develop some form of fearful behaviour. Those that didn't have the opportunity when young to savour the widest range of sights, sounds, and smells that accompany living with us will develop the most extensive range of fearful behaviours. However, even the best-socialized dogs can develop unexpected fears. My own Macy left the kitchen each time anyone opened the saucepan cupboard. Mild signs of fear and shyness, such as backing away or a worried look in the eyes, are very common. More problematic are circumstances that trigger fear-induced aggression. As many or more dogs growl and bite defensively due to fear as do due to other forms of aggression.

We make fear worse
You bring your dog to me, and it hides behind your legs. In response, you speak gently to it, stroke it reassuringly, and tell it there's nothing to worry about. That's what the "mother" in us instinctively has us do, but unwittingly what we're really doing is rewarding our dog's fearful behaviour. We're actually reinforcing the dog's fear, saying it's okay to act that way.

It's so easy to accidentally bolster shyness, apprehension, or fear. We act with the best of intentions, then wonder why our dogs continue to cower or be fearful after we've told them there's nothing to worry about. Inappropriate responses like this make fear worse.

Anything can trigger fear
The fearful or shy dog can be stressed by unfamiliar or new situations, isolation, or simply not feeling in control. A dog can easily be frightened by being asked to do something that causes apprehension, such as walking on a floor with a shiny surface. Loud noises, such as thunder or fireworks, even shouting or arguing, can

trigger fearful behaviour. So too can rough play from dogs or people. I know dogs that have been frightened by the spin cycle of the washing machine, planes flying overhead, the newspaper through the letterbox, the crackling of a log fire, or vacuum cleaners. Do search for a logical reason for fearful behaviour. Acknowledge that it has developed, eliminate the triggers if you know what they are, and develop a desensitizing plan. Get help from a qualified behavioural trainer (see page 125) who can tailor a behaviour-modification plan for your situation.

Coping with fear
Dogs have evolved these behaviours as defensive measures for coping with fear. The best ways to eliminate fear are either to remove your dog from the situation that triggers it, or to remove the sights, sounds,

A worried or nervous dog typically retreats to the security of someone it knows before barking or growling. When this happens, reassurance only reinforces the behaviour.

QUESTIONS AND ANSWERS

Do the anti-anxiety drugs that vets have, such as Prozac (fluoxetine) and Clomicalm (clomipramine), cure fear and anxiety in dogs?

No, they don't. There's simply no magic pill that will cure a dog's distress, anxiety, fearfulness, or shyness. I've seen dogs that, when treated insensitively with such anti-anxiety drugs, have become more aggressive rather than less, while they never lose their fear of the sight or sound that triggered their apprehension in the first place.

Anti-anxiety medications are sometimes useful in the first stages of a programme to desensitize a dog to whatever stimulus triggers their fear. However, they should only ever be used under the combined supervision of both the prescribing veterinarian and the dog trainer who has devised the desensitizing programme.

Use a houseline to recall your dog from underneath furniture.

smells, or events that trigger fear or stress. Ensure your dog is safe. Use the longline if you think fearfulness may induce bolting away from what frightens it. Provide your dog with some "quiet time" and the opportunity to rest physically and mentally. If your dog can't relax, encourage it with activities that involve staying still, such as chewing on a treat. Give calm exercise, including lead walking in a quiet place. As your new dog's shyness or stress diminishes, increase its free running time, but be vigilant for anything that might trigger fear – children, other dogs, sights, or sounds – and avoid them.

How desensitizing works
A good trainer can help you develop a desensitizing regime that's appropriate for your dog's specific fears. Regardless of what the problem is, desensitizing follows a structured plan. Your objective is to reward your dog for not showing fear in the presence of whatever triggers it.

When fear is over something visual – for example, other dogs or people – the critical distance beyond which your dog doesn't show fear is determined, and this distance is gradually diminished. For fear of sounds, the lowest amplitude of sound that doesn't trigger fear is discovered, and then the volume is gradually increased, always rewarding calm behaviour. Desensitizing can often be accomplished in less than a month.

Hand-shyness
Hand-shyness is very common in rescued dogs. It's often assumed that this is because the dog was previously beaten. That certainly may be the case for some dogs, but equal numbers are hand-shy because they've never experienced being stroked by people. They have yet to learn to trust human hands.

If your rescue dog is hand-shy, avoid patting its head or reaching down to stroke it. Both of these are intimidating gestures. Instead, get down to its level and, initially avoiding eye contact, offer a food treat. Never grab at your dog, and keep your movements ballet-smooth. Your initial touch should be on the chest or under his chin. Reward non-fearful behaviour with a positive tone of voice and more food treats.

Fear of loud noises

Cars backfiring, skips being loaded and unloaded from trucks, fireworks, thunder, shrieking children, shouting adults – a dog's world is filled with unexpected, inexplicable, and potentially frightening noises. Older dogs may already have a fear of loud noises, but this is a behaviour that many dogs naturally develop as they grow older.

Your pup may not notice thunder right now but can develop a fear of it later in life. While it's always interesting to know why this happens, what's more important is what to do about it. This is such a common fear that there are commercial aids you can purchase to use when desensitizing your dog to the sounds that

provoke fear. Sounds such as thunder or fireworks are available on CD either from your vet or on the Internet. The best are accompanied by detailed booklets written by behavioural vets, explaining exactly how to use the CDs. As with all forms of fear, your dog is rewarded for not showing signs of fear in the presence of the sound that triggers it.

If your dog has developed a fear of thunder, make sure you start your desensitizing programme at least a month before the stormy season. It takes a minimum of three weeks, and more often six weeks, to desensitize a dog effectively after it has developed a fear of thunder.

Fear-biters

My son's Labrador (*see* pages 20–1) Inca spent her first year of life in relative isolation, on an island where there were only two other dogs, elderly Border Collies (*see* page 54), which bit her each time she approached them.

Inca learned to love all humankind but be fearful of other dogs, and when she returned to an urban life she was frightened of other dogs. If another dog approached she cowered submissively, then raised a lip and threatened to bite. Inca had become proactive. Rather than waiting to be bitten, she was now a potential fear-biter and had to be trained to do something incompatible with biting, such as retrieving a thrown toy, when she met dogs that frightened her. Never force a fearful dog to approach what it fears, however benign it seems to you. If your dog bites out of fear, don't rely on advice in a book. Get professional help from a dog trainer recommended by a vet.

Offer food from your hand to dogs that are naturally hand-shy.

The aggressive dog

Aggressive behaviour is as normal in dogs as it is in us, and aggression can't be "cured". How aggressive your new dog is, or will be, is influenced by its parents (genetics), how its mother and breeder raised it and what its relationships with its siblings were like (very early environment), your training (early learning), life experiences, physical and mental health, and even by diet. There are many different triggers for a large variety of forms of aggression. Most forms can be managed and controlled through early learning and sensible training, if you understand the underlying motivations for threat and violence or the circumstances in which these are used.

Progression of aggression

Dogs use a variety of body postures to avoid overt aggression. It's when these visible "body language" messages fail that dogs bite. Behaviourists describe an escalating "ladder of aggression", and typically, a dog will progress through this before biting.

Usually, a dog will stop, stare, dilate its eyes, breathe faster, emit a low growl, lift one lip to show a canine, snarl, bark, snap or growl deeper, lift both lips to reveal a full display of teeth, and finally bite. Unfortunately, some dogs skip several, or even most of these stages, instead progressing from dilated pupils straight into a bite.

Don't ever rely on your dog behaving as a textbook describes aggression. Be on the watch for any subtle signs of unwanted aggression, and control it by redirecting both your dog's mind and its body elsewhere.

Aggression is as normal as eating or sleeping. The well-trained dog's natural forms of aggression are controlled through early learning and training.

Mock aggression is normal during dog play and used by dogs both as play activity and as a way of "testing" each other.

Types of aggression

To understand why your dog is behaving aggressively, you need to understand both the context in which it behaves this way and what its motivations are.

Shyness or fear can trigger pre-emptive or "defensive" aggression (*see* pages 160–3). So can pain. At the opposite end of the spectrum, bold, confident dogs can be "offensively" aggressive. These dogs pick fights with other, frequently same-sex dogs, or fight over who gets first attention from their owners.

Sex hormone is a factor in both male dominance and maternal aggression, while an inherent predatory instinct is at the root of aggression toward livestock and other animals. Some dogs become aggressive through frustration, especially during vigorous play, while others are

trained to be aggressive or inherit a greater-than-average potential to develop a specific form of aggression. For example, a type of dominance aggression called "avalanche of rage" occurs most frequently in red-coloured Cocker Spaniels (*see* pages 24–5), while it is virtually unheard of in parti-coloured Cocker Spaniels.

Aggression towards other dogs

Household aggression is much more common in same-sex pairs, especially in females, than in opposite sex pairs. Fights between females are also more severe than fights between males. Fights are

QUESTIONS AND ANSWERS

Is "aggression" in dogs related in any way to who owns them?

Of course. Most obviously, some people train their dogs to be aggressive, but there are more subtle influences. Over ten years ago, psychologists and behaviourists at Cambridge University in the UK reported that owners of highly aggressive Cockers (see pages 24–5) were more likely to be tense, undisciplined, or emotionally less stable than owners of Cockers with low levels of aggression. Danish research reported in 2003 that inter-dog dominance aggression was higher among dogs owned either by younger dog owners or by owners with limited knowledge of their breed.

more likely to be started by the younger dog, especially if she is the adult who has just arrived in the home.

Aggression toward other dogs outside the home is lower than you'd expect. My clinic is located between two busy parks with a combined area of 308 hectares (760 acres), where dogs are allowed off their leads. If there's a serious dog fight, I'm likely to see the loser, and that happens no more than once every seven weeks. A more scientific study of aggression between dogs, carried out

Older, larger, or tougher pups often try to dominate younger, smaller, or more insecure ones. Stop aggression over possessions, especially food and toys, early.

in dog parks in Indianapolis (where dogs are allowed off their leads) reported that bites were relatively rare and presented limited risk to dogs and their care-givers.

Don't avoid dealing with a problem by walking your dog only in unsocial hours. Dogs are pack animals and need the company of other dogs. Professional help reduces most problems within a few weeks.

Aggression towards people

Aggression is the most common reason for dogs to be referred to behaviourists. That doesn't mean that aggression is the most common problem dogs have; it means that aggression is the problem dog owners worry about the most. In the home, aggression can be triggered by your

dog wanting to avoid "negatives". Your dog may resort to a threat or a snap when it thinks, "I don't like it when people take things from me," or "I don't want to share my food with anyone," or "I don't like it when that child tries to pick me up," or "I don't want to move from here." This is called avoidance conditioning. A dog learns that aggression works. It prevents a "negative" from happening.

This is not dominance aggression. Contrary to what you'll read elsewhere, dominance aggression – the assertion of authority as leader of the pack – although it may occur in

wolf packs, rarely if ever occurs in domestic dogs. Your dog may behave aggressively with you over possessions or over a dislike of your handling, but not because it wants to assume leadership in your home.

Dog bites and children

Within Europe, the "home and leisure accident surveillance system" reports that children (boys in particular) under 14 are the age group that is most likely to be injured by dogs; injured usually means bitten. While older people are usually

bitten on their arms or legs, young children are bitten mainly on the head and face. In the United States, dog-bite injuries are considered a significant childhood public-health problem.

Young kids are bitten more seriously than older ones because they're more likely to stare dogs in the face. They're also more likely to try to pet or hug an attractive dog that may be frightened by their jerky movements.

Most bites happen when children are left unsupervised with a dog. Never leave young children unattended with dogs. Dog-awareness programmes, such as the Blue Dog project (www.thebluedog.org), are excellent for teaching children how to behave with dogs.

Does punishment work?

The timing of punishment, of psychologically showing a dog who's boss, is so critical that it's as easy to get it wrong as to get it right. The result in those instances when timing is a fraction out is emotional conflict for the dog. It thinks, "I love you but you scare me." You become inconsistent and threatening. Don't use punishment. If your dog is showing any form of aggression, get help from a dog trainer

QUESTIONS AND ANSWERS

Is aggression inherited?

In part, yes. Some breeds, such as German Shepherds (see pages 22–3), Dachshunds (see page 38), Staffies (see page 32), and Rottweilers (see page 42), certainly have higher odds of inheriting a predisposition toward inter-dog aggression. American research shows that household aggression between dogs occurs more frequently than average in herding and non-sporting breeds, and less frequently than average in toy and sporting breeds. Outside of the home, in the park, terriers were more likely to fight with other dogs than other groups. Whether or not this potential manifests itself depends upon who the dog ends up living with. The bottom line is that, with canine aggression, nurture is more important than nature. How you raise your dog predicts whether or not it will develop different forms of aggression.

who uses positive reinforcement techniques. There are some circumstances where, under the trainer's control, punishment may sometimes be used – not to inflict pain but for its theatrically unexpected value.

BRUCE'S TIPS ON PREVENTING AGGRESSION

- Never meet aggression with confrontation or aggression. The problem will escalate.
- Encourage early social interaction with a variety of people, dogs, and other animals.
- Ensure a varied and complex physical and social environment during the first 12 weeks of a pup's life.
- For older new dogs joining your family, use "pacifiers" to smooth the transition from kennels to your home – toys

to play with, comfortable bedding to retreat to, even dog-appeasing pheromone devices or synthetic canine-calming hormone, available from vets.
- Train your dog to control its state of arousal, to be calm and obedient.
- Train all the people who interact with your dog to be consistent and predictable in their own behaviour.
- Avoid potential bites. If there's any risk of aggression, fit your dog with a muzzle.
- Get professional help early.

Persistent dog problems

Some pups forget their lessons when life presents them with thrilling opportunities, such as joining a group of people playing ball or participating in a family picnic in the park. Older dogs may already have unwanted habits such as these; the most common ones are jumping up, pulling on the lead, or barking dementedly with excitement. In all of these circumstances, training is more complicated, because you need to eliminate a behaviour, rather than simply teach one. And unlearning is a lot harder than learning. Curing behaviour problems always takes more patience and more time than basic training; but with sensible advice from a practical and pragmatic dog trainer, problem behaviours can certainly be reduced and frequently eliminated altogether.

WHEN YOU HAVE A PROBLEM

Don't hide behind euphemisms
If you find yourself telling someone that your dog's "not terribly fond of children" or "a little hand-shy", you've got a potential problem. Don't wait until an accident happens. Your dog is not going to grow out of the problem, and in fact the more the behaviour becomes a learned response, the harder it will be to cure – so deal with it now. Get some practical advice from a sensible dog trainer.

Persistent misbehaving

If your dog is pulling on its lead, revisit how to keep it with you (*see* pages 136–7). Some dogs pull in an attempt to get away from the pull on a collar. If this is the case, a professionally fitted head harness (*see* page 151) can help put control back in your hands, because you can turn your dog's head without putting your body weight against the dog.

Renew recall training (*see* pages 128–9) if your dog tries to join in other people's activities in the park when off the lead. Don't hurry to let a dog off its longline. It needs to be 100 per cent reliable in its recall before it's let off.

If jumping up is the problem, your dog needs more training to overcome this habit (*see* pages 138–9). Make sure you and your family are consistent in your responses to jumping up and all remove the reward of your attention. Yes, it's exasperating to go back to basics, and yes, it often takes longer than you might like to overcome these unwanted habits.

If your dog won't relinquish a retrieve toy, don't use strength to get it. Exchange it for a reward of higher value – for example, a liver treat.

Seeking professional help or advice is the best way to reduce both the time involved in breaking bad habits and the frustrations you feel when a dog has persistent behaviour problems.

Noisy barkers

Generally speaking, small dogs tend to bark more than large ones, but excess barking becomes an increasing nuisance as many dogs mature, regardless of size.

Most dogs bark out of excitement or boredom, not because they're aggressive. It may sound strange, but the most effective way to train your dog to stop barking is first to train him to "speak", to bark on command and then to hush.

If your dog barks when it hears the doorbell, give the command "speak" and have someone prompt it to bark by ringing your doorbell. The reward comes when it is quiet. If it barks when it gets in the car and the engine starts, do the same, with your helper being the driver. With repetition, your dog will bark when you command "speak", without hearing the doorbell or the car engine. It's now trained to bark on command and ready to be trained to be quiet on command too.

Don't try "quiet" training by ringing the bell or getting in the car – your dog will get too excited. When it's calm, give a "speak" command, reward verbally with praise, then say "quiet" and link that command with both food and verbal rewards. Alternate "speak" and "quiet" commands until your dog responds well to both before using the commands in the circumstances that you know trigger excess barking. You will now be commanding your dog to be quiet, rather than reprimanding it for being noisy.

The most common problem

Pulling on the lead is the most persistent dog problem. If your dog still does this or has reverted to pulling, remember to be consistent about letting it know that this never, ever works. If you let it pull and it gets where it wants to get, you've unwittingly trained it to pull!

Everyone who walks your dog must be consistent and persistent. Each time the dog pulls on the lead, stop walking. You'll have to give yourself extra time, especially if you work to a tight schedule.

Use a short lead that lets your dog walk a couple of steps in front of you, and stop every time the lead goes tight. If it still pulls, call its name and vibrate its lead to get its attention. Lure the dog back to the correct position by your side, treat, and set off again, rewarding it for keeping the lead slack.

Happy dogs are inclined to jump up at our faces and "mouth" our clothes, both as play and to get our attention. Training controls these activities.

Chapter 5
Best of health

Body maintenance

Dogs don't complain. They don't dwell on what used to be or on what might have been; they live in the present. That makes them wonderful companions, but it also means that they depend upon us to notice when anything about their appearance or behaviour changes. Pain is as common in dogs as it is in us, but dogs don't cry out unless it is truly excruciating. Be observant. Watch your new dog and work out its routines. Train it to permit you to pick it up and inspect it all over. This can be fun for both of you, and checking your dog out helps keep it in good health and strengthens the relationship between the two of you. You'll spot problems while they're still small and easier to handle.

QUESTIONS AND ANSWERS

Should a dog's nose be cold and wet?

A healthy dog has a cold, wet nose, but there are also many circumstances when a healthy dog has a warm, dry nose. The nose often becomes warm and dry when a dog sleeps, for example. What's most important is change. If your dog's nose is always cold and wet and then inexplicably becomes warm and dry, look for other changes, such as a fever, that would indicate it is unwell.

Handling your dog

Get your dog used to being handled all over at home. This means you should train your dog to let you inspect it and touch it from its paws and its nose right back to its bum. Carry out a routine head-to-tail inspection at least once a week.

If there's one part of its body your dog doesn't like being touched, touch there just before a meal. The dog will learn that it gets an instant reward for acting calmly when you touch that region. If you have a small or medium-sized dog and are using a sturdy table at home to examine it on, place a rubber bath mat on it. This will help your dog to feel more secure on what is probably a slippery surface.

Getting your dog used to being handled and under your control at home will make it easier when a stranger, such as a vet or groomer, handles and inspects it.

Checking eyes

Using damp cotton wool, clean away any "sleep" that has accumulated around the eyes overnight. Look for unexpected discharge, swelling, or inflammation.

Conjunctivitis, an inflammation to the eye's membranes, may involve redness, swelling, and watery or mucoid discharge. When infected, the discharge becomes greenish-yellow, and veterinary attention is needed. Conjunctivitis can also be a

Look down the ear canal, checking for inflammation and sniffing for malodour.

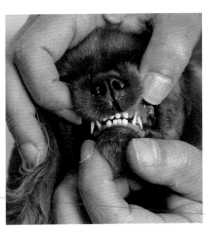

On this pup, the adult incisors have erupted but the baby canines remain.

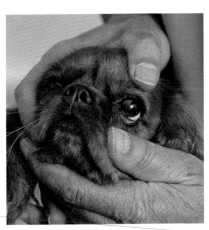

The eyes are clear and bright, with no signs of inflammation or discharge.

result of an allergic reaction, sometimes accompanied by sneezing or scratching.

Checking hairy ears

Inspect the ears for inflammation, unusual smell, discharge, or a build-up of wax. For dogs with hairy ears, use either your fingers (dipped in talcum powder to give grip) or tweezers to remove a little hair each day, immediately rewarding your dog with a food treat.

If your dog suddenly shakes its head frantically or squeals when you touch the side or the ear canal, suspect a foreign body such as a grass seed. The ear canal is so long these have often disappeared from sight before head shaking begins. See your vet the same day for help with removing the object. A little olive oil in the ear temporarily reduces pain.

Checking anal region and vulva

The anal region should be clean and odour free, with no sign of discharge or inflammation. Report any vaginal discharge to your vet immediately.

Dogs don't like their bums being examined, and it may be that this is one part of your dog's anatomy that you're not keen to examine either, but it's just as important that these bodily openings are clean and healthy as any others. Accustom your dog, using the reward system, to let you lift its tail and inspect its anal region. The skin and surrounding hair should be clean and odour-free.

With older dogs that either lick or drag their butts excessively, pay special attention to the skin regions on either side of the anus. A dog's anal sac (*see* box to the right) may become infected and abscess. In the initial stages, this causes a swelling above the anal sac, under the skin to the left or right. If an anal sac abscess has ruptured, there will be discharge or a scab at the site of rupture.

Older male dogs (and sometimes spayed females) can develop benign anal tumours. Wearing a disposable glove, occasionally feel the anal skin for the presence of hard tissue under the skin. If you feel anything unusual, contact your vet. Intact older male dogs can develop testicular cancer. Occasionally feel the testicles for symmetry and smoothness. If one feels different to the other, or one is getting larger than the other, see your vet.

Routinely examine the vulva and surrounding skin on your female dog. The vulva should be visible, with no discharge, and the surrounding skin clean with no stain. Some pups, particularly Boxers (*see* page 33) and Pugs (*see* page 36) with very muscular thighs, are born with small vulvas that can't be seen between their thighs. These dogs are susceptible to "juvenile vaginitis", a discharge-producing irritation that often spontaneously resolves when the dog has her first season and the anatomy of the vulva changes and enlarges. If you see intense hair staining or discharge or smell any unusual odour, contact your vet.

DRAGGING BOTTOMS

Anal sacs

Dogs with roundworms seldom drag their butts along the ground, but dogs with blocked anal sacs do. The anal sacs are under the skin on either side of the anus. They make a substance that is squeezed onto the faeces immediately after each bowel motion, anointing it with the "daily news", which is "read" when it is sniffed by other dogs. Blocked anal sacs are uncomfortable and can become painfully abscessed.

To empty anal sacs, wearing disposable gloves, squeeze both sides of the anus, with your thumb and forefinger, starting at four and eight o'clock and, as you squeeze, finishing at three and nine o'clock. The resulting discharge is disgusting to us but ambrosially attractive to dogs.

The anal region, including surrounding hair, should be clean and odour-free.

BRUCE'S TIPS ON DEBRIS IN THE COAT

Keep the hair between the toes clipped back (using blunt-tipped scissors) to prevent grass seeds from catching in it and then penetrating the skin. To get burrs out of your dog's hair, dab a little cooking oil around the burr; spray cooking oil works very well. This is also sometimes useful for removing gum. Don't use paint or tar remover on a dog's coat. Use mild detergent, such as baby shampoo, for water-based paint; otherwise clip the areas clean. Leave fish-hook removal to your vet, unless you can easily cut the hook with wire cutters and remove it via the cut end.

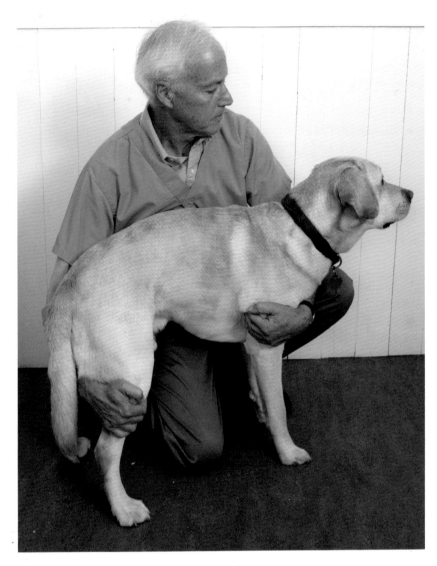

Arms around the shoulders and the rump comfort the dog and control wriggling.

or carrying it. Always muzzle an injured dog before lifting; even the gentlest of dogs might snap or bite in pain.

Observe your dog's behaviour

For a dog, life is a series of routines. Any change in these routines should make you suspicious that something is wrong.

Possible changes include less interest in playing or being with you, increased resting or sleeping, clinging, unexpected irritability, reduced alertness, reduced tolerance of exercise, apprehension or hiding, resentment at being touched, overexcitement or disorientation.

Observe your dog's actions

Watch for any changes in your dog's movements and activity, and signs such as unusual odours or changes to breathing. Any exaggerated change in breathing – such as gasping, wheezing, laboured, rapid, or shallow breathing, unremitting panting, or unusually slow breathing – warrants immediate veterinary attention.

See your vet immediately if your dog staggers or falls over, has a bloated belly,

Lifting a dog

Don't attempt to lift a giant breed such as a Great Dane (*see* page 43) on your own. This is a two-person job, with one lifting the forequarters and the other the aft, so the muscular parts of the dog's body bear the dog's weight. One arm can offer support under the ribcage, but avoid lifting under the soft belly. That can be uncomfortable to the dog, even damaging.

A small dog can be lifted by placing one hand behind the rump and the other

under the chest. For medium- or large-sized dogs, avoid placing undue pressure on either the ribcage or the abdomen. With one arm around the front of the chest and the other around the rump, draw your dog's body close to you. Keeping your back straight and using your legs to lift, stand up.

Holding a dog

Give your dog a feeling of security by pressing it to your body when holding or tries to urinate or defecate but is unable to. See your vet the same day if your dog walks in circles, has difficulty finding a comfortable position, overreacts to light, sound, or touch, is restless, very slow, or has difficulty getting up or lying down, or if you see sudden swellings anywhere on the body.

A head-to-tail body examination
Routinely examine your dog, running your hands over its body, feeling for swellings, heat, rough hair, stickiness, or any resentment that might indicate pain or annoyance at what you're doing. This simple routine takes about two minutes:
1. Run your hands over the head, face, throat, and neck.
2. Turn the head left, right, up, and down. Resistance could mean pain.
3. Run your hands over the back, sides, chest, and forelimbs, parting the hair occasionally. The skin should be clean, with minimal or no flaking dander.
4. Run your hands over the hips, thighs, abdomen, groin, and hind limbs. They should feel both firm and symmetrical. Unneutered male dogs will have a small amount of normal odourless discharge, called smegma, from the prepuce.

Monitor daily behaviour. Report increased urinating to your vet.

5. Inspect the anal region, the testicles on a male or the vulva on a female, and the tail. All should be clean, smooth, and odourless.
6. Flex each limb. There should be no resentment. If your dog replaces its leg on the ground tentatively, there may be pain there.
7. Examine the feet, pads, and nails.

Your dog's temperature
A dog's temperature is normally higher than ours, typically between 37.8°C (100.5°F) and 38.9°C (102.5°F). Never try to take your dog's temperature orally, and don't take it rectally either if it deeply resents this. If your dog has been microchipped with a thermal microchip,

Digital thermometers are inexpensive, easy to read, and accurate.

consider investing in a microchip scanner, like the one your vet has, so that you can take your dog's temperature at home by scanning it from the chip.

Dogs with low temperatures, below 37°C (98.6°F), should be kept warm and taken to the vet immediately, while those with fevers, over 40°C (104°F), should be cooled down and taken for immediate veterinary attention.

Grooming, maintenance and general hygiene

All dogs benefit from bathing. If your dog is a jumper, attach a nylon lead before bathing.

Skin and coat care

The condition of your dog's skin and hair gives a clue to general health. A dull coat or greasy or dandruffy skin can indicate internal medical problems. These changes warrant a visit to the vet.

Accustom your dog to daily coat and skin checks. Check for skin parasites, particularly fleas and ticks. Flea control treatments are good at preventing flea infestations, but even the best tick control products don't necessarily prevent ticks. The tick usually dies within 36 hours, but if you find any on your daily inspection, remove them with tweezers and a twist or with a tick remover. Fleas are good at hiding. Look for shiny black "coat dust" – evidence of infestation.

Brushing short or silky coats

A short, smooth coat such as a Pug's (*see* page 36) or a Boxer's (*see* page 33) is simple to clean. Using a bristle brush or chamois, brush against the lie of the coat at least once weekly. This cleans the coat, stimulates oil glands, and massages the muscles. Some breeds such as the Yorkshire Terrier (*see* page 34) and Maltese (*see* page 49) have long, silky coats but no protective undercoat. Be extra gentle when grooming, and avoid pin brushes that can scratch the skin. Tease out tangles each day, using a slicker brush, finishing with a bristle brush and a comb. The untidy ends of the coat can be trimmed monthly with scissors.

SHAMPOOS AND CONDITIONERS

Choose a shampoo according to your dog's coat type and condition. As a general rule, the safest and easiest shampoo to use is a low-lathering baby shampoo. Other types of shampoos are used for particular problems, especially itchy skin.

Shampoo type	Purpose
Conditioning	Good for all except wiry coats, which will be softened
Coal tar and benzoyl peroxide	Reduce itchiness by dulling nerves in the skin
Oatmeal and aloe vera	Soothe skin and reduce itching
Hypoallergenic	Usually free of perfumes or dyes
Enhancers	Colouring shampoos for show dogs
Dry	Powder that is dusted and brushed through the coat

Non-irritating shampoo, sponge, and dog towel

Brushing wiry coats

Using a slicker brush or bristle brush, groom with the lie of the coat at least twice weekly. Wiry coats can grow thick and dense, so thin out excessive fly-away hair with a stripping comb, available from pet shops. Avoid any conditioning shampoo on a wiry coat. It will soften it. There are special texturizing shampoos that maintain the coarseness and give body to wiry coat. If there is a dog groomer who knows how to strip a wiry coat – that means pull out dead hair by hand – have the coat professionally stripped three or four times each year.

Brushing short dense coats

The Labrador (see pages 20–1) has a short but very dense coat, and it's the soft, downy but thick, insulating undercoat that needs most attention. Use a slicker brush to groom with the lie of the coat at least twice weekly. During the dog's moults, brushing against the lie of the coat removes more dead hair faster. A bristle brush will then remove most of the dead hair, and finish with a fine-tooth comb, paying particular attention to the thick hair on the tail and neck.

Brushing long, dense coats

Longer, dense coats such as the Golden Retriever's (see page 26) need more attention. A slicker brush removes tangles, and a pin brush gets through the densest parts of the coat. The long hair (feathering) over the legs, chest, rear, and tail needs combing. Excess feathering should be trimmed monthly.

Washing dogs

Dog odour comes from the lips and mouth (lip-fold infection, gum infection, or odour in the breath), from passing wind (caused by gas-forming bacteria), or from the skin. The natural oil that keeps the coat waterproof also has its own distinctive odour. Skin bacteria, which proliferate when there is excess sebaceous material, modify the smell. If your dog smells, he needs a bath. Train your dog early in life to accept bathing, and for guaranteed control, use a washable nylon collar and lead to control escapes from the bathing area.

Dry the hair using a terry towel or a hairdryer on the lowest setting.

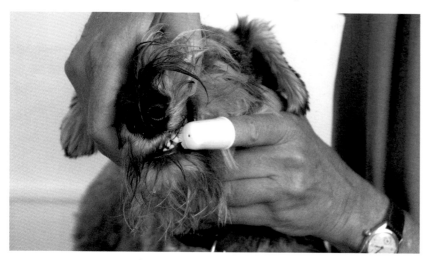

A finger brush can be easier to use than a long toothbrush.

Checking mouth, teeth, and gums

Dogs do not have bad breath, but so many have untreated gum disease that many owners assume fetid breath is normal. Preventing "dog breath" or "death breath" isn't just an aesthetic issue. Gum disease should be treated early, to prevent infection from spreading elsewhere in the body and causing more complicated problems.

Routinely check your dog's mouth, teeth, and gums for unusual odour, gum inflammation, or altered colour. Prevent calculus from developing on the teeth by brushing or rubbing the teeth and gums with a toothbrush or rubber finger brush. Avoid human toothpastes: they foam and are too strong-tasting. Palatable canine toothpastes are available.

1. Let your dog smell a food treat, then raise its upper lip and brush the tooth-gum margin of the teeth. If your dog doesn't wriggle, give the food reward.

2. Repeat on the lower teeth, reward, then do the upper and lower sides.

3. Concentrate your brushing on the upper back teeth. This is where the worst calculus and gum erosion occurs.

4. If plaque cannot be brushed off, or if an unpleasant odour is not immediately eliminated by brushing, or if there is obvious discomfort when you brush a particular area, contact your vet.

Toothpaste for dogs is flavoured and does not froth.

Choosing the right vet

It may sound odd, but as a vet I'm routinely choosing vets, either to work with me or to look after my own dogs when they need special skills that I don't have. When choosing a vet to work with, I'm not just interested in technical skills. Yes, I want a vet with lots of clinical experience, a logical approach to diagnostics, and creative surgical skills, but – I know this sounds corny – I also want one who genuinely loves dogs, who empathizes with them and their owners. The defining question when I make my choice is whether I'd be comfortable leaving my own dog in their hands.

Look for genuine interest from your vet. Your dog is an individual, not just a "case."

QUESTIONS AND ANSWERS

What do all the letters after a vet's name mean?

Generally, more letters mean more post-graduate qualifications. Interpreting the letters after a specialist vet's name can be difficult. For example, ECVIM means that vet has qualified to be a member of the European College of Veterinary Internal Medicine. ACVIM is the North American equivalent, while Dipl Clin Vet Stud is the Australian one. Because vets are a highly mobile species, you're likely to meet vets with qualifications from anywhere in the world.

Types of vets

Once upon a time, long ago, vets were Dr Dolittles, treating all creatures great and small. I'd love to be that type of vet, but the reality of modern medicine is that the omnicompetent vet is a figment of fantasy. In some regions, vets still look after both livestock and companion animals, but even these mixed veterinary practices often have one vet who concentrates on cats and dogs.

More typically, you will meet the small-animal veterinarian who only treats companion animals: dogs, cats, rabbits, other warm furries, and birds. In addition, there are the "ologists" – vets with more training in specific areas, such as dermatology, cardiology, neurology, and ophthalmology. Vets in general practice, like myself, are comfortable diagnosing and treating the vast majority of the cases we see. Because I practise in a large

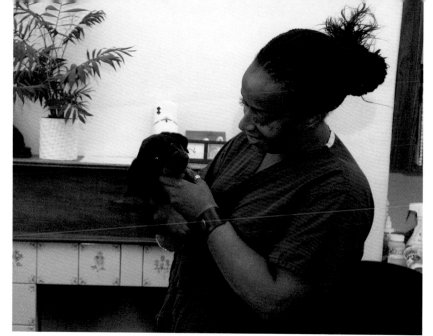

The quality of the nursing staff is as vital as the vet's abilities.

away in some regions. Consider the facilities, the location, and the cost. Profit margins don't vary appreciably from clinic to clinic. Generally speaking, you do get what you pay for: the higher the costs, the greater the investment in the staff and facilities.

Health insurance for pups

If insurance is available, get it. Pet-insurance actuarial statistics show that insurers almost invariably lose money during the first year of a pup's life, simply because naive pups are accident prone and their owners are still learning how to safeguard their new buddy's wellbeing. Insurers start making profits during the second year and usually remain in profit until a dog is over eight years old, when medical claims start their inexorable rise.

If you prefer not to give your money to an insurer, check out what a typical yearly premium is for your type of dog where you live, set up an interest-bearing account and dump that sum into it each year. I should have done that with my own dogs: within two months of each other, both Macy and Inca needed brain scans. With all the other diagnostics that were done, each cost thousands! I wish I'd followed my own advice.

city, my clients and I have the luxury of a large range of specialists to refer difficult cases to. Most veterinary colleges have teaching hospitals with staff and facilities equipped for all possibilities.

Shopping for a vet

Veterinary facilities in many countries are divided into "corporates" and "owner-operated". This division is of ownership rather than of quality. Corporate clinics are usually well equipped, often have a higher staff turnover, and follow target-based business plans; owner-operated veterinary clinics vary enormously in the quality of their equipment, often have longer-term staff, and may offer a more personal touch.

As with so much in life, you usually get what you pay for, but don't assume that the cheapest quotes for vaccinations, worming, and neutering mean that that vet is the least expensive. Discounts on these routine procedures may be offered as an introduction to a veterinary clinic.

Facilities and emergencies

Chances are there is more than one vet in your locality. When choosing a vet, visit several clinics and ask questions.

Is the reception clean and odour-free? Can you book a time to see "backstage", to have a look at the kennels and the diagnostic and surgical facilities? Do you feel comfortable there? How about your dog – is it relaxed?

Ask about ethical policies: for example, would they debark a dog as a cure for barking? Ask about referrals: any good practice should have a relaxed attitude about referring you and your dog to an "ologist".

Find out what happens when the vet and staff are not available. You should expect access to a vet 24 hours a day, seven days a week, although the emergency vet may be some distance

Home treatments

Other than shampoos, the most common home treatments involve giving medicines. I'm lucky to live with foodaholic dogs, so giving them their medicines is a treat. When Inca hears me popping her pills (for epilepsy) from their blister packs, she wakes from the deepest of sleeps and torpedoes into the kitchen because she associates the crinkling sound of the blister pack with the balls of white bread I hide her pills in. Yes, I'm a vet, and each day at the clinic I open dog's mouths and drop pills in, but for all home treatments, keep it simple. If there's an easy way to do it, use the easy way. Your aim is to ensure your dog gets its medicine, and bribery is perfectly acceptable.

Giving pills

It seems so easy when your vet shows you how to do it, but giving a pill can be a war of wills once your dog is back at home. Either it's getting better so has more strength to resist, or its confidence has returned, but getting medicine in can be vital, a literal life saver. Your simplest ploy is to hide the pill in something tasty, such as peanut butter or cheese spread.

Check with your vet before doing this, because some medicines can't be mixed with dairy products. Some manufacturers formulate antibiotics, painkillers, or wormers in tasty, chewable forms, but if these aren't available, here's what to do.
1. Command your dog to stand or sit. If your dog is excitable or rambunctious, back it between your legs before giving the "sit" command.

2. Open its mouth with one hand and turn its head upward.
3. Drop the tablet down, over the hump of the tongue.
4. Still holding the head up slightly, close your dog's mouth and massage its throat.
5. When it swallows or licks its lips, the pill has gone down.
6. Give your dog praise and rewards for good behaviour.

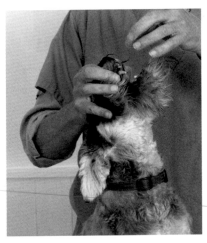

Tilt the head up and let gravity take the dropped pill to the back of the throat.

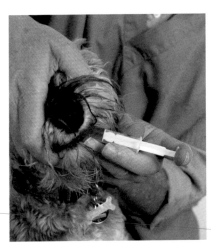

Give liquids into the side of the mouth, not squirted into the back, for safe swallowing.

Approach from behind when giving eye or ear drops. Always reward compliance.

If pill giving is futile because of the shape of your dog's face or because it is painful for it to have its mouth opened, ask your vet to provide the medicine as a liquid.

Giving liquids

Some medicines are available in liquid as well as pill form. If you are giving a liquid, ask your vet for a syringe. A 5ml syringe is equal to the teaspoon that accompanies some medicines, such as cough suppressants.

1. Load the syringe and, without opening your dog's jaws, insert the open end of the syringe into the space behind the canine teeth.

2. Tilt your dog's head up slightly, then squeeze on the syringe, ensuring that the medicine goes slowly into the mouth, not outside and off the lips. Don't squirt the medicine down the throat because it might accidentally get into the trachea.

3. Allow your dog to swallow.

4. Give praise and rewards.

Using eye and ear drops

No sensible dog enjoys having drops or ointment applied to the eyes or squirted down the ears. In either instance, clean away excess discharge with a cotton ball soaked in warm water.

1. Command your dog to sit.

2. Holding its head with one hand, bring the drops or ointment toward the eye or ear from behind so that it's not watching. You don't want to frighten it.

Using a guillotine cutter, clip the nail in front of the pink quick. Take special care with dark nails.

3. Squeeze a drop of medication onto the eye or into the ear from above.

4. After applying the medication, hold the eye closed for a few seconds to disperse the medication, or rub the ear canal so that the ear medication lubricates all surfaces.

Clipping nails

Most dogs resent having their nails cut, but small dogs in particular need regular nail clipping. So too do elderly dogs, regardless of size, that no longer exercise as much as they once did.

Only attempt to clip nails after your dog is trained to sit and permits its paws to be handled. If your dog hates having its nails done, only do one nail a night,

followed by dinner. Your vet will show you how to do this, and while it's easy to see the living pink tissue in white nails, most dogs don't have white nails. If in doubt, have a groomer or the veterinary staff cut your dog's nails.

Dealing with diarrhoea

Dogs taste life, and the consequence of this is that occasional episodes of diarrhoea are to be expected. Some of these incidents are caused by scavenging and clear up within 36 hours.

If your dog has simple diarrhoea without any other symptoms, such as vomiting, skip the next meal, encourage rest, and allow access to water. It is usually safe to use a proprietary anti-diarrhoea medicine such as Pepto-Bismol or Kaopectate. Return to feeding your dog its regular food in small amounts or give it highly digestible, bland food such as boiled chicken and rice.

If your dog's diarrhoea is anything other than simple, if there's blood in it, or if it is accompanied by vomiting, lethargy, or pain, contact your vet immediately.

BRUCE'S TIPS ON AVOIDING BATTLES

- When giving medicine, don't advertise what you're about to do. Keep it quick and professional.
- Never call your dog to you to give it medicine. Go to the dog, clip on its lead, give the medicine, and follow that with an instant reward.
- If you need to keep your dog still, secure its lead to something stable like a radiator before you medicate. Avoid tables your dog can fall off.
- If possible, give medications in treats. Check with your vet what type of treats to use; vets can supply special treats made to hide pills in.

Home nursing

Accidents will happen, and there will be times when your dog needs immediate help at home before you take it to the vet. The best approach to accidents is prevention. Keep sharp, toxic, or otherwise dangerous items out of your dog's reach. This is especially important when household activities such as birthday parties might distract you (although if my wife's dog had not swallowed a balloon at a birthday party once, I'd never have met either of them). Bleeding injuries to paws, ears, or tail tips are often the most common injuries that need immediate attention.

RISKY TIMES

Avoid crises during celebrations

- Keep poisonous plants such as holly and mistletoe berries, poinsettias, amaryllis, and hyacinths out of reach.
- Keep your dog out of the kitchen: during festivities there are too many potential accidents waiting to happen.
- Immediately dispose of gift wrapping, especially ribbons and the little bags of silica gel that come with many gifts.
- If your dog is worried by loud noises, ensure it's not frightened by festive fireworks or crackers.
- Avoid special treats: anything new might cause diarrhoea.
- A little turkey is usually fine for most dogs, but not a turkey carcass. Sharp bones can puncture intestines. Also these foods can be dangerous:
  – 65g (2¼oz) dark chocolate for a 10kg (22lb) dog
  – Grapes over 100g (3½oz) for a 10kg (22lb) dog
  – Raisins over 100g (3½oz) for a 10kg (22lb) dog
  – Stones from peaches or nectarines
  – Unshelled nuts

Cleaning simple wounds

Pads cut by glass, metal, or sharp ice are perhaps the most common foot injuries that dogs suffer. Ice injuries are usually clean, but others get contaminated by debris. Dog-bite wounds may appear small and clean, but invariably a nasty variety of bacteria are injected under the skin by the penetrating tooth. These wounds are much more difficult to clean.

1. Put a lead on your dog and command it to stand or sit.

2. For glass, metal, or ice injuries, wash the paw in clean, tepid water. A 500ml

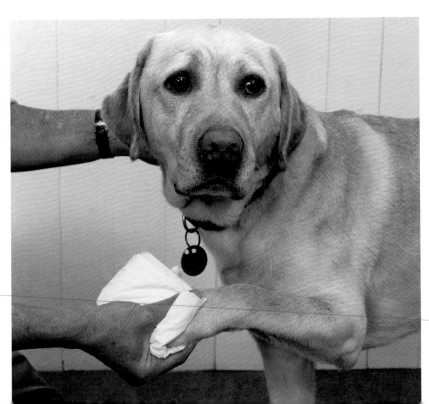

Apply firm pressure for at least two minutes to bleeding paws then bandage protectively.

(1pt) sports-drink bottle is excellent for squirting water over the injury.

3. Apply disinfectant or antiseptic. Spray disinfectants designed for use on human skin are excellent.

4. If there is a penetrating tooth wound, try to get disinfectant into the wound in order to kill bacteria under the skin. These wounds often need veterinary attention.

5. Don't use Vaseline or other oily substances to stop bleeding or prevent a bandage from sticking to the wound. If anything is applied, use only water-soluble products, such as K-Y jelly, that can be easily removed.

Controlling bleeding

Because dogs shake their heads and wag their tails, bleeding from bites, cuts, or crush injuries to these regions can turn your home into a scene from a horror film. So can bleeding paw wounds, as your dog walks from room to room leaving a smudged red trail.

1. Put a lead on your dog and command it either to stand or to sit. Using absorbent material, such as a clean cotton face cloth or, if necessary, kitchen roll, apply pressure for several minutes to the bleeding region.

2. If you are taking your dog to the vet, maintain gentle pressure on the bleeding area and keep it immobile. Prevent ear flapping or tail wagging by holding these regions against your dog's body. If a paw is bleeding, pull a sock over your temporary bandage to apply pressure and keep the absorbent material in place.

3. If bleeding is minimal, spray the area with antiseptic, apply non-stick gauze to the wound, and wrap with absorbent material followed by adhering bandage.

4. Take care that the circulation is not restricted by your bandage. More severe damage can be caused by improper bandaging than by the original injury that needed attention.

HOME FIRST-AID KIT

Vet's number

- Blunt-tipped scissors
- Tick remover
- Narrow pliers for removing objects caught in the mouth
- Rectal digital thermometer and lubricating water-soluble jelly (such as K-Y)
- Non-stick gauze pads
- Sterile cotton
- Roll of 5cm (2in) gauze
- Roll of adhesive bandage
- Antiseptic cream, wash, or spray
- Activated charcoal, to absorb any swallowed poisons
- Hydrogen peroxide (3 per cent) to induce vomiting
- Antihistamine tablets for wasp stings, nettles, or allergies
- Emergency vet's telephone number taped inside the kit

5. Ask someone to hold your dog during the trip to the vet, or attach it to a seatbelt anchor to control his movement.

Emergency muzzle

Always muzzle an injured dog when helping it; even the most gentle dog may bite when in pain or frightened. Any long material such as a tie can be used as an emergency muzzle. A dog that needs to be muzzled is invariably frightened or in pain. Speak soothingly and calmly and avoid direct eye contact. While applying a muzzle from behind is easiest, frightened dogs need to see you. Approach from the front and gently move the muzzle around the snout.

1 Approach from behind and, using whatever suitable material is available, make a loop and gently tighten this, with the knot over the dog's muzzle.

2 Drop both sides of the material down and cross them under the dog's jaw. Draw the ends up around the dog's neck and tie them behind the neck.

Serious emergencies

We never think it will happen to us, but it does. Dogs get into trouble, sometimes potentially lethal trouble, where your help is vital if your dog is to survive long enough to get to the vet. One of the most common life-threatening home risks to new pups is chewing on live wires. Minimize risks in your home, and don't forget the wriggly cables to electrical garden tools. If your dog bites a live wire, pull the plug from the mains and move him from the wire with a wooden handle before touching and giving heart massage and artificial respiration. In emergencies, don't get distracted by injuries. Look first for shock, the silent killer.

Watch for signs of shock

Shock is the failure of blood to get properly transported around the body. It is a hidden killer, and treating shock should always take precedence over treating other injuries such as broken bones. Watch out for these early signs of shock:

- Rapid breathing and heart rate
- Anxiousness or restlessness
- Lethargy or weakness
- Pale gums
- Below-normal rectal temperature
- Taking more than two seconds for blood to return after finger pressure is applied to the gums.

The signs of critical late shock are:
- Shallow and irregular breathing and heart rate
- Extreme weakness leading to unconsciousness
- Cool body and rectal temperature below 36.7°C (98°F)
- Very pale white or blue gums
- Taking more than four seconds for blood to return after finger pressure is applied to the gums.

Treating shock

- Don't let your dog wander, and give nothing to eat or drink.
- Prevent further heat loss by keeping your dog warm, and stop any obvious bleeding.
- Give artificial respiration or heart massage as necessary.
- Elevate the hind quarters to enable more precious blood to reach your dog's brain.
- Keep the neck extended and transport immediately to the nearest vet.

With the neck straight, give artificial respiration by blowing directly into the nose. The chest will rise.

Feel for the pulse in the femoral artery on the inner thigh.

Taking the pulse

A large dog may have a pulse rate as low as 50 beats a minute, while a small dog's heart might normally beat three times faster. A pup's heart rate is faster than an adult of the same size.

Monitor your dog's pulse by feeling it through the femoral artery on the inner thigh. Alternatively, if your dog is lean, monitor its pulse by placing your hand over the heart, just behind the left elbow. On smaller dogs, you can feel the heart rate by grasping the chest just behind the elbows on both sides with your thumb and forefinger, then gently squeezing until you feel the contractions. This is difficult to do on fat dogs.

Artificial respiration

Give artificial respiration only if your dog has stopped breathing. Possible causes of this include choking, near-drowning, smoke inhalation, electrocution, concussion, poisoning, diabetic coma, shock, or blood loss.
1. Place your dog on its side, straighten its neck, clear debris from its nose and mouth, and pull its tongue forward.
2. Close its mouth and place your mouth either directly over your dog's nose and mouth or, using your hand as an airtight funnel, on your hand wrapped around your dog's mouth. Blow in. You will see your dog's chest rise.

3. Take your mouth away, letting the lungs naturally deflate.
4. Repeat this procedure 10 to 20 times a minute, until the dog breathes on its own.
5. Check the pulse every 15 seconds to make sure the heart is still beating. If it's not, add heart massage.

Heart massage

Heart massage is never given alone. It's combined with artificial respiration and called CPR, or cardiopulmonary resuscitation, when the heart has stopped. Add heart massage only if the heart is not beating. When the heart stops, the pupils dilate and the gums don't refill with blood after pressure is applied to them.
1. Place your dog on its right side, with its head lower than the rest of its body.
2. On large dogs, place the heel of one hand on the chest just behind the elbow and the heel of the other hand on top, then vigorously compress the chest 100 times per minute, both down and up toward the neck.

On small dogs, grasp the chest behind the elbows with your thumb and forefinger and squeeze firmly up toward the neck, compressing the ribcage at a rate of 120 pumps per minute.
3. Every 15 seconds, stop heart massage and give two breaths of artificial respiration.
4. Continue heart massage until the pulse returns, then artificial respiration only until spontaneous breathing returns.
5. Transport as soon as possible for veterinary attention.

Use your body to support ill or injured dogs, but ensure your own safety. Even the gentlest dog may bite if it is in pain.

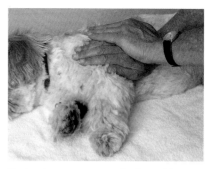

For heart massage, press firmly, pushing blood from the heart toward the brain.

Transporting an ill dog

If a dog is injured, ideally secure it on a rigid material, such as a shelf, cover with a blanket, and carry it to a car and to the vet. Realistically, you may have to make do with a blanket. Gently pull the dog onto the blanket, wrap it thickly around him, and lift the blanket-wrapped dog into the vehicle. Aim to apply as little pressure as possible directly to the body.

Preventive health care

Preventing problems is cheaper, safer, and kinder than treating them after they happen. Your dog can be effectively protected against a wide variety of dangerous or highly transmissible infections and infestations. It's irresponsible not to do so, but a more difficult question to answer is how frequently to boost the protection. Preventive medicine includes making decisions about breeding and, later in life, actively monitoring your dog's health rather than using your veterinary clinic as the local fire brigade, called upon only after problems develop.

Parasite prevention

All new dogs should be examined and treated for both external and internal parasites. The risks from parasites vary with both the season of the year and the region you live in.

Internal parasites

Pups commonly inherit roundworms from their mother, while more threatening hookworms and whipworms are less common. Tapeworms are contracted by eating infected fleas or uncooked organ meats, especially from sheep. Heartworms are transmitted through mosquito bites, while the protozoal parasite *Leishmania* is transmitted in sandfly bites. The protozoal parasites *Babesia* and *Ehrlichia* are transmitted by ticks, which also transmit the bacteria that causes Lyme disease. *Giardia* is a single-celled, microscopic, water-borne parasite, increasingly diagnosed as the cause of diarrhoea in dogs. Some over-the-counter anti-parasitic treatments can be moderately effective, but the most efficient preventive treatments for internal parasites are those available from vets.

External parasites

Some external parasites, such as demodex and cheyletiella mites, are transmitted from mother to pup shortly after birth; others, such as lice, are transmitted from dog to dog by direct contact. Irritating scabies mites transmit by direct contact but also, like fleas, ticks, and harvest mites, through environmental contamination. Flea and tick prevention are particularly important, the former because flea saliva is a common trigger of allergic

The tough flea is adapted for survival and a common cause of skin disease.

This roundworm, a most common puppy worm, is hatching from its egg.

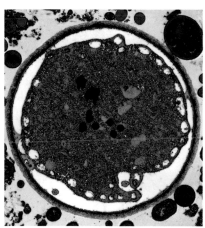

Diarrhoea-causing Giardia cysts survive outside the intestines in rivers and lakes.

This engorged tick has completely filled its abdomen with a blood meal.

skin disease, and the latter because ticks can transmit potentially lethal infections. Use preventive measures that your vet recommends are appropriate either for where you live or where you're visiting. A "spot-on" product, applied to the skin, is often effective, although sprays or collars may be needed for most efficient protection.

Infectious disease prevention

When I started in veterinary practice, dogs routinely died from infectious diseases such as distemper and hepatitis. The development of effective vaccines means that a death today is a needless tragedy. All new dogs should be given biological vaccines to protect them from infectious diseases either where you live or where you visit. Homeopathic nosodes don't work. Biological vaccines do.

Dogs should be given vaccine-induced protection against distemper, hepatitis, and parvovirus. Where needed, they should be protected from rabies and leptospirosis. Other vaccines, giving protection from canine cough (*Bordetella bronchiseptica*, parainfluenza, adenovirus) or Lyme disease (*Borrelia*) are available and used regionally.

Family planning

I've mentioned it before, but it's worth mentioning again. The life expectancy of females that are spayed before a year of age is 18 months longer than the life expectancy of females that are never spayed. That's a dramatic reason why your female should be spayed young if you're not planning to breed from her. At present there are no safe alternatives to surgery.

The life expectancy of castrated males is no different to intact males. However, the typical dog that ends up at a rehoming centre, because he's a vagrant or because his owners can't cope with him, is a young, unneutered male. Neutering males almost invariably makes them more reliable, responsive canine members of your family.

Pups can be neutered when they're quite young, but the procedure is most frequently carried out as they reach physical maturity. Neutering doesn't alter a dog's personality: in young dogs, it perpetuates the existing personality. In terms of appearance, neutered dogs may grow slightly thicker coats and, like all dogs, they are prone to weight gain if they are fed too much.

Preventive health checks

A once-a-year health check is all that's needed for most dogs. For older dogs this should include checking the efficiency of various body functions via a blood sample. Your vet should tailor health checks to the known risks within your breed and to that breed's known life expectancy.

Index

Figures in *italics* indicate captions. Those in **bold** indicate training sequences.

Useful contacts

DOG TRAINER REGISTRIES AND ACTIVITIES ASSOCIATIONS

The Association of Pet Behaviour Counsellors (APBC) members see dogs referred by practising veterinarians.
www.apbc.org.uk

The Association of Pet Dog Trainers (APDT) members emphasize positive reinforcement dog training.
www.apdt.co.uk

The British Institute of Professional Dog Trainers (BIPDT) certifies its instructors at several levels of competence.
www.bipdt.org.uk

Centre of Applied Pet Ethology (COAPE) members have completed a correspondence or lecture course in animal behaviour and follow a code of conduct.
www.coape.co.uk

The UK Registry of Canine Behaviourists (UKRCB) members see dogs referred to them by practising veterinarians, for behaviour problems.
www.ukrcb.org

The Agility Club members arrange agility classes and contests.
www.agilityclub.co.uk

British Flyball Association (BFA) gives information and produces publications about competitions and training.
www.flyball.org.uk

The Gundog Club gives information about all levels of gundog training.
www.thegundogclub.co.uk

The Kennel Club licences all canine-related competitions and provides information about organizations specializing in specific disciplines, including breed showing (ringcraft), competition and pet obedience

training, and agility.
www.thekennelclub.org.uk

DOG WELFARE AND REHOMING

Dogs Trust
www.dogstrust.org.uk

Battersea Dogs and Cats Home
www.dogshome.org

The Blue Cross
www.bluecross.org.uk

RSPCA
www.rspca.org.uk

Ulster SPCA
www.uspca.co.uk

Scottish SPCA
www.scottishspca.org

Irish SPCA
www.ispca.ie

Irish Animals is a country-based resource for dogs needing new homes.

www.irishanimals.ie

Hearing Dogs for Deaf People rescues small dogs that need good homes.
www.hearingdogs.org.uk

BREED REGISTRIES

The Kennel Club – for UK breeders.
www.thekennelclub.org.uk

Irish Kennel Club – for Irish breeders.
www.ikc.ie

Federation Cynologique Internationale (FCI) for breeds not recognized by either The Kennel Club or the Irish Kennel Club.
www.fci.be

VETERINARY ASSOCIATIONS

Royal College of Veterinary Surgeons is the registry for practising vets in the UK.
www.rcvs.org.uk

Acknowledgments

From Dr Bruce Fogle

Because I'm in clinical practice, there's never a problem finding dogs and dog owners willing to be photographed for a book project. And I can't deny that it's fun, leafing through the finished pages, seeing dogs I know well; you could even say intimately! I'm grateful to all my clients who allowed their dogs to be photographed, even those that were in for anaesthetics and minor operations.

I'm also very grateful to Hearing Dogs for Deaf People (www.hearingdogs.org.uk), a charity that rescues and recycles bright, young dogs to act as ears for people who are severely hearing-impaired. Hearing Dogs not only provided us with dogs for training shots, they also provided their facilities and their staff were just amazing. Many of them gave up their free time (they train and place over 150 dogs each year) to help with training sequences. Thanks to everyone – management and staff – at Hearing Dogs.

When it comes to dog training, Patricia Holden White and I are on the same wavelength. That's why I've been referring clients to her dog training club for over 30 years. The dog models reported back to me that Pat, together with Juliette Norsworthy and the photographer Adrian Pope, were so much fun at the photoshoots that the canine crew were sad when they finished.

It was the same with everyone at Mitchell Beazley. From David Lamb, the Publisher to Helen Griffin the Commissioning Editor and her team, particularly Juliette Norsworthy and Suzanne Arnold, the behind-the-scenes people were a pleasure to work with. Thank you.

As always, the people I spend every day with at the Portman Veterinary Clinic created time and space to help get New Dog completed. Thanks to Suzi Gray, Ashley McManus, Angela Bettinson, Lettie Lean, Hester Small, Grant Petrie, and Veronica Askmanovic for their gracious assistance.

From Patricia Holden White

New Dog is a book close to my heart, embracing as it does the emphasis on a positive owner and dog relationship as the basis for successful and happy dog ownership. Helping people to train their dogs and working with dogs with behaviour problems has made me very aware how many dog behaviour problems are actually man-made. So looking at both ends of the lead is imperative to resolving what initially may seem to be only a dog problem.

Most of my dogs are rescue dogs – and how much they have taught me! The extraordinary trainer Roy Hunter once said, "The only experts in dogs are dogs themselves". We are but observers. Observation and communication work hand in hand in the fascinating exploration of the human–canine bond. It has been a privilege to continue to work with Bruce Fogle in that exploration.

Many thanks to people who have made producing New Dog a pleasure. The staff at Hearing Dogs have been so generous with their time and dogs in their care used for photography. Thanks, too, to the members of Hammersmith Dog Training Club for participating in the photography. The staff of Mitchell Beazley and our wonderful photographer Adrian Pope have joined the spirit of fun in producing a book that we hope will guide the new dog owner through the trials and triumphs of settling in their new family member.

Mitchell Beazley would like to thank everybody – human and canine – at Hearing Dogs for Deaf People for their help and enthusiasm in hosting and modelling for the photo shoots. In particular, very many thanks to Jenny Moir and Carrie Highmore.

Thank you to all the models: Chris Allen; Becky Atkinson; Lorna Bacchus; Evie Clark; Jeremy Day; Freddie, Joshua, and Suzi Eglese; Lubca Gangarova; Mike Garner; Suzi Gray; Tom Green; Lesley Hastings; Carrie Highmore; Sarah Luxford; Chloe Morris; Theo and Molly Oakley; Nicole O'Donnell; Ingrid Ramon; Emma Richards; Karen Rigg; Darren Sparrow; Nancy Stranger.

Thank you to all the dogs: Bea; Cara; Cedar; Chelsea; Denver; Elkie; Etna; Fizz; Lacey; Maisy; Milly; Minty; Mocha; Monty; Olly; Poppy; Ramsey; Rodney; Sidney; Stig; Terry; Truffle; Umber.

Photographic acknowledgments

Mitchell Beazley would like to acknowledge and thank the following for providing images for publication in this book.
a: above, b: below, c: centre, l: left, r: right

12a Moredun Animal Health Ltd/Science Photo Library; 12b Eric Isselée/Shutterstock; 13 Jack Fields/Corbis; 14a Marc Pagani Photography/Shutterstock; 17a Jane Burton/Warren Photographic; 19 DLILLC/Corbis; 20 Jane Burton/Warren Photographic; 21 Doreen Baum/Picani/Shutterstock; 22, 23, 24 Jane Burton/Warren Photographic; 25a Octopus Publishing Group; 25b Eric Isselée/Shutterstock; 26a Lisa A Svara/Shutterstock; 26b Pieter/Shutterstock; 27 Jane Burton/Warren Photographic; 28a Octopus Publishing Group; 28b, 29a & b Jane Burton/Warren Photographic; 30l Waldemar Dabrowski/Shutterstock; 30r Octopus Publishing Group; 31 DK Limited/Corbis; 32a & b, 33a Jane Burton/Warren Photographic; 33b Eric Isselée/Shutterstock; 34 Joy Fera/Shutterstock; 35 Eric Isselée/Shutterstock; 36l & r Jane Burton/Warren Photographic; 37a Don Mason/Corbis; 37b Jean Michel Labat/Ardea.com; 38a Jane Burton/Warren Photographic; 38b John Madere/Corbis; 39l Waldemar Dabrowski/Shutterstock; 39r Wegner/Arco/Naturepl.com; 40a Dale C Spartas/Corbis; 40b Lew Robertson/Corbis; 41a & b, 42a Jane Burton/Warren Photographic; 42b pixshots/Shutterstock; 43l Rick's Photography/Shutterstock; 43r, 44l & r Octopus Publishing Group; 45 Eric Isselée/Shutterstock; 46, 47l Octopus Publishing Group; 47r, 48 Jane Burton/Warren Photographic; 49a Eric Isselée/Shutterstock; 49b John Daniels/Ardea.com; 50l Octopus Publishing Group; 50r Eric Isselée/Shutterstock; 51a & b Jane Burton/Warren Photographic; 52 Johan de Meester/Ardea.com; 53 Tracy Morgan/Dorling Kindersley; 54l & r, 55, 56r Jane Burton/Warren Photographic; 56l Shutterstock; 57 John Daniels/Ardea.com; 58, 59, 60l & r, 61r Jane Burton/Warren Photographic; 61l Rick's Photography/Shutterstock; 62 Ioannis Lelakis/Photographers Direct; 63 Jane Burton/Warren Photographic; 68 Shinya Sasaki/Neo Vision/Getty Images; 70 John Daniels/Ardea.com; 76 Roger Tidman/FLPA; 89a Arco Images/Alamy; 96b Yann Arthus-Bertrand/Ardea.com; 111r lemonlight features/Alamy; 113a Maksym Gorpenyuk/Shutterstock; 164 mediacolor's/Alamy; 176a Christie & Cole/Corbis; 186 Mike Buxton/Papilio/Corbis; 187l Clouds Hill Imaging Ltd/Corbis; 187c Visuals Unlimited/Corbis; 187r Science Photo Library.

Hearing Dogs *for Deaf People*